DRIFTING
WEST

Drifting West

THE CALAMITIES OF
JAMES WHITE AND CHARLES BAKER

VIRGINIA McCONNELL SIMMONS

UNIVERSITY PRESS OF COLORADO

Published by the University Press of Colorado
5589 Arapahoe Avenue, Suite 206C
Boulder, Colorado 80303

 The University Press of Colorado is a proud member of the Association of American University Presses.

The University Press of Colorado is a cooperative publishing enterprise supported, in part, by Adams State College, Colorado State University, Fort Lewis College, Mesa State College, Metropolitan State College of Denver, University of Colorado, University of Northern Colorado, and Western State College of Colorado.

∞ The paper used in this publication meets the minimum requirements of the American National Standard for Information Sciences — Permanence of Paper for Printed Library Materials. ANSI Z39.48-1992

Library of Congress Cataloging-in-Publication Data

Simmons, Virginia McConnell, 1928–
  Drifting West : the calamities of James White and Charles Baker / Virginia McConnell Simmons.
     p. cm.
  Includes bibliographical references and index.
  ISBN 978-0-87081-874-5 (hardcover : alk. paper) 1. White, James, 1837–1927. 2. Baker, Charles, d. 1867? 3. Pioneers — West (U.S.) — Biography. 4. Drifters — West (U.S.) — Biography. 5. Frontier and pioneer life — West (U.S.) 6. West (U.S.) — Description and travel. 7. Grand Canyon (Ariz.) — Description and travel. 8. San Juan Mountains (Colo. and N.M.) — Description and travel. 9. San Juan Mountains (Colo. and N.M.) — Gold discoveries. 10. West (U.S.) — Biography. I. Title.
  F594.W48S57 2007
  978′.020922 — dc22
  [B]

                                                            2007014683

Design by Daniel Pratt

Maps drawn by Yvonne Halburian

16 15 14 13 12 11 10 09 08 07   10 9 8 7 6 5 4 3 2 1

For "Dock" Marston, at last

CONTENTS

ILLUSTRATIONS

MAPS

PREFACE

AMONG THE MANY INDIVIDUALS AND RESOURCES THAT CONTRIBUTED TO THE research for this book, I must first express my gratitude for the assistance of the late Otis R. "Dock" Marston, a good friend with whom I enjoyed corresponding for several years, as did countless others who shared even the slightest interest in the Colorado River. His letters to me usually began with a cartoon and a salutation addressed to "Canyoneer Virginia," a form of greeting his correspondents earned through baptism in the waters of the Grand Canyon, and he concluded with a "Cheerio, Dock." He enclosed photocopies of anything related directly or indirectly to subjects of current interest, and his letters contained personal, frequently acerbic commentary about the enclosures. I was only one of the many recipients of this largesse. Recognized in his lifetime as the foremost authority on river-running in the Grand

Canyon and associated subjects, he helped all—friend, foe, or mere acquaintance—with his notes, copies of articles and letters, and references related to the Colorado River, and he was not shy about asking for assistance with his research.

At the beginning of our association, our mutual interest was Charles Baker, about whom I had produced one article, but Marston, like a sorcerer's apprentice, soon was deluging me with items about James White, who was for a short but eventful time linked with Baker and who was of much greater interest to Marston, although not to me originally.

Marston hoped that a small group—including himself, White's granddaughter Eilean Adams, archaeologist Robert Euler, and me—would write and publish an account of White's role in Colorado River lore, but I hesitated to pursue this project further, in part because of other interests but also because I felt unprepared to enter the debate about whether White or Major John Wesley Powell's celebrated expedition was first down the Colorado through the Grand Canyon. Historians already had argued this issue at great length and to little avail. By the time my interest in James White became actively engaged, the Otis R. Marston Papers, consisting of more than 400 boxes, 251 albums, 163 motion-picture reels, and roughly 30,000 photographs, had gone to the Huntington Library in San Marino, California, and Marston himself had run his last rapid. Daunted by the task of researching the Marston Papers, I turned instead to the materials about White that Marston had given to me and began to examine supplementary resources related to the history and geography through which White drifted during his lifetime, the Grand Canyon story being just one part. As others have learned, however, I found that the Colorado River is a theme that tends to captivate and dominate one's interests.

During the intervening years, my article about Charles Baker and his adventures in the San Juan Mountains had caught the attention of a few researchers whose focus was early mining history and Baker's role in it during the years of 1860 to 1861. In that article, with its brief discussion of the intertwining of Baker and White, various researchers found helpful clues about James White, as had Marston and eventually Eilean Adams, who was writing a book about her grandfather, *Hell or High Water: James White's Disputed Passage through Grand Canyon, 1867.* Such efforts are symbiotic, and I, in turn, am now indebted to Marston,

Adams, and several others. Especially, I acknowledge with high regard the exhaustive research by the late Allen Nossaman that culminated in three volumes about Silverton, Colorado. Many additional publications, such as Duane A. Smith's many books on Colorado mining and Cathy E. Kindquist's booklet about Stony Pass (now out of print), have contributed greatly to my knowledge about the history and geography of that region. In contrast, several contemporary efforts, particularly the promotional materials of tourism projects, have tended to disseminate misinformation by presenting Baker as the first or the most important figure in early mining in the San Juans.

To an even greater extent, popular references uncritically glorify John Wesley Powell, while reducing to little more than footnotes the arguable journey of James White through the Grand Canyon, if he is mentioned at all. Resurrecting her grandfather with understandable loyalty, Adams's book is biased in favor of his having traversed the entire canyon. One cannot resist speculating that incentive for her writing her book at last was either Marston's published conclusion that White did not do so or the erection of a modern, shrine-like monument to Powell at Grand Canyon National Park. Since Adams's book appeared in 2001, a few writers about the Colorado River have subscribed to the opinion that White did make the first transit, but objective scholars take a neutral stance on this issue, as I also have been forced to do.

Regardless, the prominence of John Wesley Powell in Colorado River history has perpetuated the belief that his expedition, not James White's, was first through the Grand Canyon. For his part, Marston had refused to accept the celebration of Powell's achievements in the Grand Canyon, and, ever the iconoclast, Marston went so far as to judge Powell a liar, to the amusement of the major's admirers, but, then, Marston debunked White, too. As my acknowledgments, endnotes, and bibliography demonstrate, I have limited my own discussion about Powell's explorations of the Grand Canyon because of the plethora of readily available literature on this subject. Instead, I have attempted to deal with the reasons why political and economic adversaries of Powell in the West helped keep White's cause alive.

When I did turn my attention to the life of White, I was confronted with the problem of how to situate him in history, for he, Baker, and their companions were merely examples of hordes of drifters, the flotsam and jetsam of westward migration. Their stories do not fit neatly into either popular or scholarly treatments. Biographies about such individuals are not found in conventional reference materials, and, despite my original interest in Baker, the absence of verifiable biographical data about him forced me to draw from peripheral sources. Concerning White, more information was available, but much of it was not reliable. Concerning their two fellow travelers, nothing has been found. Consequently, research necessarily turned to investigation of a variety of ancillary materials in order to place these individuals in their period in the American West.

Several repositories and their keepers aided my research. At the Colorado Historical Society's Stephen H. Hart Library, Barbara Dey expedited my work with efficient assistance, while the society's publications director, David N. Wetzel, shared useful files concerning the Thomas F. Dawson Papers. Peter E. Hanff, deputy director of the Bancroft Library in Berkeley, California, graciously verified the location of documents of Charles Christopher Parry and James White. Archivist Todd Ellison at Fort Lewis College's Center of Southwest Studies in Durango, Colorado, provided his competent help, as he has in some of my other projects. At the Archive-Research Center of the San Juan County Historical Society in Silverton, Colorado, Freda Peterson and Nicole Sharp shared files pertaining to the Baker Expedition, while the Colorado Springs Pioneers Museum's staff in the Starsmore Center for Local History, headed by archivist Leah Davis Witherow, found pertinent manuscripts by Baker's contemporaries. The staff at Adams State College's Nielsen Library lent their assistance, and Kathy Gilliam at Del Norte (Colorado) Public Library performed generous service in providing interlibrary loans.

During my visits to sites where the characters in this narrative once traveled, my investigations were abetted by several museums and special collections. My thanks are extended to Colleen Hyde, museum technician at the Grand Canyon National Park Museum archives; Willie Heitzinger at the Colorado River Museum, Bullhead City, Arizona; Don Troyer at Bent's Old Fort National Historic Site; Lola Sperra and Martha Wade at Big Timbers Museum, Lamar, Colorado; Betty Barnes and Harold Smith at Kearny County Museum, Lakin, Kansas; Dolly Ideker, librarian of Fort Dodge Museum and Library at the Kansas Soldiers' Home; Gary K. Brasher, superintendent of the Masonic Cemetery Association in Trinidad, Colorado; and George Love, for help in identifying locations on family property at Centerville, Colorado.

I am indebted to Leo E. Oliva at the Santa Fe Trail Association in Larned, Kansas, for background material about the trail; Robert McDaniel, director of La Plata County Historical Society's Animas Museum, for information about the Durango region; and Barbara Ekker of Hanksville, Utah, for lore related to mining in Utah. Jack Rudder of Alamosa shared information about military life during the Civil War period, and Frances McCullough of Monte Vista offered help concerning the era of stagecoaches and pioneer settlers. Loie Belknap Evans, publisher of Westwater Books, is especially thanked for giving me a copy of her company's out-of-print edition of Robert Brewster Stanton's *Colorado River Controversies.*

The search for archival photographs was aided by numerous capable staff people—Jessica Lemieux at the Bancroft Library, University of California, Berkeley; Cary McStay and Daniel Kosharek at the Photo Archives, Palace of the Governors, Santa Fe, New Mexico; Ruba Sadi at the Stephen H. Hart Library, Colorado Historical Society; Coi Drummond-Gehrig at the Denver Public Library, Western History Department; Susan McGlophlin at Cline Library, Northern Arizona State University; and Debbie Newman at the Arizona Historical Society, Tucson.

The helpfulness and pleasure of working with friends and family members was incalculable. Yvonne Halburian, the able creator of maps and line drawings for this and other publications, also drew the sketch of Bent's Old Fort and Baker's Bridge. My brother Marcus A. McCorison, president emeritus of the American Antiquarian Society, is to be saluted for locating a hard-to-find article from *The Outing Magazine* in which James White's letter was reproduced in 1907. Once again, my son, Thomas C. McConnell, offered comments about the manuscript as a general reader, and my daughter, Susan Sakys, was a delightful companion during travel for research.

Sandy Crooms, a former editor at the University Press of Colorado; Laura Furney, managing editor; Daniel Pratt, production manager; and Darrin Pratt, director of the press, each offered useful guidance during the long development of this manuscript. My thanks are extended to them and to all members of the staff at the press.

INTRODUCTION

ON SEPTEMBER 14, 1867, A WRAITHLIKE FIGURE EMERGED FROM THE COLORADO River at Callville, Nevada. The wraith had a name—James White. After White had recounted his astonishing tale about the ordeal that had brought him to this place, his rescuers concluded that he had floated through the Grand Canyon on a raft of logs, and when White finally recovered his strength and his wits, he also believed so. Consequently, a very ordinary drifter became a minor celebrity surrounded by controversy in the history of the Colorado River and particularly of the Grand Canyon.

According to White's story, Charles Baker, the leader of a prospecting party that included White and two others, had allegedly been killed by Indians several hundred miles upstream roughly three weeks earlier. After Baker's demise, White and another companion, one George Strole, escaped down the river on a raft, White recounted, but within a few days Strole drowned in a rapid. Thereafter, James White was the only witness to the events he related to his audiences at Callville and elsewhere. Journalists quickly spread White's tale, and today he remains part of the lore of the American West, though not without controversy among supporters and detractors alike.

The characters in this story — White, Baker, and Strole — resist simple categorization as drifters, although they offer a sample in microcosm of the minor adventurers, rogues, and nonentities who passed across the stage of the American West during the mid-nineteenth century. This group just happened to achieve transitory notoriety — fulfilling Andy Warhol's theory that "everyone will be famous for fifteen minutes" — and became identifiable figures if not authentic heroes among the anonymous host of drifters. Otherwise, those involved in the White-Baker tale had many similarities to countless others who appeared and disappeared in the opening of the West but left few if any known facts about their origins or their fates.

About this particular group we know that prior to the trio's arrival in the Southwest, the party of White, Baker, and Strole also for a few weeks had included a chap named Joe Goodfellow, whose identity, like Strole's, is impossible to trace. We know more about the activities of Charles Baker, because for a short period during Colorado's gold rush he had enjoyed a measure of fame as the instigator of a well-recorded prospecting venture in the San Juan Mountains in 1860–1861, but earlier and later information is scant until the episode of 1867, after which none exists. A Southerner, Charles Baker had set out to make his fortune and succeeded in gathering a good-sized flock of hopeful and soon-to-be-disappointed prospectors to participate in his venture in 1860. In 1867, with only a small group of novices consisting of White, Strole, and Goodfellow, he attempted to achieve what he had failed to do with a large party the first time. On the earlier adventure, his companions had cooperated until fickle whims, discord, disappointment, rumors of better locations, accidents, and the outbreak of the Civil War sent them off in other directions. Baker disappeared for a few years and returned the worse for wear after whatever misfortunes life had dealt him in the interim. Evidently a charismatic individual, he drew together his second band, a much smaller one this time, but before finding a pot of gold at the end of his rainbow, Indians terminated his activities.

One of his recruits in the second venture, George Strole, was a barely discernable follower, identifiable only by name—and that with a choice of spellings—but without face, personality, or lines to be quoted. If he was a recent immigrant from Europe, language difficulties might have caused a lack of communication. Third in this troop was Joe Goodfellow, maybe an Englishman, traveling tourist class with rough companions who did not share his fussy ways. He did not remain with the company for long before being forcefully ejected from the group and disappearing.

Fourth, and most important in the story that will follow, was James White who was in search of who knows what. About him we know the most not because he was a distinguished player in the gold rush or the settlement of the West but because of his connection with the human history of the Grand Canyon. In his perambulations through the West, he at no time demonstrated an ambition to achieve riches or to rise above the social class into which he was born. Rather, he seems to have set out to see the West, and that he succeeded beyond any expectations will become apparent in this volume. Regardless of his original, unknown intentions, he accumulated bitter experiences from which he appeared to learn little, although in the end he saw the wisdom of giving up his roving lifestyle. Thereafter, he settled in a small city in Colorado to live out a prosaic life like thousands of working-class citizens of the late nineteenth and early twentieth centuries in the West, with only occasional reminders of his moment of renown.

Many drifters like Strole and Goodfellow contributed to their own neglect in the annals of Western American history, because they were often, though not always, illiterate and thus left few written records. Even if they could read and write, as Baker did, they tended to be closemouthed about their pasts with attendant disappointments and failures from which the West was perhaps offering an escape and a second chance. For White, writing was a struggle, minimizing nonverbal autobiographical accounts, but soon after the events of 1867 others contributed an abundance of written accounts, sometimes correct and sometimes incorrect, as they have continued to do for scores of years up to and including the present.

The hope of striking it rich during gold rushes motivated many a person to set forth on a Western odyssey in the nineteenth century, but other inducements also existed. For example, in his classic *Two*

Years before the Mast, Richard Henry Dana told a dismal tale, predating the gold rushes in the West, about a "beachcomber," also called a "California ranger," whom the writer encountered on the West Coast in the 1830s. This chap had been a tailor in Philadelphia until drink and debt prompted him to depart to escape his creditors and probably ill repute as well. During his travels, he joined a trapping party that brought him to the Columbia River, but, accumulating some earnings, he proceeded down the coast to California and lost his money while regaining his overwhelming thirst. He was a pathetic figure when Dana last saw him near Los Angeles.[1]

Dana's "California ranger" was an example of many trappers, who, though sometimes portrayed as picturesque frontiersmen, lived dangerous and lonely lives far from civilization, working for uncertain profits that were squandered at rendezvous in grand debauches. In an essay, historian William H. Goetzmann examined the question of whether mountain men were "Jacksonian expectant capitalists," a phrase coined by another historian, Richard Hofstadter. Goetzmann accepted the concept that for many the fur trade was simply a means to earn cash or a commercial opportunity, with free trappers tolerating their difficult lives in order to rise beyond the economic and social status to which they had been consigned in life. Nonetheless, Goetzmann quoted the trapper Warren Ferris, who wrote that he set out from St. Louis in 1830 with mixed feelings, for he went out of "curiosity, a love of wild adventure, and perhaps also a hope of profit, for times are hard."[2] Academic arguments notwithstanding, most students of Western American history are aware that countless mountain men never reaped enough profit to move into a higher status, and many treasured their freedom too much to return to conventional society in any case. Similar ambiguity of purpose and performance among miners, too, can be seen in a comment about prospectors in Colorado's gold rush that was printed in Denver's *Rocky Mountain News* in 1860: "The few who are moving toward Mexico and Arizona [*sic*], mainly belong to that class of people who seldom remain long in any country; very good men who are among the first and most energetic to develop the resources of the country, but seldom remain long to reap the benefits of their labor."[3]

Although the prospectors described in this newspaper article were not White, Baker, Strole, and Goodfellow themselves, similar remarks could have been said about them, and Ferris's comment about his own motivations could have been applied to thousands of other drifters who headed west in the nineteenth century. The reasons were as diverse as the individuals themselves. Modern psychologists and sociologists attempt to categorize personalities and conditions that compel people to roam — for instance, they may be described as being chronically indecisive, and, indeed, in his younger years, White displayed a lack of firm plans. Other wanderers are said to have either low self-esteem or the inflated self-confidence such as the promoter Baker seemed to exhibit. Lack of occupational skills or vicissitudes of economic conditions might have caused others to take to the road. Once on their way, they often were like the picaros of early novels who blundered from one episode to another, getting into trouble through bad luck or their own faults and getting out of it through good luck or their wits. White managed to survive with good luck, but Strole did not. The fate of Goodfellow, who appears to have possessed survival instincts but poor judgment, remains unknown. Baker, the ambitious but inept planner with deplorable timing, was not rewarded with good luck, and he paid the cost with his life.

A seemingly infinite supply of potential wanderers existed in America. The typically large families in America's colonies and on subsequent frontiers exhibited a prodigious capacity to produce offspring, and as quickly as native tribes were moved out of the way, the availability of open land west of advancing settlement absorbed this growing population, the great majority of whom were agrarians, although considerable diversity existed. Colonial families spread westward, moving from New England's frontier to upstate New York, to the Firelands of Ohio, to Indiana, Michigan, Wisconsin, Illinois, and Iowa, generation after generation. Additional emigrants came from the Middle Atlantic and Southern colonies, crossed the Appalachians into Tennessee and Kentucky, then Missouri and Texas, where immigrants from Europe soon joined them. Strole and Goodfellow might have come from families who were part of these movements or were individuals who themselves had left the Old World on their own to seek their fortunes. Southeastern states contributed many westward migrants, both before and after the Civil War, with Baker reputedly among them.[4] Nothing indicates that anyone among our four drifters, however, wished to take up land in the West and become a farmer, despite abundant free land and opportunities that expanded vastly after the enactment of the Homestead Act in 1862.

Adding to curiosity and a desire for "wild adventure," the Panic of 1857 exacerbated the economic necessity that caused many to head west.[5] Only limited opportunities were available to young men in rural, preindustrial America in the nineteenth century when the majority of the nation's population engaged in subsistence farming. Although there were jobs as crossroads merchants, as innkeepers, as blacksmiths, on stagecoach lines, and in livery stables, occupations other than tilling the soil were limited for young men in rural America. Basing our supposition on national statistics in the absence of further biographical information about Baker, Strole, and Goodfellow, we might safely assume that these three came from rural, agricultural backgrounds. If the families of Strole and Goodfellow were recent immigrants, they had possibly located first in a city and then had lived on a farm, before they set forth, fleeing plow, civilization, and or even the law. James White was an exception, as we know that his father was a carpenter, and James reached his maturity in an urban setting, the modest-sized but growing town of Kenosha, Wisconsin. Most likely, he had no hope of being financially or educationally capable of entering the commercial world or a profession. He might have chosen to become a craftsman like his father; or, in a Great Lakes port town like Kenosha, he could have worked in drayage, on a Great Lakes steamship, or at some other unskilled job. Nevertheless, in his own good time, he turned his back on Kenosha and Lake Michigan and set forth to see the West— probably out of "curiosity, a love of wild adventure, and perhaps also a hope of profit" like Ferris—although White's only working experiences until then were as a carpenter's apprentice and handler of horses or mules.

A military career was an option for some young men both prior to and following the Civil War, but not for the quartet in our narrative, it appears. During the Civil War, when millions joined the conflict, White signed up with a volunteer company in California, as did many other wanderers, and Baker is said to have seen service with the Confederate Army. In any case, neither White nor Baker remained in military service after 1865. In the next few years, during the Indian campaigns, military posts in the West became meccas for civilians like White, Strole, and Goodfellow who found work and recreation there.

Meanwhile, Baker, down on his luck and camping nearby, contemplated his next plan to get rich, needing only some gullible companions to help bring to fruition his dream of striking it rich. Baker succeeded in recruiting the other three for this purpose in 1867.

Like tidal waves, flowing and ebbing, thousands of Fifty-Niners had washed into Colorado at the time of the Pikes Peak gold rush, and earlier more thousands of Forty-Niners had swarmed into California. Such famous migrations as these were spurred by economic and personal motivations, undeterred by the forbidding geography of the American West and the challenging routes through it or around it. During California's rush, some undertook a lengthy sea voyage around Cape Horn to San Francisco, but most made arduous treks across plains, mountains, and deserts. Whether for explorers, trappers, and traders or for pioneers, gold seekers, and drifters, the most conspicuous paths west of the Mississippi and across the Great Plains paralleled the Missouri, Platte, and Arkansas Rivers. But eventually the weary, transcontinental travelers were forced to cross either arid landscapes without adequate water supplies or mountains with rugged topography. Although some traders, defying threats of starvation, thirst, and unwelcoming natives, were venturing over the sear Southern Route along the Mexican border or, more commonly, over the Spanish Trail through the Great Basin and the Mohave Desert to California, the more northerly Platte River offered an avenue for many more overland travelers to the West Coast, the Northwest, and Utah in the 1840s.

Down the immense, dry expanse west of the Rocky Mountains ran the Colorado River. On a modern map, portions of this artery might appear to afford a satisfactory route for travel, but on the land its true nature quickly corrects such notions. Not far from its source its strength is sufficient to have forced passages through mountains and mesas before it reaches the inhospitable basin country. There, in southern Utah the river is augmented by its largest tributary, the Green—itself of such volume that it once was thought to be the main stream. Beyond this confluence, the Colorado River slices ever-deeper chasms through barren rock until it disappears between the foreboding walls of the mysterious Grand Canyon. Soon after the river again emerges at the western end of the Grand Canyon it cuts south to the Gulf of California. Thus, any potential use of the Colorado River as a transcontinental route to or from California does not exist, although the lower portion of the river opens the possibility of access to and from the sea, and during the 1850s and 1860s a few formal expeditions and informal enterprises pondered the Colorado River's practicability as a navigable stream. The canyon itself was occasionally considered as a route for railroad construction, but never for long.

When the aspirations of the majority of gold seekers turned to sand and gravel in California, the ebb tide carried hundreds of failures eastward on assorted trails across the deserts and mountains in the general direction of home. Still reluctant to abandon their dreams, these persistent souls examined trails through the Southwest and around the Colorado and San Juan Rivers as they moved eastward and watched for any gleam of ore in streambeds as they went. Some of the prospectors who originally had seen gold in Georgia found traces in the area of present-day Denver and ignited the Pikes Peak gold rush.[6] Like variations on a theme, the siren song continued to lure disappointed but persistent prospectors to try their luck wherever strikes were rumored then and later—California, Nevada, Pikes Peak, South Park, the Upper Arkansas, the San Juan Mountains, the Blue River, Idaho, Montana, the San Juan River, Prescott, the Grand Canyon, Glen Canyon, El Dorado Canyon, the Northwest, Cripple Creek. And the seduction of a bonanza was not confined to the American West. Alaska, Mexico, South America, and Australia still drew prospectors like magnets even as the twentieth century was born, and in the American West isolated operations like those on the San Juan River and in the Colorado River's Glen Canyon still beckoned to diehards.

Although solitary figures were the exception, a few, preferring their own company to the competition and rowdiness found in mining camps, were tucked away here and there with their gold pans and sourdough, oddities about whom stories were told around campfires. Most, though, joined together loosely with groups of former strangers for as long as mutual protection, communal effort, or whim required, then fell away until changing circumstances led them to regroup with others. Short-lived business ventures, organized to capitalize small mining and milling operations, offered jobs to some, who, like driftwood, lingered in eddies for a while before moving on and vanishing.

To say that they were entirely forgotten would be incorrect, however, for some families whom they had left behind remembered them, wrung their hands, and occasionally waited for the return of their prodigal sons. A reminder appeared in the *Rocky Mountain News* in 1861: "Information Wanted. — Of John H. Culligan. When last heard from he was in Denver City. Any person knowing anything as to his whereabouts will grant to his mother a kind favor, by addressing a line to P. L. G., *Times Office,* Chicago, Ill. If this meets his own eye he will answer it in person."[7]

The pull was not always mutual for many nomads who were never able to adapt to conventional society and continued to roam from one place to another until ill health or age weighted down their feet and the Pearly Gates welcomed them to a permanent resting place — sans eulogy, sans monument, as seemingly occurred to Baker and Strole. Others took jobs and disappeared into the masses of humanity that made up new settlements in the West. After several years of drifting, James White settled down in Trinidad, Colorado, with a wife, worked as a drayman, and sired numerous offspring. For a half century in Trinidad, he lived a life not unlike the one he might have known in Kenosha, Wisconsin, had he remained there, although, because of his role in Colorado River lore, he escaped the anonymity shared by most settlers of towns large and small, and he assuredly had some memories unlike those of his neighbors. In imagination, one can picture the very different memories of Joe Goodfellow, living out his days in an unknown place. And what of Baker and Strole if their fates were not as White, the sole surviving witness, described them?

Individuals such as these men, however, are usually omitted in published accounts about Colorado's territorial history. Although figures vary greatly for the early years of the gold rush, it has been estimated that 25,000 to 30,000 thronged into Colorado Territory in 1860, although only a small fraction of their names and experiences have appeared in publications, and those usually briefly, like flotsam washed ashore by a flood before floating away into obscurity. The history of the American West has slighted this cast of supporting characters who wandered across the stage, whereas a few more successful or at least more conspicuous people, deemed by historians to be more worthy of posterity on the printed page, were given the lead roles. Some of these men, and occasionally women, did find a fortune, large or small, in the mines. More often, though, they made money *from* miners, accumulated capital and prestige, established schools and churches, practiced law and medicine, created a body of laws to benefit their own interests, and had their names carved on tombstones.[8]

Meanwhile, countless unknown people, toting their belongings on their own backs, horses, or mules, vanished. Their obscurity has deprived researchers, writers, and readers of many tales that lie between the lines of the often-recorded dramas and has left countless stories untold, hidden behind the stage scenery. Refusing to be pigeonholed in academically contrived models about the opening of the West, these were real people with their own reasons for doing whatever darned fool thing came into their heads, and their presence should not be overlooked.

Resources for learning about some of these people and their experiences can be found in the publications and manuscript collections about pioneer settlers located in local libraries and museums. Often, unfortunately, researchers will find pioneer accounts to be tainted with folklore and reported with a dollop of wishful thinking rather than with trustworthy information, as the appendix to this book demonstrates. Reflecting the not-uncommon tendency of old-timers to gain personal luster by claiming association with well-known events or names, like Charles Baker or James White, some narrators tended to inflate their own activities. Adding to this human tendency, the mystique of the Grand Canyon has encouraged lively emotional, rather than objective, debates about exploits of figures like White and Powell for well over a century.

Folklore does not require a rewriting of history, but fascinating stories offer new insights about migration in the West and the motivations and experiences of the wide diversity of those who participated, some of whom eventually became settlers—the matrix of pioneer settlement—while others simply disappeared. We should acknowledge that these wandering souls could be found in large numbers wherever and whenever the right conditions existed. In the American West of the mid-1800s, the place and the time were right. People like James White and Charles Baker, George Strole and Joe Goodfellow, warrant a few lines in the story. What follows tells their tale.

DRIFTING
WEST

ONE

SEDUCTION

JAMES WHITE, AT AGE THIRTY, WAS GETTING PAST THE SPRINGTIME OF LIFE WHEN he set out in 1867 to strike it rich in the San Juan Mountains with Charles Baker, George Strole, and Joe Goodfellow. White had already been drifting around the West for six years, experiencing a variety of adventures and calamities, but he had still missed out on prospecting with a party of gold seekers. And one bit of wisdom that he had still not learned, despite several opportunities to do so, was the proverb "Believe nothing of what you hear and half of what you see." Neither had his fellow seekers of treasure.

Baker, the leader of their venture, was speaking an approximation of the truth when he told a ragtag audience at Fort Dodge in southwestern Kansas that he knew quite a lot about the mining country in Colorado Territory — firsthand, not just from rumor. What he did not tell them was that he left with no reward but with some opprobrium after his previous venture. He had joined the Pikes Peak gold rush in 1860 when hordes, brimming with optimism about their golden future, flocked to the mountains. Some say even more than 30,000, many with "Pikes Peak or Bust" emblazoned on their wagons, had rushed west. They swarmed into the placers around Denver, Auraria, Clear Creek, Gregory Gulch, Boulder, and South Park, believing that all that was required was a pick, a shovel, a gold pan, and possibly a sluice and rocker knocked together on the spot to equip a prospector for making his fortune overnight. A map? Gushing with promises of easy rewards, guidebooks offered approximations of geography and trails, and old Indian paths were soon worn into roads by packtrains and wagons.

As prospects near the Front Range were staked, the streambeds and gravel bars farther on in the Upper Arkansas River Valley beckoned gold seekers. There they tried their hands first around Cache Creek, near today's Granite, and next at California Gulch, near the later silver mines of Leadville. Among the hopefuls at the gold diggings in 1860 was Charles Baker. Others included people like Horace and Augusta Tabor and Stephen B. Kellogg. An account by Augusta Tabor offers an unvarnished picture of life at placers in the Upper Arkansas. The Tabors had arrived in Denver from Kansas in 1859 with a small baby, and, after sampling the placers around Idaho Springs, they headed farther into the mountains. She wrote:

> When we got to Cache Creek we stopped one month. My husband whip-sawed some lumber to make sluice boxes and put them in. We found plenty of gold but there was so much black sand and we did not know how to separate it. . . . I would work all day long picking it out with a little magnet, and when night came I would not have a pennyweight it was so fine. Afterwards those mines turned out to be very rich, if we had stayed right there we would have had enough. It is owned by capitalists now, 20 miles below California Gulch. . . . We were the first there. . . . Three gentlemen, Nathaniel Maxey, S. P. Kellogg [Stephen B. Kellogg], Mr. Tabor and myself and baby.[1]

After the Tabors and their companions left Cache Creek and moved up to California Gulch, where others were experiencing more successful panning, Horace and Augusta in due time accumulated "a nice little fortune," as she wrote. Other early prospectors were not so fortu-

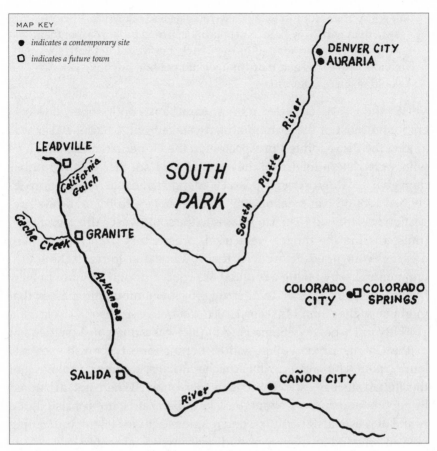

MAP KEY

● indicates a contemporary site

◻ indicates a future town

DENVER CITY
AURARIA

LEADVILLE

California Gulch

SOUTH PARK

South Platte River

Cache Creek

GRANITE

Arkansas

COLORADO CITY ● ◻ COLORADO SPRINGS

SALIDA ◻

CAÑON CITY

River

Prospecting in the Upper Arkansas River region, 1860.

nate in finding gold, but men, ill-equipped for the rugged life, found a measure of comfort if they could inveigle a woman to cook for them. As Augusta pointed out:

> Really the women did more in the early days than the men. There was so much for them to do, the sick to take care of. I have had so many unfortunate men shot by accident, brought to my cabin to take care of. There were so many men who could not cook and did not like men's cooking and would insist upon boarding where there was a woman. . . .
>
> I never saw a country settled up with such greenhorns as Colorado. They were mostly from farms and some clerks. They were

3

all young men from 18 to 30. I was there a good many years before I saw a man with grey hair. . . . Thousands turned back. We met them every day and they advised us to go back; but we started with six months provisions and thought if we did not find anything here we would go on to California.[2]

As thousands crowded onto stream banks and slopes, latecomers found most of the ground already staked out. Charles Baker was among the disappointed prospectors in the Upper Arkansas diggings who were determined that they would find another location rather than give up. Rumors, gossip, and sometimes reliable information circulated around camps about the next best place to try, and one suggestion was the San Juan Mountains to the southwest. Although rough trails crossing the ranges were tried, prospectors from the northern diggings concluded before long that it was easier to reach the southern mountains by taking a roundabout route through Abiquiú in New Mexico Territory rather than struggling over mountain passes that might be higher than 11,000 or 12,000 feet above sea level.

Fifty miles north of Santa Fe, Abiquiú was a dusty little settlement in the Chama River Valley with a population of Spanish-speaking landowners, Ute and Jicarilla Apache Indians, traders, employees of the Indian agency, and U.S. Army personnel. When not disrupted by reports and rumors about Navajo Indian raids, life consisted of a round of seasonal agricultural and religious activities, with the trading post and the Indian agency providing grimy social centers.

When gold was discovered in Colorado in 1858, the news came as no surprise in Abiquiú. For nearly a century before the Pikes Peak gold rush, rumors had circulated about minerals in the neighboring San Juan and La Plata Mountains. In the mid-1800s, these peaks were in Utah Territory, a technicality easily ignored because New Mexico possessed the nearest and most feasible access into the region. But, deep in the land of *poco tiempo,* Abiquiú was hardly an incubator of adventurers bent on exploiting the mountains' mineral wealth. For one thing, Indians to the west and north of the Chama River Valley habitually behaved in an unfriendly manner. Moreover, in the 1700s, when Abiquiú first was settled, the Spanish government had restricted exploration and trade, although local men occasionally undertook surreptitious ventures ending sometimes with a summons to appear before a magistrate and pay fines. As a result, until after Mexican inde-

4

pendence in 1821, history records few names of traders or prospectors who actually traveled beyond the Chama River Valley.

In the 1700s, however, a Ute Indian had brought some silver to Abiquiú to trade, making the presence of precious metals in the mountains known. This lump of silver purportedly passed into the hands of an artisan in Santa Fe, who fashioned two rosaries and a cross from it. Thus, when Juan Maria Antonio Rivera's expedition of exploration was authorized to travel northwest from Santa Fe in 1765, not only was the presence of silver known but the party also was hoping to locate its source. Their route was the old Indian trail that became part of the Old Spanish Trail, through the Chama River Valley to the region of present-day Durango, Colorado, and farther west. Rivera passed the southern flank of the nearby range that he called the *Sierra La Plata*, the "Silver Mountains," and his journal entry from July 5 reveals that, after crossing the Animas River to its west bank, his party visited a Ute village where he hoped to find Cuero de Lobo, an Indian who previously had shown him a piece of silver. Cuero de Lobo was not there, but the Indians told him that Cuero's daughter, in another village, could provide information about the source of the silver. Unfortunately, the woman was not in a congenial mood. She lied that Cuero was dead and that she did not know where the silver had been found. Informed about her duplicity, Rivera continued on in search of Cuero de Lobo, but in vain.[3]

Not many years later, in 1776 the expedition of Fray Francisco Atencio Domínguez and Fray Silvestre Velez de Escalante set out on the same route that Rivera had traveled. With hearts firmly fixed on the work of their church, particularly the goal of finding a route between Catholic missions in New Mexico and California, the two padres did not waste time searching for silver. Single-mindedly, they ignored an Indian guide who previously had been with Rivera and who told them about a nearby vein that had, he claimed, been found in 1765. After 1776 it would have been indeed surprising if Spaniards less spiritually motivated than Escalante and Domínguez had not searched for silver in the La Platas and San Juans, following the route of the Spanish Trail. Escalante and Domínguez's intended goal, California, also eluded them, but during their return to Santa Fe, blocked by the impediments of the canyon country, the padres forded the Colorado River in Glen Canyon at an Indian passage that became known thereafter as the Crossing of the Fathers.[4]

5

Exploration did not follow for decades, however. After Mexican independence, trade and travel through Abiquiú increased, as did U.S. military forces during and after the Mexican War. In the 1840s the Army of the West, en route to California, marched down the Gila River, crossed the Lower Colorado, and reported the natural resources they saw. In the late 1840s and 1850s, surveys for transcontinental railroads were undertaken by expeditions of John Charles Frémont, John W. Gunnison, and others, so possible routes through the West were becoming known, along with frustration about the obstacle posed by the Grand Canyon. By the late 1850s, Lieutenant Joseph C. Ives was probing the Lower Colorado River and Captain John N. Macomb was looking at the upper reaches.

Propagandists for American expansion, with the support of capitalists and politicians, were touting the West's glorious resources and economic opportunities, with one of the enthusiastic spokesmen being William Gilpin, who participated in the U.S. Army's Indian campaigns in New Mexico and had led troops from a garrison at Abiquiú into the San Juan Mountains in pursuit of Navajo raiders. In the Chama River Valley he most likely heard local chatter about minerals in the mountains, and he, in fact, saw some minerals firsthand while he was in the field. Thus, when the Pikes Peak excitement exploded farther north, Gilpin was eager to assert that the southern mountains also possessed precious metals. In 1858 he proclaimed them to form a "metalliferous band of metals" and "a veritable arcana of the Mountain Formation and its metalliferous elements."[5] Such bombast would help propel Gilpin into the office of governor of Colorado Territory when it was created, and it fanned excitement among prospectors.

California's gold rush also had helped to spread interest in the region. A portion of the throng of Forty-Niners had passed westward through the Four Corners region and, following similar routes a few years later, were drifting eastward with their tattered outfits, panning streams and examining gravel bars as they went. (One of these itinerants was "Captain" John Moss, who had been working for San Francisco's mining investors around the Lower Colorado River. After seeing something of promise in the La Platas in 1856, Moss established Parrott City in the La Platas in the 1860s, while he was in the employ of investors at San Francisco.) These Forty-Niners did, in fact, spot some color. Famously, other prospectors on their eastward trek from

6

California discovered gold around present-day Denver and inaugurated the Pikes Peak gold rush.

When word about the Pikes Peak rush reached New Mexico, the southerly region awoke to its own opportunities at last. Prominent among the boosters was the territory's *Santa Fe Weekly Gazette*, eager to tout the area's commercial establishments, which might benefit economically. News soon traveled to Abiquiú, where a few residents looked forward to profiting from the traffic that they hoped would pass the doorsteps of the trading post, the center for exchanging the exciting news. Until then, this establishment had conducted business primarily with local folks, Indians, the agency, and traders on the Spanish Trail who had few other options than to purchase whatever merchandise was on hand and to pay whatever price was being extorted.

Henry Mercure, a French Canadian, was one who quickly recognized the commercial opportunities that the mining excitement would bring. With his name sometimes appearing as "Henri" or even "Don Enrique," he was the younger brother of a merchant, Joseph Mercure, of Santa Fe who had stores in Taos and Abiquiú. The brothers did business with Indian agencies, a profitable opportunity for merchants wherever agencies existed. The Mercures recognized that in the mining excitement, Abiquiú's adobe village could be a place where prospectors would gather and, of course, purchase supplies.[6]

Another fellow who hoped to gain from the rush was Albert Pfeiffer. After emigrating from Germany in the 1840s, Pfeiffer had worked his way west by hiring on with a freighting outfit on the Santa Fe Trail. He spent a few years in Santa Fe, where he and Henry Mercure became friends and where Pfeiffer met the lovely Antonia Salinas, whom he married. Thanks, no doubt, to his friendship with Kit Carson, who was the Indian agent at Taos, Pfeiffer became agent at the subagency of Abiquiú. In the Pfeiffer household in the Chama River Valley were Antonia's child from a previous marriage and the infant son of Albert and Antonia, plus several adult servants and young Indian captives who also were domestic workers, as was typical in the homes of northern New Mexico.[7]

In the late 1850s, Pfeiffer's agency at Abiquiú was serving Capote and Tabeguache Utes and Jicarilla Apaches, who received rations and idled away considerable time there. From time to time the agent was also called upon to lead expeditions to locate those who failed to report dutifully and to retrieve stolen livestock from Navajos who plagued the area's rancheros, but he spent many tedious hours tending to paperwork required by the superintendent in Santa Fe. Like many Indian agents, Pfeiffer kept a bottle handy in his desk drawer to assuage boredom and a thirst that would eventually make him a full-fledged alcoholic.

His strengths, however, were his knowledge of Indians, the San Juan Mountains, and outdoor skills, honed during his pursuit of his wayward subjects. These talents served him well when Captain John N. Macomb, leading an expedition of the U.S. Army's topographical engineers in the summer of 1859, called upon Pfeiffer to accompany him on his survey to locate a route for the passage of troops through the region. From Abiquiú to the hot springs at Pagosa in Colorado and then west toward the Animas River, Pfeiffer accompanied Macomb. With them also went Henry Mercure, an interpreter named Neponocio Valdez from the agency, and others of the village. Their route was the now-familiar Spanish Trail.

After Pfeiffer and his friends had left the expedition, Captain Macomb's report says, "[We] passed along the southern base of the mountain group known as 'Sierra de la Plata'; hence in a northwesterly direction for about one hundred and twenty miles, over gloomy barrens." Along the way, geologist J. S. Newberry climbed onto Mesa Verde, described the sweeping landscape to the west, but missed spotting the archaeological wonders for which the mesa later became famous. Printed with Macomb's report, Newberry did, however, provide information about copper mining near Abiquiú and the hot springs at Pagosa, as well as archaeological ruins in the area of the Animas River. About the geology of the La Plata Mountains, Newberry wrote that metalliferous veins existed and asserted that, "doubtless," silver and gold existed there:

> At least there is better promise of the discovery of the precious metals in these mountains than in any others we have visited since leaving the Rio Grande. The name given by the Spaniards to this great sierra, Silver Mountains, would seem to indicate that at some time silver had been found there, but I cannot learn that any definite knowledge is possessed by the Mexicans or the Indians of the existence of metallic veins such as would justify their choice of a title so significant.[8]

Pfeiffer, Mercure, and their neighbors had a pretty good idea of the silver's significance and of the presence of gold besides. They also understood that the road past their village from the confluence of the Chama River with the Rio Grande and on northwest to the mines would enhance their own economic opportunities, and they recognized that the Spanish Trail beyond Abiquiú was inadequate for the hordes whom they anticipated to arrive as soon as the mining fever heated up. A road suitable for wagons loaded with provisions and equipment would be needed, and a go-getter could charge tolls just for hacking down a few trees, prying out the largest rocks, filling the deepest holes, and throwing down some logs across streams for bridges. Moreover, storekeepers along the way would profit.

In the path of newcomers in the Rockies, there were, in addition to obstructions like trees and boulders, Native Americans who objected to having their homeland invaded by prospectors. A letter published in Denver's *Rocky Mountain News* in November 1859 reported a warning from Kit Carson:

> I was requested by Kit Carson, Government Agent for the Ute
> Indians, to say to the miners here that he hoped to visit this region
> next spring, with several leading "braves" of the tribe, to conclude
> a permanent peace between them and the whites. He deems this
> very desirable, as the Utes are the most dangerous of the mountain
> Indians, excellent shots with the rifle, and if hostile, will be likely to
> destroy many small prospecting parties and solitary travelers next
> season.[9]

Disregarding such warnings, during the spring of 1860 the *Santa Fe Weekly Gazette* printed notes that Pfeiffer and Mercure provided about gold deposits they saw during their travels in the San Juans, and the resulting publicity spurred prospectors to hurry south from the placers in Colorado. While Santa Fe's newspaper and commercial enterprises boosted the interests of its region, editorials in Denver's *Rocky Mountain News* regularly discredited its rivals to the south, where prospectors and business might be lured away from the boom in its own area. Golden's *Western Mountaineer* also was keeping its readers abreast of news from the southern mountains.

Among the prospectors who were hearing these good tidings was Charles Baker, one of the hundreds of disappointed prospectors at California Gulch. Augusta Tabor was only partly correct in lumping

9

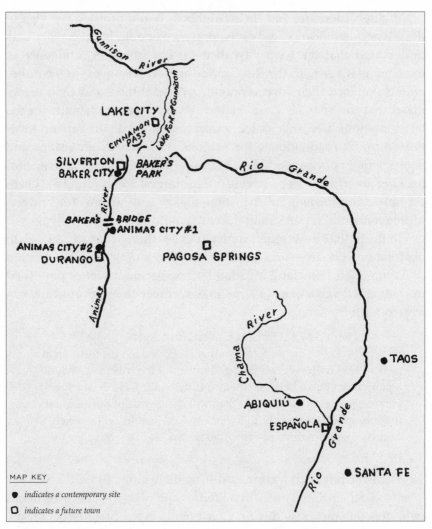

Activities in southern Colorado and northern New Mexico, 1860–1861, related to prospecting in the San Juan Mountains.

defeated prospectors as "go-backs" who went home. Like many others, when Baker gave up on California Gulch, he did not go back to wherever he had come from, but he continued to look elsewhere, as did other thwarted gold seekers who went north, west, and south in their quest, venturing to the nearby Blue River and farther afield throughout the Rockies, even across the Colorado Plateau. Some looked over the prospects in New Mexico's distant Gila River country and silver prospects in Arizona, destinations that Baker must have filed away in his head for future reference if the mountains failed to pan out.

One of the most ambitious of the explorations made by resolute prospectors in 1860 was a roundabout journey down what was then called the Grand River, the portion of the Colorado River north of its confluence with the Green. At this point, they gave up and eventually wound back through the northern San Juan Mountains. In a lengthy report that appeared in the *Rocky Mountain News,* D. C. Collier extolled the minerals as well as the rugged scenery of these mountains. Although handicapped by cold and stormy weather in the San Juans, Collier reported that he and his companions saw many quartz seams. "Innumerable lodes cropped out on either side" of the headwaters of the Rio Grande, he said. His report caught the attention of prospectors who were still lingering in the camps around Denver, South Park, and the Upper Arkansas during the autumn of 1860, hoping for something better.[10]

Such news inspired faith in the "great central gold belt," theorized by professed experts to be a 300-mile-long band running on a southwest-northeast tangent through Colorado's mountains. In addition to the portions of the territory originally inundated with prospectors, this zone included the headwaters of the Gunnison River, the San Juan Mountains, and the La Platas. During the summer of 1860 these areas began to entice disappointed prospectors as well as some who had enjoyed enough success to whet their appetites for more. Among the former was Charles Baker, and among the latter was Stephen B. Kellogg, Augusta Tabor's acquaintance from Cache Creek and California Gulch.

An account of these beginnings was reported from Lake City, Colorado, in the *Weekly Rocky Mountain News* in 1877. The sources for the newspaper article were S. B. Kellogg and Mrs. Tom Pollock, who were in a party that joined Baker in the San Juans in 1860–1861. (Several years later this rather well-known newspaper article was repeated by Frank Hall without attribution in his *History of Colorado*). It related:

> In 1860 California Gulch was swarming with placer miners; among
> them were S. B. Kellogg & Co., who owned some of the rich ground
> and took out large amounts of gold, and Charles Baker, a rest-
> less, impecunious man who was always in search of something

new. He entertained extravagant opinions of the richness of the country beyond, and at last prevailed upon Mr. Kellogg and F. R. Rice to outfit him for a prospecting expedition. He set out in July, 1860, to explore the San Juan country, — meaning the country along the San Juan River. Six men went with him, of whom three were Cunningham, Bloomfield and Mason. The names of the others are forgotten. Baker reported to Kellogg from time to time, and finally that they had found diggings that paid twenty-five cents to the pan.[11]

Years later Kellogg himself summed up his opinions about Baker with the comment that he did what he did better than anything else — promoting an enterprise for others to subsidize with provisions and labor, but, so far, Baker still enjoyed the confidence of his backers. Somewhere else, this charismatic individual might have been found successfully selling patent medicine or newfangled Singer sewing machines. Today, he might be a motivational speaker. In 1861 he was organizing prospectors to find riches at new diggings.

Baker's original group consisted of twenty-one who started out from the Upper Arkansas and split into two parties in the Gunnison River area, with Baker and six companions going south to investigate the Lake Fork of the Gunnison River, then considered the main source of the Gunnison. (Lake City and its silver mines, which boomed several years later, are on the Lake Fork of the Gunnison.) From there, Baker and his cohorts crossed the alpine heights of Cinnamon Pass into the drainage of the Animas River, El Rio de Las Animas Perdidas, the "River of Lost Souls," as Spanish explorers had named it. Calling the San Juan Mountains the La Platas, Baker reported finding quartz leads all the way from the Lake Fork down the Animas in gulches and gravel bars where rich gold mines would be located. Baker's enthusiastic companions were sufficiently convinced by the prospects that they decided to return during the winter of 1860–1861 with a larger enterprise, which became known as the Baker Expedition.

When Baker and his little band arrived in late summer 1860, they were not discoverers but followers of a vanguard that already was ensconced on the Animas River. By early autumn 1860, Baker made his way from the Animas River to Abiquiú in the Chama River Valley. There he encountered Henry Mercure and, soon, Pfeiffer as well. These gentlemen were reputed to be the principal sources of information for others who had passed through the settlement during late summer and early autumn. From Abiquiú, Baker sent an enthusiastic report about the activities to newspapers, which circulated this information in Santa Fe, Denver, and Golden. In this account he pointed out that access from the north was not suitable, but in the southern portion of the region wonderful opportunities existed not only for mining but also for agriculture. He advocated that the area should be reached from New Mexico, and he described the steps that he and others were already taking to establish legal claims:

> In the absence of Mr. A. H. Pfeiffer, the Indian Agent, I met with a cordial reception from H. Mercure, who kindly furnished me with all the necessary information, and in ten days after we reached the mines, about one hundred and seventy-five miles distant from Abiquiu, over the only good practical road to this district of Country — organized in accordance with the usual mining customs — claimed a town site in a beautiful park in the center of the mining district, and organized it [Baker City, in Baker's Park, where Silverton later came into existence]. Having accomplished the object of our mission, and the falling snow and scarcity of provisions warning us of the necessity of departing, a portion of my men returned directly to Abiquiu. A few others and myself went to San Miguil [San Miguel River], thence to the Dolores and Rio de los Marcus [Mancos River]. Here learning that Mr. A. H. Pfeiffer had kindly consented to accompany Capt. Dodd's company in quest of me, I found them upon the Rio de los Animos, stopping at the base of the mountain in consequence of falling snow. . . . [At] the upper margin of a magnificently beautiful agricultural valley of great extent, is located Animos City, at present containing a population of from three to five hundred men. [This location was about ten miles north of a later town that also was called Animas City, adjacent to today's Durango.] At the Pogoso (the great Boiling Springs) [Pagosa Springs] is claimed and organized the city of Pogoso. [This claim was made by the local men who accompanied Macomb.] On all the tributaries of the Rio San Juan, and upon the Rio San Juan itself, is to be found a large extent of arable land.
>
> There will not be less than twenty-five thousand Americans engaged in mining and agricultural pursuits upon the waters of the Rio San Juan within a year from the present writing, and perhaps double that number. Justice to New Mexico requires that the territory should be the direct beneficiary of the development of these mines. If you desire the city of Santa Fe to be a mining metropolis,

13

and a point upon a great national life of commerce, you occupy that natural position, but prompt and energetic action is necessary to secure it. You have to compete with capital, energy and men familiar with these things.

The establishment of a private mail from the mines to a connection with the United States mail, to be succeeded by a reliable express for the transmission of gold, is an immediate necessity. It will be either by way of Denver City or by way of Santa Fe. The people of Santa Fe can say which route will be selected.

Very respectfully yours,
CHARLES BAKER[12]

Author Marshall Sprague has proposed that Baker was promoting New Mexico because his sympathies lay with Confederate interests.[13] Although some New Mexicans might have had such inclinations, they surely were not shared by Pfeiffer, who served faithfully in the U.S. Army in subsequent years and was a business associate of Baker. The Captain Dodd referred to in Baker's letter to the press joined the Union forces during the Civil War. What can be said with confidence about Baker's ambitions is that he hoped, even expected, to make his personal fortune. Unquestionably, New Mexico Territory was hoping for a similar outcome for its commercial interests, too.

Meanwhile, Colorado's *Western Mountaineer* and *Rocky Mountain News* were mentioning the departure of many prospectors to the southern mines. Most used the route passing through northern New Mexico. Observing that several large groups of prospectors were heading to the San Juans, the *News* reported in mid-October that a "Mr. Marshall" came into the office to show nuggets from the San Juans before he headed back. A few days later thirty set out, and within a week T. G. Mark was leading seventy-five south. On October 24, Richard Sopris wrote home from Fort Garland in the San Luis Valley that his party of sixteen had arrived at the fort safely and that another group, including Doc Arnold, had come in "in excellent health and spirits." These prospectors were able to purchase goods at the sutler's store at Fort Garland. Although the Sopris group traveled from the fort by way of the most common route, southwesterly across the San Luis Valley and then to the Chama River and Abiquiú, the Arnold party crossed Cochetopa Pass to the Gunnison and the headwaters of the Lake Fork of the Gunnison and then to the Animas River.

Possibly some of these itinerants had heard Baker's enthusiastic reports by word of mouth before they appeared in newspapers or from other sources. At any rate, Baker's name soon was appearing in the printed stories, and some of these reports took on a distinctly negative tone, for prospectors were beginning to send back discouraging observations about what they found in the San Juans. Whereas Baker had claimed that the diggings yielded twenty-five cents to the pan, others grumbled that they were finding only four or five cents' worth, and, of course, Denver's press was pleased to repeat any such disparagements about the rival mines to the south.

As headquarters for the boom, Abiquiú also came in for some harsh criticism in the press, even in Santa Fe. Baker had written that Albert Pfeiffer and Henry Mercure were the important men to see not only for directions to the mines but also for supplies, but Abiquiú's competitors claimed that supplies should be obtained at Santa Fe or Taos because of the inferior inventory at Abiquiú's trading post. Predictably, the *Rocky Mountain News* also did its best to debunk the village. In one of its stories, the *News* wrote that the traders had promoted their village as a means of selling excess goods that were on hand due to slow sales among local residents. Another sarcastic appraisal read:

> Abiquiu is a miserable Mexican village with supplies, and the very worst starting point at which to start over the mountains. Taos, on the north [sic], or Santa Fe, on the south are either much better. They [the trading post in the Chama Valley] are obliged to send to Santa Fe for supplies. Unbolted flour was ten dollars per 100 lbs. Mr. S. [Sopris] describes the country as the most dreary, God-forsaken one he ever saw. He thinks it must be the one which was offered by his Satanic majesty to tempt the Savior, and that it was no wonder he refused it. A number of small parties had come in after them, and all had banded together for mutual protection, and organized an independent company, sixty or seventy strong, with which to penetrate the Navajoe country.[14]

"Navajoe Country" meant, most likely, the San Juan River region, where prospectors might encounter hostile Indians, but such was the ignorance or naiveté of gold seekers. Danger existed even along the Chama River route that led close to Navajo territory and into the lands occupied by Ute Indians, about whom Kit Carson had warned. For protection, prospectors recognized the importance of banding together for mutual aid on the trail, and a number of parties lingered at Abiquiú, where they gathered supplies and courage and saw to the needs of their livestock, wagons, and mining equipment before moving on.

Meanwhile, traffic was increasing to the mines north of Abiquiú during the autumn, and a passable road was becoming an immediate necessity as well as an attractive opportunity for investors. When David McShane arrived at Abiquiú in the fall of 1860, he noted that wagons could go no farther, and oxen then were pressed into service as pack animals. To alleviate transportation problems, in late 1860 Pfeiffer, Mercure, Baker, and others organized the Abiquiu, Pagosa, and Baker City Road Company.[15] Legislation for it was passed in Santa Fe and signed by the governor in December.[16]

Several of the ambitious incorporators of this enterprise had personal business interests that would be furthered by this undertaking. After Pfeiffer and company traveled with Macomb's survey, they had incorporated the Pagosa Town Association and staked out a square-mile townsite, where they expected that mining development would spur settlement. Indeed, squatters eventually began to live around Pagosa Springs, while Pfeiffer protested to no avail. Of course, Baker also wanted to provide a road all the way to his own townsite, Baker City in Baker's Park, the proposed terminus of the road and titular seat of a proposed San Juan County. Although he had claimed land for his town by following the procedures for filing a mining claim, claim jumpers could easily pull up the stakes he had planted if he failed to get his settlement started quickly. At Conejos in Colorado another organizer of the road was Agent Lafayette Head — Indian agent, flour miller, and store owner — who stood to benefit from having travelers pass through the San Luis Valley to reach Abiquiú. Having been a trader at Abiquiú previously, Head knew all about a shortcut from Conejos through the hills to Tierra Amarilla on the Chama River, but the longer route had business advantages. Still another investor in the toll road project was George Bute, who sent word to the press about the road's progress. He told of the laying of "bridges," although, in fact, the bridges consisted merely of a few logs across streams like the Pinos River.

One of these bridges was located at Animas City, where the river narrowed between rock ledges to provide support for a few sturdy logs. This span was given the name Baker's Bridge. Frightening as the crossing might have seemed, it was an important one. Over the years,

Within a few years, a new Baker's Bridge replaced the original log crossing of the Animas River, and three more increasingly solid spans followed. The first Animas City was on the east side of the river near the first crossing. Author's collection, drawing by Yvonne Halburian, based on photos in La Plata County Historical Society Collections.

at least four bridges have replaced the original Baker's Bridge, the location of which is on County Road 250 near Pinkerton Hot Springs, north of the mouth of Hermosa Creek. Animas City was located on the east side of the Animas River near this bridge and consisted of tents and a few brush shelters in late 1860. Beyond this point, anyone going to the mines went on foot with packtrains until winter's snow dictated the use of backpacks, snowshoes, and sleds.

Neither the approach of winter nor disagreeable reports in Denver's newspapers deterred determined gold seekers. Remembering the enthusiasm about the southern mines, Wolfe Londoner later reminisced that "a man named Baker, who came up with glowing accounts of immense deposits of gold in the streams of the San Juan . . . went around throughout the mining camps and told his story and got a great many converts."[17]

Londoner, more loquacious than particular about facts, was operating a store at Cañon City at the time. In later years he boasted that in the autumn of 1860 "at least 5,000 miners" passed through his town. Some of these travelers might have been latecomers who were heading into the mining camps of South Park and the Upper Arkansas, which Cañon City served as a supply town, but the number claimed by Londoner still appears inflated. Nevertheless, his fellow boosters began constructing a road southward to Fort Garland in the San Luis Valley as a "shortcut" to the San Juans.

As Londoner described the emigrants, they outfitted at Cañon City and left "in very good style" with mining tools, quicksilver, pack animals, wagons, nice mule teams, and enough provisions to last them through the winter. "It was those men who had made a great deal of money during the first year of the mining excitement in the mountains where they had struck good diggings, and they laid out all their gold dust for supplies, thinking all they had to do was to go down and strike 'Baker's Park,' as we called it, and dig it up by the shovel full."[18]

Some who planned to go to the San Juans wisely holed up at places like Denver or Taos to await spring, but diehards, who otherwise might have passed for sane men, wanted to arrive as quickly as possible in order to stake out claims before the rush that was expected after winter snows melted. Although Baker said that 300 to 500 people were at Animas City in the fall of 1860, another person expanded the population to 1,000, still leaving a great many of Londoner's 5,000 unaccounted for. Some may have continued beyond Animas City with their pack animals, but, as snow became deep during the winter of 1860–1861, traffic to Baker's Park dwindled, while prospectors who went back and forth between the placers and Animas City kept the snowy trail packed to whatever extent was possible.

Ignoring meteorological realities about the San Juans and the pessimistic warnings of the *Rocky Mountain News*'s editor that snow already was accumulating in the San Juans, a party of at least 100 men, women, and children headed for the San Juans in December 1860. This star-crossed enterprise has become known as the Baker Expedition.

Although Baker was the principal promoter, he was not its actual leader on the trail. Two of the men in the group were Kellogg and Rice, previously introduced as grubstakers for Baker's earlier reconnaissance in 1860. Kellogg had such faith in the enterprise that he sold a good claim in California Gulch for $17,000, or so he said, and rushed back to Wisconsin to fetch his wife, Abby, and their ten-year-old daughter so the family could take part together in the grand adventure in the San Juans. Mrs. Rice also joined her husband. Because he was a respected figure in Denver, Kellogg's enthusiasm probably convinced some others to participate, but editor William Byers at the *Rocky Mountain News* may have felt misgivings when he reported on December 7, "Our long time friend, Kellogg, has our thanks for a beautiful quartz crystallization from the San Juan mountains, laid upon our table yesterday." Byers may have feared that he never would see his "long time friend" again.

On December 14 the Baker Expedition left Denver, and on December 31, seventeen days after their departure, "C.W." (C. Wiltse) wrote a letter in Abiquiú that roundly criticized Baker and his promotion of the San Juans. The letter, however, did not appear in the *News* until mid-January, long after the party was on its way. C.W.'s letter began, "Reports from the San Juan (Baker) mines are at present very discouraging. Stock has fallen one hundred and fifty per cent at least, and there are few here who believe that there is anything there to pay."[19]

Continuing with his report, obtained from twenty-three experienced men, C.W. said that they had seen "prospect holes, a large bar and several gulches staked off, a saw pit, and a harness which Baker had left" in the Baker's Park area. At the "big hole," where prospects had been touted as ranging from $2.50 down to $0.35, the men knew they were at the right place because it was identified by a ditch that was about 100 feet long. Panning there yielded "three very fine specks" worth about twelve cents.

Another group that came into Abiquiú from Animas City reported that they had found only worthless diggings. As C.W. wrote, they believed "that Baker is either deceived himself, or the most outrageous deceiver that ever lived." Moreover, the debunkers could not believe rumors that Baker and his friends had spent $3,000 to get a charter for their toll road and then another $2,000 on groceries to take to the mining country. C.W. himself sympathized with the prospectors who had found Baker's diggings to be worthless:

> [They had] traveled six hundred miles to learn the truth of the reported discoveries. Many had spent their last dollar, and consequently would exert the last extreme to succeed; and they have come out so perfectly well satisfied that no report, however well intentioned, will induce them to return.

19

Merely a flat space between the San Juan and La Plata Mountains in the early 1870s, when this photograph was made, Baker's Park became the site of the town of Silverton when lode mining drew hundreds into the area in 1874–1875. Courtesy, Denver Public Library, Western History Collection.

This result has naturally created a very bitter feeling against Baker; and unless he shows some better discoveries, from which he has made his wide spread reports, he will have to take very good care of himself, or there will be less of those who bear the name Baker.

Our own party have camped here [at Abiquiú] and sent in to ascertain from Baker himself, where he has any other discoveries; and if he has, which we think very doubtful, to go on, and if not to return, considering ourselves badly sold; and I shall return, with the resolve never to believe another report of gold discoveries from a human being, but to set them down immediately as lies—base, unfounded lies—and will be correct ninety nine times out of every hundred. If this is a humbug—and there is but little doubt about it—it is a severe one, and disastrous to many.

This country will be thoroughly prospected next summer, and it is my opinion if there is anything to be found, it will be down in the Navajoe country; and that is barely possible. The disappointed miners are, many of them, turning their attention to the Navajoes, and are trying to raise a party, and probably will bet quite a number to go down there principally for the purpose of plunder.[20]

In a letter printed in the *News* on December 12, Richard Sopris also commented that some of the prospectors had "organized an independent company, sixty or seventy strong, with which to penetrate the Navajoe country." Another correspondent sent the *News* a negative report in January 1861. He said that he had gone to the diggings in the area of Baker's Park, where he found some claims and holes and a drainage ditch, but he learned of no rewards in the form of gold. Disenchanted prospectors were abandoning Animas City, he said, while a rumor appeared in the *News* that Baker had been hanged.[21]

Unaware of these dismal reports, the 100 or more men, women, and children of the Baker Expedition were plodding southward to New Mexico. They had left Denver with ox teams, wagons, provisions, gold pans in which to collect their fortunes, and enough equipment to "dig it out by the shovel full," as Wolfe Londoner described them. Providing the bulk of the provisions, wagons, and oxen was Thomas Pollock, a.k.a. "Noisy Tom," a Fifty-Niner who had already been a carpenter, ferry operator, blacksmith, hotel owner, and stockholder in Auraria's town company, as well as Denver's first hangman. Accompanying him was his sixteen-year-old bride, daughter of the Reverend John Milton Chivington. In addition to the wives of Pollock, Kellogg, and Rice, several other women and children, too, were part of the expedition. One couple, F. A. and Mary Melissa Nye, brought along their two children.

The fact that the expedition was a family affair suggests that the San Juans offered, at least in rosy imagination, not only the promise of a fortune in gold but also a land where people hoped to remain to establish farms, towns, hardware stores, schools, and all the other accoutrements of civilization just as soon as the prospectors struck it rich in the mines. These people pictured themselves as pioneers, not common drifters. Although several would, indeed, become solid citizens of Colorado in good time, it would not happen until long after the San Juan Mountains had tempered their zeal for prospecting. Benjamin Eaton, for instance, became a developer of irrigation for agriculture in northeastern Colorado and a governor of the state, and Charles Hall, having seen all he wished of prospecting, became a prominent rancher in South Park, where he produced salt for silver mines.

Ignorant of the discouraging reports that were being printed in Denver, the Baker Expedition began to encounter trouble long before

21

it reached the mining country. Intending to travel southwest toward the Rio Grande and Chama Rivers, they spent two weeks crossing from the Huerfano River to the San Luis Valley by way of Sangre de Cristo Pass, where they had to cut trees for a path for their wagons and to gather forage for their famished stock. Next, in the wide, bitterly cold valley below, they were forced to burn some wagon beds to build fires. It was March by the time they reached Conejos, where they could replenish supplies. When the expedition reached Abiquiú, they were forced to leave their remaining wagons and to continue north to Animas City with pack animals. On April 1, several miles beyond Animas City, they at last arrived at a beautiful, sunny slope at Castle Rock near Cascade Creek, and here with joy they set up an encampment called Camp Pleasant. Originally intended as only a temporary layover to allow the party to recover sufficiently to continue to the placers, Camp Pleasant became a base for the women, children, and a few of the men.

As soon as they had recovered, about fifty or sixty determined men set off from Camp Pleasant with packs of provisions, picks and shovels, and some pack animals, floundering through the last snow-covered miles to Baker's Park. It was hard going even in April. When a group with David McShane had attempted the trek from Animas City earlier in the winter, with each man carrying about 100 pounds on his back, the snow was anywhere from four to seven feet deep, he said. The Baker Expedition's men lost some of their animals, which fell from the precipitous trail to their deaths, and the shovels intended for digging up gold "by the shovel full" were used for digging through snow on paths that quickly filled again with fresh drifts. Finally, at Eureka Gulch, eight miles northeast of Baker City, they found Charles Baker himself, along with several other hardy prospectors, living in brush shelters and working the placers.

Baker and his companions had been busy. They had laid out eleven districts with 200 claims in each, but little actual gold had been collected in the riffles of sluice boxes that the prospectors had constructed with whip-sawed lumber. Disparagers stated that the Eureka diggings were yielding only about fifty cents a day, and nearby Cunningham Gulch had netted less than two dollars for nine men in a week's work. In Baker's defense, one must concede that placer mining in several feet of snow presented special challenges, and few locations could pose more challenges than the San Juans in winter, particularly when snow-fall was heavy. Still, the prospectors wanted some indication of success to lift their morale, but none came.

Back at Animas City and Camp Pleasant in the winter of 1860–1861, food was becoming almost as scarce as gold. During the previous autumn, Albert Pfeiffer had assured the gold seekers that he would be looking in and bringing supplies from Abiquiú, but he failed to appear until late winter. Livestock was butchered, whether or not by the legitimate owners. The only storekeeper at Animas City priced his merchandise exorbitantly and sold it only on a cash basis, until an uprising by miners, with no cash and unsatisfied appetites for food and alcohol, ran the merchant out of town and distributed his goods among themselves. Most accounts of this incident, citing the *Rocky Mountain News,* identify the storekeeper as Manuel Armijo and say that he merely had gone to Santa Fe to obtain more provisions. Another version, citing the *Santa Fe Gazette,* refers to him as "Mr. Ortiz of Santa Fe," from whom 200 sacks of flour were forcibly appropriated by the miners. Yet another claimed that he was simply a man who put in a garden and managed to produce a few vegetables for his neighbors who were living in about seventy-five cabins. If so, he had made remarkably good use of the sun's warm rays, and a large number of cabins had sprouted in someone's imagination.

Tom Pollock had brought a large supply of food with the expedition and had distributed it to feed many in the party during the journey from Denver. When Ute Indians threatened hostilities, he gave them what they demanded and took four Navajo children in exchange. With his supplies exhausted, he then set out for Santa Fe to obtain additional food and took some of the captive children with him. He gave or traded the children to various people, including Albert Pfeiffer. A drifter at heart if not in fact, "Noisy Tom" was gone for two months, during which time the Civil War began. When Tom returned empty-handed to Animas City, everyone had left except his wife, Sarah, and "an invalid prospector," who were surrounded by a camp of Ute Indians. He explained that he had been threatened by Indians during his return trip and had been forced to give up everything to them. For her part, Sarah told a dramatic tale about preserving her virtue during Tom's absence by shoving a hot flatiron into the face of an Indian who attempted to force his attentions on her.

The Baker Expedition produced other memorable, and more verifiable, stories. For instance, Charles Hall became separated from companions with whom he went north into the Uncompahgre region. Suffering greatly and nearly starving to death when found, he was nursed back to health by Mary Melissa Nye, an example of the service that women in mining camps performed. Hall not only survived his ordeal but also married the former Mrs. Nye in due time. They settled at the Salt Works Ranch in South Park, a tranquil ending to their traumatic experience in the San Juans. Their granddaughter, Antoinette Perry, for whom the theatre's Tony Awards are named, may have inherited her flair for drama from them.[22]

As for Charles Baker, rumors circulated about his being threatened by hanging at Animas City. If one can believe John Turner, an elderly pioneer who contributed information many years later, Baker had attempted to play fair with all prospectors. Turner said that Baker drew lots for only fifty claims, each 200 feet square, in Eureka, Cunningham, and Mason's (Arrastra) Gulches for the prospectors whom he was representing. The same benign John Turner also explained that, indeed, Baker had been threatened with hanging, but the entire affair was simply a good joke of no consequence. Everyone, including Baker himself, Turner said, got a jolly laugh from the incident.

Robert J. Bruns, who compiled Turner's story along with other pioneer narratives, described Baker in the following generous terms: "Many reliable and trustworthy men, who followed the excitement, and saw Baker every day, assure me that he was a quiet and unassuming man; of superior intellect and capacity, melancholy and imaginative; a pleasant, fluent, and plausible talker at times, but in no sense a schemer; and thoroughly honest and sincere in every respect though somewhat enthusiastic."[23]

A considerably less charitable description from George Gregory stated that "Baker was as near a maniac as anything I can compare him to, insisting to his friends to go into country where there was nothing, and as I believe, to lead people over the Toll Road which he is interested in, and build up the towns they have located. Not one of which, except Animas City, has a house, and that has but about twenty log cabins. Provisions are very high, and are in fact high all through [New] Mexico."

While expressing his own good fortune that he had sufficient food with him, Gregory described the hardships of others who went without bread for weeks.[24] In addition to their need for provisions and their inability to locate good placers, there was constant fear of Ute and Navajo Indians, especially the former. The superintendent of Indian affairs in Santa Fe was correct in warning miners that his charges were displeased with the influx of prospectors into their territory.

The final blow had come when Manuel Armijo returned to Animas City from Santa Fe with garbled news about the outbreak of the Civil War. Animas City's residents were about evenly divided between Union and Confederate sympathizers, but, whatever their loyalties, most began to leave immediately. Many were only too happy to say good riddance to Baker and the San Juans for any reason, and joining the army of either side was their new cause. By July, Animas City was deserted.

Evacuees from the San Juans crossed the high mountain passes in assorted groups during the spring and early summer of 1861. A few decided to pursue will-o'-the-wisps in the Navajo country or in southwestern New Mexico's Silver City region and beyond, pursuing opportunities that C.W. had suggested in late 1860. Others set off to Colorado's Blue River country, but the majority headed toward civilization and the few comforts and security that wartime offered.

During their flight some endured hardships that added to their bitterness about the venture, but, fortunately, no verifiable deaths are known to have occurred, despite tall tales to the contrary. With the winter's deep snow thawing, streams rose and trails turned to mud, increasing the normal difficulties of travel. Few pack animals remained, and provisions were scant. Wolfe Londoner, ever the colorful narrator, described the exodus of prospectors through his erstwhile supply town, Cañon City, as follows:

> Until late next spring [1861] we could get no news from them
> at all. There were heavy snows in the San Juan Mountains and
> ranges down there. About the first week in May some of them
> commenced straggling in. They had lost their plump and ruddy
> appearance; their nice mining boots with red tops to them had dis-
> appeared; of their mining shirts there was only a scrap or a button
> or two left, and they were, taking them all in all, a sad and weary
> crowd who had come afoot across lots and were picking their way
> back to their earlier haunts, the mining camps. Later they came in
> larger numbers but mainly in the same condition, everything gone.
> They had lost their animals in the mountains, some of them [the

animals] had died, a great many of them had been lost and were never heard of again, starved to death in the mountain ranges of the San Juan.

What little profits the merchants of Canon had made in outfitting them in the previous fall, they gave back to these people in food and clothing and helping them to the camps of Tarry-all [in South Park] and California Gulch. Most of the inhabitants of the once great city of Canon, then emigrated to the mountains, leaving but a very few behind to guard the vacant stone warehouses and dwellings which had been built during prosperity.[25]

By July 4, everyone had left Animas City. It has been said that a small handful of diehards, Charles Baker among them, hung on in the San Juans until fall before drifting on to unknown adventures. The *Cañon City Times,* however, reported on June 10, 1861, "We had the pleasure of a visit from Col. Baker on Thursday, who was on his way to New Mexico, to appoint deputy marshals to take the census."[26] Precisely what this census might have been, if it did exist, raises a question, a possible answer being that it referred to recruitment of Southern sympathizers for the Confederate Army. An unconfirmed rumor reported that Baker was seen that fall at Cañon City with Andrew Peedee, one of the prospectors from Baker's Park. Although many of his contemporaries speculated that Baker joined the Confederate Army, there is no verifiable evidence that he did so, nor is there information concerning his whereabouts again until 1867.

Adding to the general disappointment for the other prospectors was the discovery that they were too late by the summer of 1861 to locate decent claims at any of the established mining camps in Colorado, where the ground was already staked. Kellogg, who claimed to have sold a productive claim in California Gulch to finance Baker's explorations, tried repeatedly to locate another good claim. With his wife and daughter, he was listed as a miner, living at Granite, in Colorado's census of 1870 and possessed real value of $10,000, but in 1877, when he was interviewed at Lake City, Colorado, for the account that appeared in the *Weekly Rocky Mountain News,* he was said to be a justice of the peace. Next, the Kellogg family went to Leadville, and shortly afterward they moved to Buena Vista, Colorado. Were it not for his attachment to his long-suffering family, one might call Kellogg and many other married men like him drifters.

Although Charles Baker and other prospectors of 1860–1861 were disappointed, this view of Sultan Mountain and ore dumps in 1874 reveals the riches that existed in the area. Courtesy, Colorado Historical Society, no. J754, William Henry Jackson photo.

Baker, of course, was eventually proved correct for insisting that there was gold in the San Juans, but what he saw had washed down from soaring peaks and had been deposited in streambeds and gravel bars. When he staked his claims, he chose well, for a few years later those same gulches would prove to possess immensely rewarding lode mines, but largely of silver rather than gold. The placers, in contrast, never yielded fortunes. Lode mining, smelters, improved transportation, and significant infusions of capital would be required before the San Juans yielded their riches. The presence of recalcitrant Native Americans also had to be resolved before the development of mining, whether of gold or of silver, could commence on a large scale. Despite a little prospecting later in the 1860s and early 1870s, more than a decade would pass before the mineral wealth of the San Juan Mountains was reaped. Argonauts like Baker failed to recognize this treasure in silver in 1860–1861.

Still vainly seeking his El Dorado, in 1867 Baker drifted back to Eureka Gulch's placers with James White and George Strole as his new recruits, a story that will be recounted in Chapters 3 and 4.

THE EDUCATION OF A DRIFTER

IN THE SPRING OF 1861, WHILE CHARLES BAKER AND MANY OTHER DISAPPOINTED prospectors were abandoning mining camps in Colorado Territory, James White was setting out from Wisconsin for the West. He was belatedly following a half dozen men from Kenosha, who during the previous year had bestowed their hometown's name on Kenosha Hill, also known as Kenosha Pass, southwest of Denver. White's former townsmen were among the thousands from throughout the country, especially the Midwest, who flocked across this pass into South Park. By 1861, when White was getting started, the promising ground at Colorado's placers had already been claimed, a few prospectors had been killed by Indians, and the majority of latecomers were on their way out, leaving the rewards to those few who were fortunate enough to have found good diggings early in the game or were stubborn enough to persist.

White cannot be said to have been terribly eager or ambitious about trying his luck in the West, or he would have started sooner. He was twenty-three years old when he finally departed the shores of Lake Michigan, and why he left then is not known. He might have been escaping some unpleasantness within his family circle or the fetters of domesticity, for he was of an age when men were settled down for better or worse with wives and babies to provide for, but it is not known whether White even had a sweetheart back in Wisconsin. Quite likely, lack of employment and the outbreak of the Civil War combined to turn the young man's yearnings toward something new and different.

Only sketchy information can be learned about James White's family and his early years. His parents, Daniel and Mary, began their family's westward journey from Connecticut when the Erie Canal was being built. James, the youngest of twelve children, was born in Rome, New York, in 1837. Called the "Big Ditch," the Erie Canal connected the Hudson River to Lake Erie and opened the region around the other Great Lakes to settlement and trade. As migration moved west, so did the Whites to the future site of Kenosha, Wisconsin, where investors were deepening a harbor on the shores of Lake Michigan to develop economic opportunities. As a result of this enterprise, Kenosha soon was on its way to becoming a thriving community with plenty of work for James's father and his sons until the nation's economy collapsed in the Panic of 1857. The Midwest was especially hard hit, and work was scarce. Even families with a milk cow, some chickens in the backyard, and a kitchen garden were hard-pressed to make a living beyond the barest essentials during this economic depression.

Twenty years old when the economy failed, James had been working as an apprentice to his father and perhaps had done some drayage work, too, for many years later he would turn to the latter occupation. In any case, it seems safe to assume that his activities were physical, for he was not well-educated. Kenosha could boast of having the first school in the state, but James seems to have spent no more of his childhood in school than was absolutely necessary. A letter written by him in 1867 demonstrates that he possessed, at best, rudimentary skills in writing.[1]

Exacerbated by the depression, Colorado's gold rush gave thousands of economically challenged males a good reason to pull up stakes and head west. In 1859, as a result of the mining excitement, many had left their homes to improve their fortunes, and more followed in 1860. Some with wives and families intended to return home after they had accumulated enough gold dust or had given up the search, whereas others never quit traveling once they had loosed their tethers. Those who delayed their departure for Colorado until 1861 missed their golden opportunity to strike it rich in the first wave of mining. Like them, James White had waited too long before he left Kenosha.

When he departed for the West, his meager fortune permitted him to ride a train only as far as St. Joseph, Missouri, the terminus of the Hannibal and St. Joseph Railroad at the time, but he was seeing the world. He had ferried across the mighty Mississippi River, and at St. Joseph he witnessed the spectacle of hundreds of wagons, oxen, mules, and thousands of their owners encamped by the Missouri River while they stocked up on provisions and replaced lost or broken equipment before setting out for Colorado, Nevada, or California. He knew that he would have to attach himself to one of these companies, for he could not afford the luxury of stagecoach transportation to his next destination, Denver.

Fare from St. Joseph to Denver was $100. Mark Twain's *Roughing It* reveals that in the summer of 1861 the author (Samuel Clemens) and his brother Orion each paid $150 with another $50 to be paid later for their total stagecoach fares from St. Joseph to Carson City, Nevada, traveling in a Central Overland and Pike's Peak Express Company stage, but, as Clemens described their journey, it could scarcely be called a luxury trip.[2]

Like hundreds of other impecunious travelers milling around St. Joseph, White managed to tie on with a wagon train, a safer way to travel than by attempting to cross Indian country alone. From St. Joseph most favored the route that swung northwest to the heavily used Platte River Road and from it down the South Platte to Denver. This road was shorter and usually safer than dropping south to take the Santa Fe Trail along the Arkansas River. Shorter routes like the Smoky Hill Trail, lying between the two main roads, were considered by wise travelers at this time to be too isolated, too dry, and too infested with hostile Indians. We can assume that the wagon train with which White traveled took the northern route.

What he thought of this part of his journey is unknown, but the romanticist Walt Whitman surely had a different trip in mind when he composed his poem "Song of the Open Road," which reads in part:

Afoot and light-hearted I take to the open road,
Healthy, free, the world before me,
The long brown path before me leading wherever I choose.
Henceforth I ask not good-fortune, I myself am good-fortune.[3]

Tramping all day and sleeping at night under the wide sky, or under a wagon in the mud when it rained, might have appealed to Walt Whitman, but hitchhikers like White soon had their delight in the "open road" quenched. If their paths were lighthearted at the outset, their high spirits soon were dulled by tedium and torments.

White's party probably was not a tidy ribbon of canvas-covered wagons such as artists picture. True, many trains were primarily made up of conventional covered wagons, commonly light ones, but there also were riders on horses and mules, along with people trudging on foot behind them. Although mules drew some wagons, they were out-numbered by oxen, which tended to be less likely to wander away while grazing at night and had the good manners to fall in beside their regular partners under the yoke with less fuss in the morning. Also, when necessary, they could be butchered and eaten as "beef" along the way, if necessary, or sold at the end of the journey. They plodded steadily at about two miles per hour, an agonizingly slow pace for any-one in a hurry but an advantage for the travelers on foot.

When an Overland coach carrying the mail rocked past, it kicked up dust in the faces of the common folks in the wagon trains, but coaches had their own disadvantages. Racing along at eight or ten miles an hour, day and night, with horses or mules being changed in less than five minutes at relay stations, passengers might have welcomed an oppor-tunity to sleep on the ground. The menus offered during short breaks at meal stop stations were less than appetizing, usually featuring rancid bacon according to Mark Twain, whereas the meals with a wagon train might be varied with fresh antelope, sage hen, jackrabbit, rattlesnake, or a succulent prairie dog floating in a kettle over an open fire.

Even when they started out, travelers with a wagon train were clad in wardrobes bearing little resemblance to those seen in daguerre-otypes and photographs of the period, for which a man arrived at a studio cleaned up and wearing a clean shirt, a floppy bow tie, a top-coat, and a silk hat of his own — or borrowed them from the studio. The majority of people in a wagon train were young men lacking means or reason to dandify themselves, unless fancy garb happened to be what a fellow was wearing when he was run out of town. On the road, some walkers limped along in threadbare broadcloth suits and plug hats, but most wore woolen trousers tucked into dusty boots, homespun woolen shirts, possibly vests, long or short coats, and hats — wide-brimmed, narrow-brimmed, tall or flat, plug or cap — to keep the infernal dust and bugs out of their shaggy, lice-infested hair. They seldom owned more than one complete set of spare garments.

Although hitchhikers like White were permitted to walk behind the wagons in the dust or possibly beside them, climbing aboard for free ride was not allowed. A walker might be allowed to toss his gear into one of the wagons only if he could pay a little cash or proved to be a good enough volunteer to warrant the favor. If he was accompanying a train without paying anything, he was expected to help with the physical work, such as gathering sagebrush or buffalo chips for the campfire, making camp, breaking camp, rounding up livestock, hitching teams, hunting game, fending off Indian attacks, shooting snakes, and whatever other necessity arose.

In the absence of a description from White himself, another's account of such a trip in the early summer of 1861 will have to suffice. The Methodist preacher John L. Dyer, well-known in Colorado's Rockies as the "snowshoe itinerant," possessed a small amount of cash and respect, entitling him to a few comforts that a common drifter like James White could not expect. We pick up Father Dyer's story in eastern Nebraska:

> At Omaha . . . there was a train of eighteen wagons starting for Pike's Peak. One of the men agreed to board me across for fifteen dollars, and haul my carpet-sack and gun. I was to walk. We set out for six hundred miles, as it was called. . . .
>
> There were a few soldiers at Fort Kearney. I exercised myself with two or three trips out to the Bluffs, four or five miles. I wanted to see a buffalo, but never got sight of one, much less a chance to shoot one.
>
> About seventy-five miles below Julesburg, we came to a house made of cedar logs, just built, and it was on Sunday. Our train

stopped, and my company asked if I would preach they could get the privilege of the house. It was so arranged. There were others there besides our company of twenty men, which made in all forty very attentive hearers. After it was over, our boys concluded I was disgraced, for it was a house of ill-fame. I replied that if it was, I had had forty whore-mongers to one woman. They did not bother me anymore. Those who live in glass houses must not throw stones.

We frequently met with Indians. The poor creatures had learned to swear. What a pity the white men had not better manners than to teach them to blaspheme!

One day we came to a station where there were a number of camps, and a lot of drunken men tearing around. . . . Here a drunken man came into our corral and claimed one of our oxen. Swore he would have him, holding his gun at ready. I stood at one end to help, and had a big ox-gad. He ran toward me. I raised the gad and told him to get out of there, and made at him, and he got out at the nearest gap.[4]

Swaying along in his coach, Mark Twain had few opportunities, except at stations, to observe scenes such as this one. He did mention Julesburg, also called Overland City, 470 miles from St. Joseph. Julesburg was "the strangest, quaintest, funniest frontier town that our untraveled eyes had ever stared at and been astonished with," he commented. After observing a hilarious buffalo hunt, Twain crossed the Platte in a mud wagon that had replaced his coach, and from there his Overland route continued west rather than turning toward Denver, as Dyer's wagon train did. Resuming his own account, which was no kinder than Twain's description of Overland City, Dyer wrote:

We reached Julesburg, and there took the cut-off — a new road — which a company had opened, having bridged two or three sand-creeks with poles, and put up a toll-gate, and of course advertised the cut-off. . . . The trail was not yet worn smooth, and it seemed long and tedious.

[We] were all foot-sore, as well as the oxen, and nothing to break the monotony. The day before we got through, we stopped to water the cattle. I asked my team-boss if I should make some coffee. He was mad, because one of his oxen was not likely to get water, and swore at me. My offer was gratis, for I had not agreed to do anything, but had done many little things to assist the boys. . . .

Now we came to the last night on the plains. I had two pairs of pants, about half worn. I had left my pocket-knife and purse in the pocket in the pair that was in the wagon that night, and when I took them out, found the contents all gone. Well, the loss was small, as it was less than two dollars and a-half; but it was all I had, and I was consoled in the fact that I was no worse off than I would have been if it had been five thousand dollars. We stopped two miles up Cherry Creek, above Denver. I took what I had in my carpet-sack, and with my gun on my shoulder, walked into town.

More inclined to action than to philosophizing, James White might not have accepted the theft of his possessions with such equanimity had he been in Father Dyer's situation. When White arrived in Denver, probably broke or very nearly so, he found a place where the streets were muddy or dusty, depending on the weather, and filthy with the droppings of horses and oxen. The town bristled with Indians, mountain men, squaw men, teamsters from New Mexico, prospectors, freighters, blacksmiths, wheelwrights, liveries, and crowded saloons. The rowdy Elephant Corral was a bar–hotel–brothel–dining room–gambling hall, with a corral where the owners of livestock could leave their animals and redeem them after carousing, if they had any money left. Denver boasted a few fancy clubs with tables run by sporting men and stores with exorbitant prices, none of which White could afford. Instead, White probably headed for one of the saloons where trail-weary drifters, busted by the Pikes-Peak-or-Bust, could get a whiskey, a meal, and place to flop, all under the same canvas roof.

Discovering that he could not afford to stay there for long, White was soon on his way into the mountains, but he had come too late to stake a good claim in the diggings, if he ever had entertained such fantasies. Besides, provisions were dear in the camps for someone without a productive claim to pay the storekeeper. Without much delay, White pushed on to Nevada's Virginia City. Although his path from Colorado is unknown, it is likely that he passed through Salt Lake City, where other travelers would have warned him about the Great Basin's desert of alkali and sand that lay ahead. And to prepare for this ordeal beforehand, it was advisable to quench one's thirst with the illicit Mormon drink called "valley tan," which was not too hard to find.

At Virginia City, newcomers like White discovered a wide-open city spawned in the Comstock Lode's excitement. Night and day, gambling parlors, prostitutes, and profanity greeted millionaires, thieves,

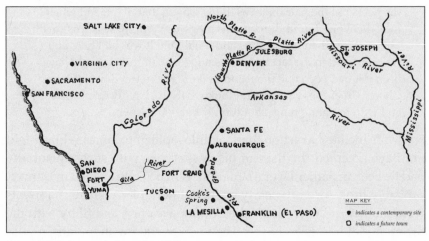

James White's travels in 1861–1865.

murderers, and penniless drifters. Without much effort, White could have located a job as a teamster, or he could have shoveled ore at a silver mine or a gold mine, at a stamp mill or a smelter, and, if a worker was desperate enough, he could even shovel sawdust on a saloon floor or manure at a livery stable.

By September White was ready for something different. A Union Army recruiter arrived in Virginia City from California with an offer of $100 plus a bonus after three years of duty for anyone who would enlist, and White signed up. For down-on-their-luck drifters, such a decision seems to have stemmed from expediency more than fervor about the war. Conscription did not exist in the Union until 1863, so White was not a draft-dodger, in any case. While looking forward to having a little cash in his pocket, White enjoyed the questionable privilege of riding to Sacramento in the Pioneer Stage Company's coach, jouncing over the high Sierra Nevada. The road, an old Indian trail, had been used by the Pony Express and next by the Overland Mail, before it was churned to a fare-thee-well by hundreds of freight wagons hauling mining equipment and supplies to Virginia City from Sacramento and ore from the Comstock Lode to California's reduction works. Arriving at Camp Union in Sacramento, White officially enlisted as a private in the Fifth California Volunteer Cavalry, Company H.

If White's purpose when he left home was to see the world, he was fulfilling his plan, for he beheld the Pacific Ocean soon thereafter. First,

View from Alcatraz Island across San Francisco Bay, 1870, showing the shore battery at the fort where James White stood guard in 1862. Courtesy, Colorado Historical Society, no. 1206, William Henry Jackson photo.

according to Eilean Adams's account, White's regiment was stationed for a short time at Camp Wright, a camp that military historians place at an exceedingly windy location near the San Jose Valley. His next stop included a panoramic view of San Francisco Bay, California's largest and most spectacular harbor, for he was stationed at Alcatraz Island. An excess of rain in 1861 and 1862, however, might have dampened his enthusiasm about the post. To protect the port and the city from Confederate raids, this island at the Golden Gate had become the site of a military fortress when the Civil War began, and, as it turned out, a few Confederate adventurers actually were incarcerated there. More importantly, an ordnance depot was located at this well-defended site, and here James White stood guard in the rain and fog.

Since he remained at Alcatraz for only a few weeks, White had few opportunities to sample the pleasures and perils of San Francisco. It was then a city of more than 50,000, with a Chinese population of about 3,000 who would have fascinated an ogle-eyed young man from the Midwest. But he must have heard how Forty-Niners poured in during the gold rush, often leaving their abandoned vessels in the bay in their haste to reach the mining country around Sutter's Mill. Before long, White and his company left Alcatraz Island and sailed from San Francisco Bay to San Diego.[5]

San Diego failed to inspire White to describe its fine bay and its sailing ships. History tells us, though, that at the time when he was there, the village of small adobe buildings was dominated visually by its mission, and the wooded hillsides around the town had been stripped for firewood. White's company remained there only a brief time before they left behind the blue vistas and cool breezes of the Pacific and set off across the desert during the summer of 1862.

Following the California Road, White and his comrades slogged to their first destination, Fort Yuma. The Army did not provide suitable uniforms for the climate or for appearance, but volunteers were permitted to wear civilian clothing if they could afford to buy it. Those who could not were forced to wear the military's dark woolen pants, flannel underwear (usually worn without shirts), and slouch caps that offered little shelter from the sun or rain.[6] White's experience might have been better than that of some others, for he had been assigned to the quartermaster corps as a teamster, perhaps entitling him to ride across the scorching desert.

When reached, Fort Yuma offered no respite from heat. Located on a bluff overlooking the Colorado River, the site's original function had been to control troublesome Yuma Indians and to serve surveyors of the boundary between Mexico and the United States. Until the Civil War interrupted exploration, government expeditions had passed through the region, newly acquired as a result of the Mexican War. When the Civil War prompted the Army to build a more permanent fort, the commandant had tried in vain to warn his superiors that little danger could be expected from either Indians or Confederates, and, besides, the site was inhospitable with temperatures sometimes soaring to 120 degrees. Regardless, the new fort was constructed, neatly enough but devoid of shelter from the sun. An often-repeated joke, already old then and still being told today, claimed that when a soldier from Fort Yuma went to hell, he was so cold that he sent a request back to the fort for his blankets.

The decision to build the fort at this location, however, was far from frivolous. The fort was on the west side of the Colorado River, and a town called Arizona City, later Yuma, with a landing and sup-

Steamboats and the ferry at Arizona City (Yuma) on the Lower Colorado River with Fort Yuma on the bluff on the west side of the river, where James White served in 1863. Courtesy, Arizona Historical Society, Tucson, Library/Archives Department, no. 17685, George H. Baker lithograph.

ply depot were located on the east side. When the troops were not consuming whiskey from the village, they could watch the ferry, which made this point the center of activity for the entire region. Most military personnel, cargo, and civilian emigrants heading westward followed the Gila Trail, which funneled traffic down the Gila River to its confluence with the Colorado at Arizona City and from there usually to Los Angeles. Hoping to prove the river navigable, the U.S. Corps of Topographical Engineers sent Lieutenant Joseph C. Ives in 1857 to learn how far a boat might penetrate the mysterious "Big Cañon" of the Colorado River. Ives brought a disassembled, ironclad paddlewheel, *The Explorer,* to the mouth of the Colorado and reassembled it, while another boat carrying Army supplies made the venture a competition and beat *The Explorer* through the Black Canyon. In early 1858, however, *The Explorer* reached the Black Canyon, where it struck a rock, later known as Explorer Rock, and the vessel's voyage ended. Some of the crew then continued in a skiff and reached Las Vegas Wash. Ives also led a contingent overland and reached the

39

Colorado at Diamond Creek, where he came to the conclusion that the river could be ascended only with great skill and famously observed that the eroded landscape was valueless. Meanwhile, Ives's cartographer, Friedrich W. von Egloffstein, produced the best map of the region that existed up to that time. While White was at Fort Yuma with little else to while away his time, he might have listened to some tales about such events as he watched a few paddlewheeled steamboats and barges on the river below the fort. They were serving mining camps upstream as far north as El Dorado in the Black Canyon, where drifters from California's El Dorado and other camps were now seeking their bonanza. These vessels also delivered supplies to Fort Mohave, which had recently been reactivated near today's town of Needles, south of the Black Canyon.[7]

In the 1860s other operators above the Black Canyon also hoped that steamboats would be reaching places like the mouth of Las Vegas Wash and Callville, six miles east of that wash. Call's Landing, as it was known originally, was established in 1864 by a Mormon elder, Anson Call. He built a warehouse and corrals there for supplies that could be shipped upstream to Mormon outposts like St. George, as the Church of Jesus Christ of Latter-Day Saints was hoping that transportation on the Colorado River would provide them with better access to southern Mormon missions than overland routes could, but these ambitions proved to be unsuccessful.[8] Possibly White heard some grandiose chatter at Fort Yuma about the future of boating on the Lower Colorado River and its possibilities for transportation, but he did not hear then about a place named Callville. White left Fort Yuma in 1863, a year and a few months before Anson Call established the landing that would play an important role in White's life in 1867.

Resuming its march from Fort Yuma in February 1863, White's outfit made the trek up the Gila River and then east to Tucson, a town unlike any White had yet encountered. A jumble of brown adobe hovels on narrow streets, the town was filled with burros, government wagons, miners, children, dogs, chickens, mescal, monte games, and peccadilloes that a soldier's blinding headache might mercifully erase from memory, given enough time. From Tucson, White's company again headed east on the Southern Route through Apache country. Previously the Army and the Apache Indians, led by Cochis and Mangas Coloradas, had engaged in bloody battle, but White's outfit was spared encounters with them, as Fort Bowie had been recently constructed to control the Indians frequenting nearby Apache Spring and Apache Pass in the Dragoon Mountains, and tranquility prevailed for the moment. After passing through this area, White's Company H continued without incident to Fort Cummings at Cooke's Spring. This location boasted a constant spring of water, where the Butterfield Overland Mail had operated a station until the station was destroyed by Apaches in 1861. In 1863 the Army was constructing an impressive adobe fort there for the purpose of protecting emigrants, and it was hoped that mail service might be restored before long, too. This location, where White's company remained only a short time, is northeast of present-day Deming, New Mexico.

From Cooke's Spring, White's company continued to the Mesilla Valley. In the 1850s a small post called Fort Fillmore had been established there, but it was abandoned when Confederates occupied the town of Mesilla in 1861. The fort next was reoccupied by California Volunteers in 1862, and here James White found himself herding government livestock in the Mesilla Valley in 1864. He always seemed to arrive after the excitement had passed. The only relief from the heat and boredom came during cool evenings, when the troops could sit around camp, telling tall tales and ribald jokes and playing a few hands of cards at the end of another day.

By late summer 1864, their hot, dry journey brought them to the hot, dry post called Camp Franklin at present-day El Paso, or then simply Franklin, Texas. This intermittent military camp, sometimes known as the Post at El Paso, was first established in 1848 at the close of the Mexican War. Its purpose in the 1860s was to prevent Confederate incursions or whatever other disturbances might occur along the border with Mexico. The camp's location moved around in the area of El Paso, until it finally came to rest as Fort Bliss. When Baker's company reached Camp Franklin, the troops were expecting to be sent on to New Mexico's Fort Sumner at the Bosque Redondo Reservation, where thousands of Navajos had been rounded up by Kit Carson and Albert Pfeiffer during the Navajo campaign. Perhaps because of dwindling personnel or mounts, White's Company H officially became part of the First California Volunteer Infantry, Company E, at this point. As luck would have it, though, the troops remained at Franklin long enough for White's military service to come to an ignominious end.

During his service with the cavalry, devoid of action and glory, White had endured seemingly endless guard duty and tending the government herd. He was looking forward to the conclusion of the monotonous assignments in only a few more weeks when his three-year tour of duty would end. With a discharge and some scrip in his pocket, he would be able to say goodbye to Army life. Instead, White's Army career was about to end with an event, about which this man, normally of few words, spoke vigorously in his later years.

Probably every man in White's outfit was ready for something besides marches, regulations, and menial assignments, and just across the Rio Grande lay the town of El Paso del Norte in Chihuahua, beckoning bored soldiers in the dark of night to relieve their loneliness and their monumental thirst. Furthermore, an enterprising individual needed little imagination to see that money could be made by finding a way to bring these pleasures to the camp itself. One night, intending to make a trade for whiskey at a store on the Mexican side of the river, someone broke into Camp Franklin's storeroom and stole 200 pounds of coffee. The difficulty of transporting this amount of coffee, returning with whiskey of equivalent value, and then consuming such a quantity of liquor must lead one inevitably to the conclusion that the coffee-whiskey scheme involved several conspirators. As White later related during his account of the event, the coffee was confiscated at the border by customs. Then, when the storekeeper in the Mexican village, who was an Army deserter named Butshoffsky, arrived at the customs house to claim the coffee, he had to pay double the normal duty and received only seventy-five pounds, but, worse for all, the coffee caper was uncovered.

Back in camp, three or four soldiers, including White, were arrested and accused of having stolen the coffee. A small boy was sent to Camp Franklin to identify the alleged thieves because Butshoffsky declined to come across the border at the river to identify them for easily understood reasons. White protested his innocence and a comrade supported his alibi, but when he was instructed to write his own defense on paper, he was unable to accomplish this task because he could not write well enough, as his granddaughter explained in her biography.[9] He was tried by court-martial and found guilty three years to the day after his enlistment, the day that he thought he would become a civilian again.

In the 1860s, young trees enhanced company quarters at Fort Craig, where James White was incarcerated in the stone guardhouse in 1864–1865. Courtesy, Palace of the Governors (MNM/DCA), neg. no. 14514, U.S. Army Signal Corps photo.

Sentenced to a year of hard labor, White was taken up the old Spanish Camino Real for imprisonment at Fort Craig, about forty miles north of the town called today, ironically, Truth or Consequences, New Mexico. Fort Craig, constructed on the west side of the Rio Grande in the 1850s by the U.S. Army to protect New Mexico Territory from Apaches and Navajos, became important when thousands of New Mexico's volunteers camped in and around the site during the Civil War. Despite their numbers, in February 1862 they failed to block an invasion by Confederates from Texas under General Henry H. Sibley and were defeated during the nearby Battle of Valverde. Sibley then continued north to victories at Albuquerque and Santa Fe before being routed at Glorieta Pass, where the Confederate invasion ended.

Almost all of Fort Craig's buildings and fortifications were adobe, with an outer wall surrounding the layout. Exceptions were a stone guardhouse and a stone wall around the cemetery where nearly 500 soldiers were buried after the Battle of Valverde. The choice of stone as a building material for the prison was practical, for adobe could easily be gouged and breached by a prisoner with a will to escape, but, fitted out with a ball and chain, James White would not have gone far, even if he had had the will. The fort's treeless site on an elevation near the often-dry Rio Grande was at the northern end of the Jornada del Muerto, the "Journey of Death," where many a traveler had perished from lack of water. Without shackles, a strong individual might have made it north twenty miles to Socorro, but, with escape ruled out, White and his fellow convicts were forced to perform their hard labor, whether it was prying rocks out of the Santa Fe–El Paso road, digging clay to make more adobe bricks for a new storehouse, carrying rocks for the wall around the cemetery, or chopping cottonwood from the bosque for firewood. Fortunately, it was not yet summer, when temperatures could soar to 100 degrees and higher, but the dank guardhouse was bone-chilling at night, summer or winter. It was not a happy time for James White.

Suddenly in April, after only five months of imprisonment, however, White's misery ended with the close of the Civil War. Hundreds of thousands celebrated the cessation of battle, but their joy could not have exceeded that of the Union Army's prisoners who were promptly granted amnesty and released. White went back to El Paso, where he not only became the possessor of an honorable discharge but also of his bonus, permitting him to purchase a horse and an outfit. As a volunteer, he would not have been eligible for a pension, which in later life he could have used to good advantage. In the spring of 1865, he was at least a free man, though an embittered one, when he rode away to Santa Fe and on to Denver.

The Denver of 1865 was hardly recognizable as the same place it had been in 1861. Fire in 1863 and flood in 1864 had wiped away many of the early crude structures, which were being replaced with brick ones. Denver was taking on the prerequisites of an ambitious city that intended to be the capital of the territory, and even of a state if some had their way. By autumn, White was convinced that he had seen enough of Denver and the West. Together with a family heading east, White left, perhaps planning to return home to Wisconsin, but he got only as far as Atchison, Kansas.

THREE

HORSE THIEVES

JAMES WHITE HAD ACCUMULATED A MULTIPLICITY OF EXPERIENCES, FEW OF WHICH he would have wished to repeat, by the time he arrived at Atchison, Kansas, in late 1865, but he still was unready to turn his back on the West. Instead of returning home, White took a job in Atchison with the stage company of Barlow, Sanderson and Company, work that brought him to Fort Dodge in 1866, where he would meet Charles Baker, George Strole, and Joe Goodfellow. If "accident counts for much in companionship," as Henry Brooks Adams once said, the adage would be verified by this meeting and their adventures together.[1]

In the spring of 1867 the four put their heads together in hopes of improving their lot, and, as footloose individuals often did in the migration west, these casual acquaintances formed a small band to search for gold in the Rocky Mountains.

With the exception of Charles Baker's career in 1860–1861 and James White's in 1861–1865, nothing is known about how these drifters were engaged prior to the intersection of their paths, and how they met is a matter of speculation. Even White's statements about his occupation are ambiguous. According to the short life story to which he signed his name many years later, he was driving stage at Fort Dodge, and in an interview in 1907 he said his run was between Fort Dodge and Cimarron Crossing, though his words did not specify his actual job.[2] At any rate, White said that he became acquainted there with "Capt. Baker, also George Stroll [sic] and Goodfellow." The other three left no known written records about their occupations or their meeting one another.

White probably thought his fortunes were improving when he took a job with the stage company. If he indeed was a driver for Barlow and Sanderson's Santa Fe Stage Company, which held the contract to deliver mail, he was earning a whopping thirty-five dollars a month. The run that White claimed to have had was nearly ninety miles between Fort Dodge to the Upper Cimarron Crossing of the Arkansas River, or twenty-two miles west of Fort Dodge if he meant the Middle Crossing. The latter was near the present towns of Cimarron and Ingalls, Kansas, where the hazardous, dry route turned toward Santa Fe. At this crossing the stage line had a swing station consisting of a couple of adobe buildings where teams of horses or mules were changed. At the Upper Crossing, about sixty-five miles farther west, the Cimarron Cutoff crossed the Arkansas and headed south toward the Cimarron River and on to Santa Fe. Either route meant a dry, hazardous run that any driver should have been glad was not his own, and because of Indian unrest at the time, the trip along the Arkansas to the crossings was risky enough. With the advantage of proximity to a water source at least, the stage company's coaches, government supply trains, and many other travelers continued west from the Upper Crossing along the Mountain Branch of the Santa Fe Trail on the north side of the Arkansas.[3]

Not all stage company employees at the Upper Crossing's Bluff Station held the exalted position of stage driver, of course. Most employees were tending the equipment and livestock, changing teams, feeding and watering them. Crude comfort but scant security existed at the station. Originally, the stage line's Bluff Station was merely a

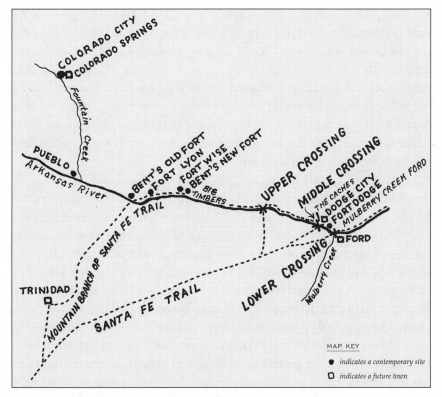

Route from Mulberry Creek to Colorado City.

dugout with an earthen wall surrounding it for protection, although in time the station acquired a few adobe houses, stage barns, and a good-size corral for horses and mules.

Milling around were military escorts, often drunk, on assignment from Fort Dodge to protect stages and wagon trains or to engage in reprisals against Indians after raids. The soldiers often found themselves assigned to the latter duty, for livestock was regularly stolen at all the crossings, whether Upper, Middle, or Lower. Most wagons in the trains on the Santa Fe Trail were drawn by reliable but agonizingly slow oxen, whereas mules, although sometimes used because they were faster, were unpredictable and excitable. Travelers with wagon trains camped near the crossings, rested, made plans, gathered courage to commence, or regrouped after the feat was accomplished. While crossing the river, slow-moving wagons offered prime targets for attack.

Wagon trains and stages nervously endured the long hours on the trail between the crossings, too. They experienced attacks by Indians, blizzards in winter, wind, dust storms, downpours, clouds of mosquitoes, thunder and lightning, rattlesnakes, and jackrabbits that might spook teams unexpectedly. Oven-like heat in summer replaced below-zero cold in winter. Often the road became impassable when the ground—a wide skein of ruts, carved and kneaded by about 3,000 wagons and 25,000 oxen—became a mire of seemingly bottomless mud after a thaw or a rainstorm.

Native Americans, however, were the most worrisome hazard in the mid-1860s. Along with raids by Kiowa, Comanche, and Apache bands, there were the Arapaho and Cheyenne who were wreaking vengeance for betrayals and brutalities such as the Sand Creek Massacre, for insufficient and inferior rations, for epidemics of deadly diseases that white people had introduced to the indigenous peoples, for hardships after travelers destroyed vital timber, water holes, game, and the once-plentiful prairie grasses that were being stripped away by livestock. Thousands of newcomers were settling in the eastern portion of the territory that the Santa Fe Trail crossed, but western Kansas, where more than 100 white people were killed in 1867, remained unattractive to homesteaders and town founders because of Indian attacks on wagon trains, stages, stations, and livestock.

To protect the great volume of travelers on the trails after the Colorado gold rush had begun, a string of widely spaced military posts was established along the Santa Fe Trail, and after the close of the Civil War, additional posts were established. One of these posts was Fort Dodge, where White, Baker, Strole, and Goodfellow met up. Theoretically, Fort Dodge appeared to be strategically placed, as it was just west of two main branches of the trail, the Dry Route and the Wet Route, but the fort was scarcely capable of protecting itself. The home station for Barlow and Sanderson's Santa Fe Stage Company at this location had been burned in 1864, and in 1865 Indians not only killed several travelers on the trail but also stole all but ten head of animals from the fort.

At first this isolated outpost was little more than a warren of dugouts in the riverbank with a wall of earth surrounding them. Lack of water elsewhere accounted for the choice of location, and lack of building materials accounted for the decision to create dugouts. With

This sketch of Fort Dodge during its construction appeared in Harper's Weekly, *May 25, 1867. The stone structures built in 1867 were remodeled over the years and augmented by more modern facilities. Used by the U.S. Army until 1882, the property is now occupied by the Kansas State Veterans' Home near Dodge City.* Courtesy, Denver Public Library, Western History Collection, no. Z-4073, Theodore R. Davis sketch.

the post's filthy conditions, disease was rampant and medical care was essential, but even the hospital was merely a soddy. In 1867 a few more permanent structures of lumber and stone began to be built with stone quarried five miles north of the fort, where stonecutters and haulers provided good targets for Indians.

Not surprisingly, drunkenness was a common problem at isolated forts, largely thanks to the presence of a sutler's store. Without a town anywhere near Fort Dodge at the time (Dodge City, seven miles west of the fort, did not defile the landscape until 1872), the store was the social center for idle soldiers, civilian lingerers, dusty drifters, and curious Indians. Built in 1866, the store at Fort Dodge immediately became a constant source of trouble for the commandant, who vainly attempted to control his soldiers' drinking by restricting the sale of alcohol to limited evening hours. Patrons were also drawn to the store's more innocent and essential inventory, such as beans, flour, sugar, coffee, dried apples, wild game meat, tobacco, shirts, boots, blankets, nails, knives, and whiskey—depending on what had come in on a trader's wagon

James White, Charles Baker, and their companions can easily be imagined mingling among the patrons of the sutler's store at Fort Dodge as it appeared in Harper's Weekly, *May 25, 1867.* Courtesy, Denver Public Library, Western History Collection, no. Z-4073. Theodore R. Davis sketch.

or in barter with customers. Here also was the likelihood of finding female companionship of questionable pedigree. Cash for purchases was scarce, so the sutler often accepted weapons, pelts, or other items, either legally owned or stolen, for his goods.[4]

Besides Army personnel, a hodgepodge of about 100 civilian employees worked at the fort. The size of Fort Dodge's garrison varied from day to day and year to year, with the average number being about 200 during 1866, increasing in 1867 to about 300, minus deserters. The stage company's workers camped nearby, as did Santa Fe Trail travelers awaiting an escort, and whenever a stage or wagon train arrived, driver and guards were sure to need a drink and a chew. For this motley assemblage, loafing at the sutler's store was the most common pastime, for there were few other opportunities for recreation nearby except shooting rattlesnakes, wolves, and bison.

In his sweaty shirt, run-down boots, and dusty hat, James White would have been easy to overlook among the other customers milling around the place, unless he was, as he claimed, a stage driver. This personage was a notable figure on the trail, with a heroic reputation, reinforced by Hollywood's B-movies. Other than his status as a stage driver and the strength of his stocky frame, White was nondescript. He was of medium height, medium bland face, medium blond hair, and medium blue eyes. A stolid young man of few words, he generally hoarded them for correcting misguided persons who disagreed with him, for although he was short on education, like thousands of frontier individualists he was long on self-confidence.

It seems possible that in this dingy trading post, White first encountered Charles Baker and the other two who were fated to become their companions on the road. White needed little persuasion to seek new surroundings, and Baker was a man with talent for persuading an audience that he had a surefire idea. By 1867, however, Baker's enthusiasm and silvery tongue, which had lured large numbers of followers to the San Juans in 1860, appeared to have lost some of their power, for he found only three men — White, Strole, and Goodfellow — to accompany him on the trail of his next scheme.

Charles Baker had changed in many ways since leaving the San Juan mining camps, although it is impossible to identify the causes of his changes. At the very least, he appeared to have been ill-suited to the grubby life he was living around the Santa Fe Trail. Neither his contemporaries nor later researchers have been able to discover what he had been doing after he left the San Juan Mountains in 1861, although lack of information did not prevent fanciful biographical statements about him. Occasionally, old-timers in Colorado said they knew him, while exposing their ignorance by calling him "Jim" or "John." In his old age, even James White called Baker "Jim." Most were inclined to believe Baker was a Southerner from Virginia or maybe Georgia, possibly because his speech hinted of Southern origins. Some claimed he had participated in the Mexican War, others that he served the Confederacy during the Civil War after he left the West in 1861, but my search of military records of several states has failed to find support for any such assertions. A Lieutenant Charles Baker appears in the records of Waul's Legion in Texas, but records show that this man died in 1862. The National Park Service lists fifty Confederate Charles

Bakers in its Civil War Soldiers and Sailors System, one of whom — or none of whom — might have been a prospector before the war. Both before and after the San Juan debacle, people called him "Captain," a commonly used nickname, as even White proposed once when he was speaking about Baker's identity. "Captain" was a title often bestowed on anyone who displayed a knack for leadership, and a few years after Baker's death, or disappearance by other unknown means, some yarn-spinners who professed personal acquaintance promoted him to "Colonel." White said that he never heard Baker mention anything about serving in the Confederacy, but White, whose memory was increasingly unreliable as he aged, contradicted his own statement on another occasion.[5]

Possibly, Baker was, in fact, one of many Southerners who, suffering economically after the war, returned to the West to seek better fortunes. Whatever else Baker might have been up to, it is apparent that he had not found a successful calling by early 1867. In 1907, White said that he, Baker, Strole, and Goodfellow all were working for Barlow and Sanderson, but in 1917 White said Baker was trapping at Mulberry Creek when they met. (Readers are forewarned that many things that White said at one time or another varied, rendering his authority dubious.) The mouth of Mulberry Creek was a dozen miles southeast of Fort Dodge at the Lower Cimarron Crossing, where Indians often camped, as did travelers who followed the Lower Crossing. A trapper earned little profit on the plains of Kansas in the 1860s. He might have found a small number of beaver, but more likely he made his living trapping muskrats, coyotes, and rabbits, whose pelts would have been of poor quality in the spring season. Sometimes a trapper might have brought some wolf skins to the sutler's store as wolves were detested as predators on livestock belonging to the fort, the stage line, and wagon trains. In any case, it definitely was time for Baker to be moving on to find the gold he knew was waiting for him somewhere in the West, and he needed companions.

The origins of Baker's other two recruits, George Strole and Joe Goodfellow, are a mystery, although their names suggest that Strole might have been of German extraction and Goodfellow of English. White said that these two had been in St. Louis, but then White also said once that Baker had been there, working as a boatman on the Mississippi. Such a statement, however, did not provide specific information. In those days, nearly everyone in the area had been to St. Louis, the transportation and commercial hub for the valleys of the Mississippi and Missouri Rivers. It had suffered economically during the Panic of 1857 and next was torn apart by opposing loyalties during the Civil War, but hundreds of young men were picking up jobs again at the docks and on riverboats after the war. Moreover, this city was the gateway where thousands of travelers entered the Trans-Mississippi West. Whatever roles these hordes had played during the war and its aftermath, no one talked unnecessarily about the recent past. It was better that way. Chances for a better future, beckoning on the western horizon, were what people preferred to discuss.

Idlers around Fort Dodge might have heard Baker's sweet talk as he extolled the opportunities of getting rich in the mining country of southwestern Colorado Territory. White, Strole, and Goodfellow, though, were the only ones who took Baker seriously enough to fall in with him. White said in 1907 that all four had quit their jobs with the stage company in spring 1867 to head west on a prospecting trip. White's physical ability would have complemented Baker's mental agility, and Strole proved to be a steady follower, whereas Goodfellow seems to have been the odd man out from the beginning. The one characteristic they all shared was an itchy foot.

They did not start west until spring's rain and warmth encouraged grass to grow along the trail to feed their horses, and then a late snowstorm delayed them a while longer, during which time they decided that they would need more horses for their venture. The date given by White for their start was April 13, or sometimes simply mid-April. He said that their departure point was Upper Cimarron Crossing, not Fort Dodge, although his various tales have discrepancies. When Robert Brewster Stanton interviewed White at Trinidad, Colorado, in 1907, White described their dramatic departure:

> My particular companions at this time were George Strole, Joe
> Goodfellow, and Captain Baker, as he was generally known.
> Although we called him Jim Baker, his real first name was never
> known to any of us. Early in April 1868 [1867] we four decided to
> leave the Stage Company and go west on a prospecting trip. In order
> to supply ourselves with means of transportation, we decided to
> steal some horses from the Indians who were camped on Mulberry
> Creek, about one hundred miles east of [Upper] Cimarron Crossing.

We left Cimarron about the middle of April and went east about one hundred miles to Mulberry Creek, where the Indians had a band of horses. That is, Captain Baker, George Strole and I did. Joe Goodfellow started with us but only went half way and then turned back. [Goodfellow is said to have remained at The Caches, a few miles west of Fort Dodge.] He joined us again a few days later, on our trip west. We three, Baker, Strole and I, hid in the willows along the stream all day until about nine o'clock that night when the moon came up so we could see the horses. We started toward the camp, and although the dogs in the Indian Camp began to bark, we each succeeded in catching a horse and mounting. We rounded up the band and cut out some thirteen head and drove them fast as we could gallop away up the river [the Arkansas] towards Colorado City [in Colorado Territory], which was our destination.

The Indians from whom we had stolen the horses did not over-take us, but we learned afterwards that the next night they attacked the stage barns at Cimarron and drove off thirteen head to replace the ones we had taken from them. [The version of 1917 says that fourteen horses were stolen, and yet another version speaks of the theft of stock by Indians as taking place at Fort Dodge instead.] Joe Goodfellow rejoined us. And when we had traveled two or three days, Goodfellow wanted to divide the stock equally between the four men of the party. Although Baker was captain of the party, he said that he only had one voice in the matter, but that he would put it to a vote. Baker asked me if I was willing to give up one third, and I told him I was not. Then he asked George if he would give up one third, and George said no. We argued the thing out but we could not agree with Goodfellow, but we all four went on together to Colorado City.[6]

White said that they were chased for a day and a night by the Indians without being caught. Presumably, he, Baker, and Strole each had a horse to ride from the Upper Crossing down to Mulberry Creek. After mounting one Indian pony apiece and cutting out thirteen (or fourteen), they might have had a total of nineteen or twenty, a large number for three men to herd as they raced upstream, and Goodfellow also probably had at least one mount of his own.

Justifying this theft, Baker claimed that Indians had stolen his horses at Mulberry Creek. White's accounts made no apology for the raid on the Indian camp. To him, the episode might have seemed compatible with the eye-for-an-eye ethic that prevailed during this period of emigration and settlement of the West. Although arguments for military campaigns focus on depredations by the "savages," incidents like the White-Baker-Strole raid also helped to enflame trouble. Throughout the 1860s, Indians retaliated against white people and vice versa in a seemingly endless round of raids, one side or the other taking vengeance for past injustices.

In early 1867, cholera in Indian villages kept western Kansas a little quieter than usual, but a raid took place in April at the Upper Crossing, where thirteen horses were indeed stolen from the stage barns, possibly in retaliation for the horse theft at Mulberry Creek. As spring turned to summer in 1867, hostile Indians increasingly threatened travelers on the Santa Fe Trail. In the angry atmosphere, hostilities continued in western Kansas in 1867, and in one noteworthy attack, a Mexican wagon train lost nearly 300 mules. A well-documented scare, in which a nun died, involved the Most Reverend Jean Lamy, bishop and later archbishop of Santa Fe, whom Willa Cather celebrated in her novel *Death Comes for the Archbishop*.[7]

In response to the turmoil, the Army undertook a campaign on the Great Plains. Although General George A. Custer had managed to disgrace himself during this campaign, nevertheless it culminated in the Treaty of Medicine Lodge, whereby several Plains tribes unwittingly signed away their claims to lands between the Arkansas and Platte Rivers. By then, Baker and his companions had put hundreds of miles between themselves and the hazards of life on the prairie. Following the Army's campaigns, conditions were considerably safer when White returned in 1869 to work for Barlow and Sanderson.

In April 1867 the three horse thieves rejoined Joe Goodfellow, who was waiting for them at The Caches, a well-known campsite on the Santa Fe Trail, about ten miles west of Fort Dodge. The name derived from an incident in 1822–1823, when a severe snowstorm forced a small party to camp on an island in the Arkansas River for several weeks. When their livestock died during this delay, the travelers dug caches (pits in which to hide their goods) on the north side of the river, and the party continued on foot when weather improved. The area was named for these pits, which were visible for many years after the goods were retrieved.

Beyond The Caches the foursome rode west, past Middle and Upper Cimarron Crossings and then along the Mountain Branch of the Santa Fe Trail into Colorado Territory. Their route ran through the area known as Big Timbers, a forty-five-mile-long tract of trees that once outlined the Arkansas from east of today's Lamar, Colorado, to Las Animas near Bent's Old Fort. Of this former woodland, only a few hundred cottonwoods still remained when gold seekers passed in 1859, and the enormous trees were nearly gone by 1867, as was the once-lush grass nearby. The destruction of Big Timbers by traders and travelers was one of many causes of anger among Cheyenne and Arapaho Indians, who had formerly used the area for camping, gathering wood, grazing their horses, and trading with mountain men who also camped there. As a result of this depletion of firewood, even the logs from cabins and stage stations disappeared as quickly as they were abandoned, so the team of four prospectors probably found not even vestiges in 1867.

Although the Mountain Branch passed some other well-known sites that were occupied at the time, James White's account made no mention of them. For instance, about eight miles west of today's Lamar, William Bent's stone trading post, called Bent's New Fort, stood on a bluff on the north bank of the Arkansas in Big Timbers. Built in 1852 after the abandonment of his larger, better-known post, Bent's Old Fort, his new establishment was not as successful as its predecessor, as the fur trade had been waning for several years. A few years before the Baker-White party passed the new fort, Bent had leased it to the U.S. Army to use as a commissary, and a mile to the west the Army had built additional structures, calling the entire facility Fort Wise, later known as Fort Lyon No. 1. The name Fort Wise is well-known because of its relationship with the Sand Creek Massacre of 1864, which occurred about thirty-seven miles northeast of the fort. What the Baker-White party would have passed in 1867 was a place in transition, for, following a destructive flood in 1866, the Army began to build Fort Lyon No. 2 twenty miles to the west and was preparing to move there.

With their remuda of stolen Indian ponies, it is quite possible that Baker, White, Goodfellow, and Strole thought it wise to skirt the Army installations, about which White said nothing. Nor did White say anything about Boggsville, the nearby hamlet where Tom Boggs (brother-in-law of Kit Carson's wife) and John Prowers had established homes and were irrigating ranchland. It is difficult to imagine travelers avoid-

In the 1860s, the remains of Bent's Old Fort served as the home station for Barlow, Sanderson and Company's stage operations. In the upper right, the fort is shown as it originally appeared. Author's collection, Yvonne Halburian drawing.

ing such places where supplies and a little socialization could be had, but White was silent about them.

Nonetheless, White deemed Bent's Old Fort worthy of mention. Located 140 miles west of the Santa Fe Trail's Upper Crossing, Bent's Old Fort was the most famous of the Bent trading posts. The adobe fortress, built by brothers Charles and William Bent and their partner Ceran St. Vrain in 1833, was about eight miles northeast of today's La Junta. Fur trappers, many being the legendary figures of the Old West, and several Plains Indian lodges, especially Arapaho and Cheyenne, rendezvoused and traded at the celebrated fort, which was also a magnet for wagon trains on the Mountain Branch of the Santa Fe Trail. By 1847, when Charles Bent, then the new governor of New Mexico Territory, was murdered in an uprising at Taos, New Mexico, business had been falling off with the waning of the fur trade. Also, the U.S. Army had become an unwelcome guest, with its horses and mules denuding the short-grass prairie around the trading post. The Army offered to buy the fort, but William Bent refused the offered price and chose to abandon the place in 1849, burning and destroying part of the structure with explosives as he departed.

In 1861, Bradley Barlow and Jared L. Sanderson obtained permission to use what remained of the fort as a home station. With some of the ground-level rooms still existing, Sanderson shored up remnants of the walls and he and his wife moved into the structure. The stage company continued to run coaches down the Mountain Branch southwesterly toward Raton Pass until 1880, but Bent's Old Fort marked the farthest west along the Arkansas River that Barlow and Sanderson carried mail at the time, for another company had the contract to carry it from there to Denver.[8] Although James White said no more in his accounts than the fact that he and his companions went to Bent's Fort in 1867, one can imagine them staying long enough to relax and gossip with stage company employees, some of whom they might have known, before moving on. Two years later White had an opportunity to become better acquainted with this area when he again worked for Barlow and Sanderson.

Beyond Bent's Old Fort, the four horse thieves passed the mouth of Timpas Creek where the well-worn Mountain Branch veered to the southwest toward a new settlement called Trinidad, before crossing Raton Pass and continuing down to Santa Fe. In 1867, a little north of Raton Pass, Trinidad with its stage station was just coming into existence. One day, after the rough little settlement and James White both had matured a bit, White would make his home in Trinidad.

But for now, he and his companions remained on another well-traveled road up the Arkansas River, over the gently rising prairie, mile by mile toward the mountains, a blue mirage on the horizon. In the distance, Pikes Peak came into view, still glistening white with a blanket of melting snow. Leaves on cottonwoods along the river would have been greening, and a few fields were plowed at scattered ranchos in readiness for the corn, beans, chilis, and wheat that were irrigated with ditch water. In late spring, the Arkansas, which fed the acequias, would have been running brown and full with snowmelt from the distant mountains.

At Pueblo, where Fountain Creek met the Arkansas, the four men were about a day's ride from the mountains. This fledgling community was not a major attraction yet, although it was the closest thing to a real town that the four men had seen since long before their days at Fort Dodge. A few Fifty-Niners, recognizing that there were better prospects for earning a livelihood in supply towns than in placers, had given birth to Pueblo. Several years earlier at this location, an adobe post called El Pueblo had attracted trappers, traders, and tramps, but Ute and Jicarilla Apache Indians killed most of the polyglot occupants of El Pueblo in 1854, and the site had been abandoned. When the four horse thieves arrived, Pueblo offered a few shops, a cluster of adobe structures, houses, and even a school and some entertainment, but White made no mention of the place in his various accounts.

From there, the foursome easily could have continued west up the Arkansas to Cañon City and the San Juan mining country, or they could have dropped south to the Huerfano River and thence into the mountains. In the Huerfano area, they might have been welcomed by some of the settlers who were Confederate sympathizers during the War Between the States, but the foursome had a different route in mind. Leaving the Arkansas, they headed north up Fountain Creek to Colorado City, at the foot of Pikes Peak. White's biographer Eilean Adams has said that they were seeking a "gateway" to the San Juans, but they were taking a roundabout detour instead.

Their journey from Mulberry Creek to Colorado City had covered little more than 300 miles, some of those at a fast enough pace to escape pursuing Indians; yet, the trip had taken about a month. At an average of about ten miles a day, the excursion can best be described as leisurely, and they were still in no rush when they arrived at Colorado City.

There, Baker ran into a few men he had known in 1860–1861 in the San Juans. Having been swept to the mountains with the rush to Pikes Peak or Bust, they had constructed a few cabins at the foot of the peak before riding the wave of prospectors into the San Juan Mountains. When the tide abruptly receded, they settled in their shelters below Pikes Peak and began to lay out a supply town. Colorado City offered the best route at the time to the mining camps around South Park and the Upper Arkansas River Valley, and the ambitious founders aspired to rival Denver. Rough-hewn though it was, Colorado City even succeeded in luring the territorial legislature to meet in one of its little log buildings in 1862, but the legislators had scurried back to Denver after only a few days. Nevertheless, the little town soon boasted of having a few hundred cabins, shops, small farms, a flour mill, scenic wonders like the Garden of the Gods, mineral springs a couple of miles to the west, some stalwart defenders of civilization who served in the militia at the Sand Creek Massacre, a Methodist church, and a Catholic church.

Like early prospectors throughout the West, the citizenry of Colorado City was cosmopolitan. For instance, there was the Frenchman,

Anthony Bott, one of Baker's old acquaintances from his San Juan prospecting days, who had donated land for Colorado City's Catholic church. A German, George Bute, who had invested in the Abiquiu, Pagosa, and Baker City Road Company with Baker and others, had settled down in Colorado City and become clerk and recorder of El Paso County. Another acquaintance from the San Juan debacle was the Scotsman David McShane, a farmer north of town, who soon would become chairman of El Paso County's Board of Commissioners.[9] A participant in the San Juan expedition, Noisy Tom Pollock had purchased land around the nearby mineral springs at Manitou from his father-in-law, Colonel John M. Chivington, but Pollock, who still kept busy in many enterprises in many places, appears to have been absent in May 1867. Even though some other prospectors of 1860–1861 denounced Baker for enticing them to the San Juan placers, his acquaintances at Colorado City appear to have held no grudge. McShane later went so far as to embellish the hero of the San Juan fiasco with the title "Colonel."

At Colorado City, Baker, White, Strole, and Goodfellow had opportunities to hear discouraging news about placer mining in the mountains but more promising rumors about activity down the San Juan River and the Lower Colorado or around Prescott, Arizona, where some of the prospectors of 1860–1861 had gone. Anywhere that there might be some excitement worth following up was worth hearing about. The three horse thieves sold a mule for $200, and Goodfellow bought two horses and a colt from the stolen Indian remuda, so the party had sufficient funds with which to buy supplies for the trail — probably things like flour, coffee, sugar, beans, side pork, pick axes, shovels, gold pans, candles, tobacco, maybe a fresh pack of cards, new shirts or boots, and, of course, whiskey.

Having sold some of their livestock, the four adventurers might have had enough cash left over to indulge in a bath and to enjoy the town's entertainment, a few hands of poker, and some ladies of the night, although Baker, White, and Strole figured that their recreational activities weren't worth discussing, and Goodfellow may have been too finicky to indulge.

In the latter part of May, after a week or so they were ready to leave Colorado City and head up Ute Pass to the mining country.

DISASTER

THE PHRASE "SEEING THE ELEPHANT" WAS POPULAR AT THE TIME OF THE GOLD rushes in the nineteenth century. Its implication was that the beholder had seen as much as he could tolerate of the strange creature. A brief glimpse of the elephant was enough to prompt many prospectors to give up and go home. Depictions of elephants began to appear on some of the wagons that had started out so optimistically with "PIKES PEAK OR BUST" emblazoned on the canvas.

A popular jingle of the day began:

It was six men of Indostan
To learning much inclined,
Who went to see the Elephant
(Though all of them were blind)
That each by observation
Might satisfy his mind.[1]

In the rest of the verse, each blind man reaches out his hand, touches one part of the elephant, and in his mind's eye imagines something very different from what his companions are picturing, none of which resembles an elephant at all.

In 1860–1861, like many other prospectors, Charles Baker had a glimpse of the elephant, and during the years 1861–1865, James White had several peeks, but neither had yet seen the entire beast from head to tail. Undaunted, White, Baker, Strole, and Goodfellow set forth in the spring of 1867 en route to discovering how the creature appears when it is on a rampage.

They left Colorado City for the mining country in May. One account offers a precise date, May 25, for their departure, although others refer more broadly to late May. White once said that Baker made notes in a little book as they went along, but unfortunately for subsequent chroniclers, this record did not survive the journey and, most unfortunately for Baker, neither did he. White noted that Baker had a compass, too, which also disappeared.

As White narrated years later, the four men set out on foot with their packtrain, though often a party of prospectors would have had a string consisting of one mount for each man and one pack animal to carry his gear. Each man usually had a rifle or a shotgun in a scabbard and a revolver in a holster. Subsequently, White claimed to have two revolvers, so he was well-armed.

The route passed the mineral springs at Manitou, followed Ute Pass, where they gained a couple thousand feet in elevation quickly, and then swung around Pikes Peak's shoulders and through the hills toward South Park. This route, closely following today's U.S. Highway 24 west from Colorado Springs, was a notably indirect way to reach the San Juan Mountains, but it might have been chosen to allow investigation of the diggings in the Upper Arkansas River Valley. It was also safer than taking a more southerly route along the Front Range where Indians were conducting raids at this time.

The route had been merely a steep trail in 1860, but by 1867 Anthony Bott, Baker's old acquaintance, had made a number of improvements. He had carved out a grade in Ute Pass to create what might be called a road to South Park, although it was still rough and boggy in places, but travel through the largely uninhabited region was easier than it had been for prospectors only a few years earlier. Like many others

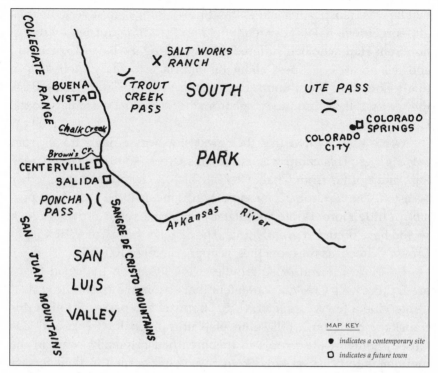

Colorado City to Brown's Creek.

who undertook similar improvements in the early years of the territory's existence, Bott charged tolls from travelers on his thoroughfare, unless they succeeded in detouring around the tollgates. After crossing Wilkerson Pass, the men descended into the sweeping, grassy basin of South Park and began to see hints of human settlement, like Sam Hartsel's fine Hereford cattle grazing on the open range. The livestock was intended to be sold as meat in markets in Denver and in the dwindling mining camps of the region, but passersby most likely enjoyed some steak dinners, too, free of charge.

On the west side of South Park, Baker and his cohorts could easily go a couple of miles out of their way to see Charles and Mary Melissa Nye Hall at their Salt Works Ranch, and White told Robert Brewster Stanton, during the interview at Trinidad in 1907, that the team of prospectors camped at the Salt Springs. This place was worth seeing, for Charles Hall had set up pans there to evaporate the salt that he was transporting across the "Snowy Range" to silver refineries at Georgetown. Baker apparently had no fear of an unfriendly reception from Hall, who had suffered greatly during the Baker Expedition, and felt no awkwardness about his marriage to Mary Melissa Nye that followed it. From South Park, using the easy Trout Creek Pass, they crossed the Mosquito Range from the South Platte drainage to the Upper Arkansas.[2]

White told Stanton that their next stop was a day's travel from Salt Springs. This camp was at Brown's Creek, south of Trout Creek Pass and not far from Chalk Creek, which he mentioned on another occasion. The trip from Colorado City had taken about a week, or possibly a little more, White speculated, so the arrival at Brown's Creek would have occurred in early June. The distance from Colorado City to Brown's Creek, as the crow flies, is approximately 100 miles.

By 1867, a dozen or so families were living on the small farms around Brown's Creek, a settlement that acquired a post office called Centerville a few years later. (U.S. Highway 285 passes through this transitory place on a hill south of Nathrop, Chalk Creek, and Gas Creek.) Some of the people in this area had originally come to the mountains to prospect but, like many others, turned to their former occupation of farming when they noticed that they could better provide for themselves and their families if they directed their energies toward producing potatoes, flour, and hay instead of panning for elusive gold. In the mid-1860s, farms were scattered along the Arkansas on the grasslands in the lee of the majestic Sawatch Range, and, in fields between today's Buena Vista and Brown' Creek, water was flowing through small irrigation ditches.

Some of these settlers are remembered as respectable pioneers, but others were troublemakers who took part during the 1870s in a malevolent feud called the Lake County War, or sometimes the Gas Creek War. (Lake County then included lands that became Chaffee County and other counties to the west.) During those troubled times, property was burned, people were murdered, and some decent families were forced to seek safer homes. Among the more peaceful neighbors at Brown's Creek were the families of Galatia Sprague and Jacob Ehrhart, who were criticized by some of their ne'er-do-well neighbors as being too self-righteous. Whatever one's conclusions about these events, it is tempting to comment that the ugliness of human nature did not com-

View of the Sawatch Range from the Centerville Cemetery, near Brown's Creek. Photo by author.

pare favorably with the beauty of the landscape around Colorado's Chalk Creek, Gas Creek, and Brown's Creek. While they were there in 1867, James White and Joe Goodfellow also evinced the spitefulness that seemed to plague the area.

Jacob Ehrhart's son, T. J. Ehrhart, composed a letter in 1916 for Thomas F. Dawson, detailing what happened at Brown's Creek in June 1867.[3] Ehrhart wrote that his parents had moved into a one-room cabin at Brown's Creek in 1866, near twelve other families who were living in the area "six or eight miles square." That fall the men got together and built a one-room, log schoolhouse, a structure that was on the east side of today's U.S. Highway 285. Galatia Sprague taught at this school during the winter. In 1867, James White and his cold, wet companions took shelter in the schoolhouse when a late spring snowstorm struck. They remained for a few days until conditions improved enough to permit travel. The schoolhouse had no floor, but it did have a fireplace at one end where the men could warm themselves and cook.

While preparing to move on after weather improved, White used the fireplace to bake bread. Baking bread over coals required some effort, though not much skill—simply stirring up flour, salt, and water and browning it in the bottom of a prospector's gold pan—to make enough unleavened hardtack for the trail. Loaves would be an unheard-of luxury, requiring a heavy Dutch oven, which few prospectors carried. During his Army career, White would have become well acquainted with hardtack and learned that it was best dipped in coffee, bacon grease, and hunger to render it palatable.

It is useful here to interject White's information that was given in 1907 to Stanton concerning the prospectors' preparations for departure and a fight that ensued on the morning after the baking of bread:

> Baker had put me in charge of the pack animals. We had one mule in the outfit and put two hundred pounds on the mule and packed the other animals equally. That night near Salt Springs [Brown's Creek] I took 25 pounds of flour off Goodfellow's horse and baked most of it into bread. The flour not used I put back on the horse, and was going to put the bread on the horse also, when Goodfellow said the bread ought to be put on the mule. I said it ought to go on the horse because I had taken the flour off the horse.
>
> We quarreled over it. We drew our revolvers and passed five shots between us. I hit Goodfellow twice, shot him once in the leg and once in the arm. We disarmed him, and put him on his horse and I took him to a house. I told the woman to take care of him, that he had two or three hundred dollars and two horses, and that he would pay her when he got well. As we parted he said to me that when he saw me again he would kill me, and I told him when he saw me to go ahead and shoot. I bade him good-by and left him, and Baker, Strole, and I went on our journey.[4]

Ehrhart's description of what he witnessed as a young boy, almost fifty years prior to the writing of his letter to Dawson, differs in only a few particulars:

> On the morning after the weather had settled, the party was packing up to move, and I, as a boy, was very anxious to go from the cabin we occupied over to witness the breaking up of camp, but my mother objected to me going over, and I stood at some distance from our cabin watching operations and heard a number of revolver shots and saw that there was considerable excitement and activity among the men at the schoolhouse and the pack animals. Very soon afterwards some one from the camp—I believe Capt. Baker [or White according to his own account]—came to our cabin and stated that one of the men had been wounded in the foot, and wanted to leave the wounded man somewhere where he could have care and attention, and we having but one room, he was directed to a neighbor's farther up the stream by the name of Sprague [Galatia Sprague], where he went and made arrangements to leave the

injured man, whose name was Joe Goodfellow. The remainder of
the party then proceeded on their way.[5]

Violence over a petty matter like whether to load bread on a mule
or a horse is difficult to understand unless a clash of personalities,
primed with a little whiskey no doubt, had been building since the episode in Kansas when Goodfellow had been a slacker during the theft
of Indian ponies and then resisted paying for a share of the animals.
In contrast, White appears to have performed his portion of work and
then some throughout the journey. In the Old West, there was room
for nearly every sort of person except someone who regarded himself
as better than others or who failed to pull his own weight when necessary, and Goodfellow appears to have fit both categories. Not only did
White figure that he had good reason to do what he did, but he also
proved to be the better marksman.

Later, when White's exploits had expanded dramatically beyond
the mere baking of bread and the shooting of a quarrelsome companion, interviewers generally heard nothing about this episode. At first
White omitted it and said merely that he, Baker, and Strole were traveling together when they left Colorado City. This omission was later corrected in 1869 during a meeting with General William Jackson Palmer,
who wrote in a letter afterward:

> The fourth I had never heard accounted for, and had often won-
> dered why White had never referred to him. One gentleman in my
> presence threw doubts upon the whole story, because this last indi-
> vidual was never accounted for — I availed myself of this opportu-
> nity to ask White the question direct — "What became of the fourth
> man." He hesitated a moment and then said "I shot him" — It was in
> a quarrel on the Arkansas in which he said the other had given the
> first and repeated provocation. This accounted for his never having
> mentioned him before.[6]

Subsequently, White made no effort to conceal the story about
Goodfellow. Apparently Joe Goodfellow recovered, but without yet
having tried his hand as a prospector, he had seen enough of the
elephant and disappeared. White said that Goodfellow went "back
home" after his recovery at Brown's Creek, but no solid evidence of his
whereabouts after their separation has been found. In the U.S. Census
of 1870 a thirty-year-old butcher named Phillip Goodfellow is listed

in Fairplay, and P. J. Goodfellow appears as a member of a jury in Lake County, but other clues for finding Joe Goodfellow have failed to surface.

By mid-June at the latest, the three remaining members of the Baker party were on the trail out of Brown's Creek with about 200 miles still remaining before they reached Baker's destination in the San Juan Mountains. When they started, they would not have idled, for settlers in those days had a fondness for frontier law and order that inspired them to pursue folks who shot others, but even without dawdling along the way, the trek would have required another two weeks or so.

The trio traveled down the Arkansas to Poncha Springs and over Poncha Pass into the San Luis Valley, then up the Rio Grande by way of Wagon Wheel Gap to the headwaters of the river. Passing through the broad, flat San Luis Valley, they might have seen scattered farms belonging to Spanish-speaking settlers and a few other newcomers who also were taking up land by then, but White mentioned none of them nor the year-old village of Saguache. Logically, most travelers would have stopped at Otto Mears's store there for another sack of flour or a bottle of whiskey. Although Mears was not yet famous, he later became so after he turned his limitless energies to the building of toll roads and railroads that penetrated the San Juans.

The route of Baker, White, and Strole reached the Rio Grande at Loma, a cluster of adobe buildings on the north side of the river. A few years later, another town called Del Norte was established across the river on the south bank as a supply center for the San Juans' booming silver mines, which did not yet exist. From Loma the three prospectors went up the Rio Grande through meadows and narrowing valleys toward Wagon Wheel Gap and Stony Pass. Wagon Wheel Gap, where the river is confined between cliffs, was named for a wagon wheel that was found by early pioneers, who speculated that it might have been broken when people were escaping the San Juan debacle in 1861. In their desperate condition, however, it seems unlikely that anyone dragged a wagon over Stony Pass.

In the headwaters of the Rio Grande, White, Baker, and Strole crossed Stony Pass on the Continental Divide and descended to the Animas River drainage and Eureka Gulch, or "Rickey Gulch," as White called it. The trail over Stony Pass can best be summed up in the word

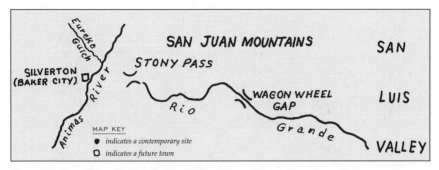

Stony Pass and Eureka Gulch area.

difficult, although it would later become the route most frequently used in the 1870s to reach the San Juan mines, prior to the arrival of the Denver and Rio Grande Railway's narrow-gauge trains at Durango and Silverton. In the 1870s, during the San Juan mining boom, some crude improvements in the Stony Pass route were made, with the route then veering over the slightly lower Cunningham Pass—a name recalling one of Baker's companions of 1860–1861. In the final descent to the valley of the Animas River, the trails from Stony and Cunningham Passes joined and passed through Cunningham Gulch, an area where rich lode mines later yielded their treasure.[7]

In early July 1867, Baker, White, and Strole were at the diggings on the Animas. White was sure that on the Fourth of July they were in camp at Rickey Gulch, as he called Eureka Gulch, which lies four miles northeast of the foot of Cunningham Gulch. In both Eureka and Cunningham Gulches, Baker had staked claims in 1860–1861, and he still had faith in them, especially in the one at Eureka Gulch. White reported that he saw the handsawed sluice boxes that Baker said he had made during that earlier time. Particularly, White recalled that they dug a long ditch, 150 by 15 feet, a chore that must have reminded him bitterly of his hard labor at Fort Craig. He said that the three prospectors "stayed in this neighborhood about a month, prospecting," but their efforts were not rewarding. Convinced of the futility of further work in the placers, the three packed up and left.

When Major E. M. Hamilton came through this region in 1871 on a military reconnaissance and saw prospect holes and full containers of whiskey around Cunningham and Eureka Gulches, he speculated that weather or hostile Indians had forced some prospectors to beat

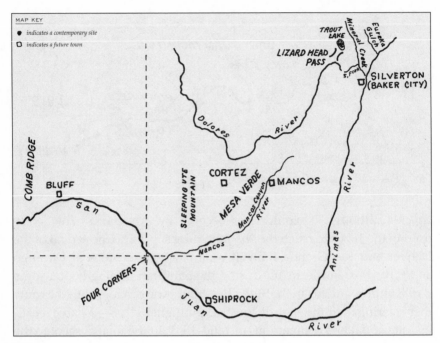

Route from Eureka Gulch to Comb Ridge.

a hasty retreat. Suggestions that these prospectors might have been White, Baker, and Strole are tempting, but more likely the containers belonged to other prospectors who came into the area afterward. Weather was not a factor in mid-summer that would have caused the men to leave, and White made no mention of a storm or of Indians here. Moreover, a picture of White leaving whiskey behind is difficult to imagine.

From the information about their prospecting, the party's whereabouts can be traced until approximately late July. During the three and a half months after they left Mulberry Creek, Baker had been leading his companions on a journey that covered at least 600 miles of prairie and mountain. The decision of the leader and his two companions to leave Eureka Gulch after a mere month is reminiscent of Kellogg's description of Baker as a "restless, adventurous, impecunious man who was always in search of something new," and now other diggings, farther on, beckoned Baker. Among these locations, the headwaters of the Dolores River looked inviting. White later said that they

went to the Dolores River and the Mancos River, the same geographical region that Baker visited, according to his newspaper story in 1860,
when he wrote about having been to the Dolores, Mancos, and San
Miguel Rivers. If one can accept that both Baker and White understood
the geography correctly, the Baker party in 1867 went from Baker's
Park to Mineral Creek and then up South Mineral Creek, a dozen miles
or so as the crow flies, to Trout Lake in the drainage of the San Miguel
River, for a brief stay. From there, they crossed nearby Lizard Head
Pass to the south, thence down the Dolores to the Mancos, and eventually to the San Juan River.[8]

White abbreviated his description when he said in 1916, "We
went down the Animas about 5 miles, crossed over into the Mancos."
Going down the Animas about five miles would have taken them into
Baker's Park. From today's Silverton in Baker's Park it is only two
miles to Mineral Creek. Based on an interview with White in early
1868, the botanist Charles Christopher Parry wrote this version of the
trek: "[Prospecting at Eureka Gulch] being only partially successful,
they continued farther to the west, passing the Dolores, and reaching
the Mancos, which latter stream was followed down to the main valley of the San Juan."[9] White also mentioned to Parry that they camped
at a lake for a couple of days and fished. Although the San Juans and
the La Platas both offer many lovely lakes where the three men might
have enjoyed a holiday, Trout Lake had long been famous among trappers and prospectors for a similar respite. Among all his vague memories, White later recalled distinctly his two pleasant days of fishing.

Another location soon made an unforgettable, if slightly inaccurate, impression on him. This place was Mancos Canyon, through
which he, Baker, and Strole passed in 1867. For years afterward he
remembered seeing some of the famous Ancestral Puebloan (Anasazi)
ruins of Mesa Verde. South of the town of Mancos, Colorado, Mancos
Canyon takes its sinuous course south, along the east side of the mesa
before turning west along the south side of the mesa. In the southern
portion of Mesa Verde National Park, a visitor on Chapin Mesa looks
down upon the Mancos River as it wends westward before passing
from sight through the Ute Mountain Tribal Park.

The journey of White, Baker, and Strole is noteworthy, for it pre-
dates by a few years any of the more widely accepted "first" reports
about Mesa Verde. White told his daughters about Mesa Verde, and his

Following a trail to the San Juan River in 1867, White, Baker, and Strole traveled through Mancos Canyon at Mesa Verde. Courtesy, Denver Public Library, Western History Collection, no. 1238, William Henry Jackson photo, 1892.

story was repeated in 1917 to Thomas Dawson, who himself had a serious interest in Colorado's history and prehistory. White's description, as repeated in Thomas F. Dawson's booklet, *The Grand Canyon*, reads: "At the head of the Mancos we saw a large lookout house, about 100 feet high, which was built of cobblesotnes [*sic*]. Farther down the canyon we saw houses built of cobblestones, and also saw small houses about 2 feet square that were built up about 50 feet on the side of the canyon and seemed to be houses of some kind of a bird that was worshiped."[10] It is impossible to understand what the hypothetical "worshiped birds" might have been. Possibly White saw small granaries that appeared to him to be bird cages, or he might have seen rock art depicting a bird. Possibly he saw the "Eagle's Nest" ruin, so high and seemingly inaccessible to humans that investigators later bestowed its descriptive name.

White, Baker, and Strole preceded the widely acclaimed "discoverers" of Mesa Verde of the 1870s and 1880s, but the three prospectors' observation in 1867 was not the first. Navajo and Ute Indians who occupied the region certainly had seen the ruins, although they avoided the mysterious houses and towers built by "the dead ones," as Utes called them. Similarly, Paiute people wandering through this area had most likely seen the haunting ruins of the Anasazi. Early explorers, however, had narrowly missed the site. In 1776 the Domínguez-Escalante Expedition came upon the remains of a small pueblo near the Dolores River, though not the spectacular Mesa Verde ruins. A more egregious oversight was that of Captain John N. Macomb and his topographical engineers in 1859. Following the Old Spanish Trail after parting company with Albert Pfeiffer, Macomb's men camped at the Mancos River, and their geologist, John S. Newberry, climbed Mesa Verde, admired the sweeping view of the Colorado Plateau to the west, and descended without having spotted the remarkable prehistoric ruins. Some of the disappointed Forty-Niners working their way eastward from California probably came through Mancos Canyon and saw the ruins, though, and malcontents from Baker's diggings, including Doc Arnold, are known to have entered the area in late 1860 or early 1861 when they were heading to the Southwest.

The Hayden Expedition's members later spotted the archaeological site in 1875, and miner John Moss of Parrott City led the expedition's photographer, William H. Jackson, back again to investigate the ruins on his own time. Others who came were the geologist William Holmes and journalist Ernest Ingersoll. Jackson, Holmes, and Ingersoll published detailed descriptions, and next the Wetherills famously spread the word about their own discoveries, resulting in plunder by collectors and archaeologists of many stripes. James White's early impressions of the ruins did not come to light for several decades and were generally overlooked by the public then.

The Jackson-Holmes writings, being considerably more precise, reveal how little White recalled about Mancos Canyon in his later years. Jackson's description of the old Indian trail that he followed through the canyon is of special interest here. As Jackson wrote, the canyon was about 200 yards wide, sometimes more, sometimes less, with the stream meandering from side to side. It was densely bordered with undergrowth, willows, and "thorny bushes," often causing the team to scramble along a narrow path on the "treacherous" bank. The sandy trail was strewn with broken potsherds. When Jackson and his companions climbed to examine alcoves and stone houses on the canyon's wall in 1875, they found them already looted.[11]

Beyond Mesa Verde, White said simply, "We followed the Mancos down until we struck the San Juan." As Baker, White, and Strole progressed past Mesa Verde, the terrain opened out. They left behind the yellow-gray, striated cliffs and spires of rock, views of the dark juniper and piñon pines on the mesa, and entered the broad, arid San Juan Basin with Sleeping Ute Mountain looming to the north. Far behind were the crystalline mountain streams, tall evergreen forests and groves of pine, the mountain lake where they had fished, the disappointing diggings at Eureka Gulch, the calamity at Brown's Creek, and the trail across the prairie to the Rockies. They were entering a world of sand and stone.

According to White, the party was heading to the Grand River as they descended the Mancos toward the San Juan River. (Until 1921 the Colorado River above the confluence with the Green River was officially called the Grand River.) Whether White had any useful knowledge about these regions seems unlikely, although he might have overheard conversations about them during his earlier wanderings. More likely, Baker had picked up information from prospectors and now intended to investigate the Colorado, Grand, or Green. Or perhaps he and his companions were planning to seek gold in the San Juan River

The San Juan River near Bluff, Utah. Photo by author.

country, the area where some of the disgruntled prospectors had indi-
cated they were headed when they left Baker's diggings in 1860 and
1861. In 1867, prospectors from Arizona were turning their attention to
the San Juan River again.

Leaving Mancos Canyon, the Mancos River runs about thirty miles
across open country through sand, yucca, and prickly pear cactus to
the confluence with the San Juan River in the Four Corners region,
where Colorado, New Mexico, Arizona, and Utah meet. At this point,
the men crossed the San Juan to its south (left) bank. As White later
related, he and the other men then went down the San Juan "as far
as we could and then swam our horses across and started over to the
Grand [Colorado] River."[12]

Knowing where they crossed the San Juan, in which direction they
crossed, where they intended to go after the fording, and how much
time elapsed afterward are significant matters when one attempts to
understand what happened subsequently, but since such information
was never ascertained, the saga becomes a tangled knot. Dates and
distances are important, but the accounts given by White to various

persons are conflicting and confusing. White told Stanton that he and his companions left Mancos Canyon about the first of August. This estimate seems to be fairly accurate within a few days, although White also said that the trip from Baker's Park to the San Juan took three days, an amount of time that is too brief to allow for the 150 miles from Silverton to the mouth of the Mancos, plus two pleasant days of fishing along the way. Also, his statements in a letter to his brother in 1867 and in the account given to C. C. Parry that appeared in print in 1868, saying that they followed the San Juan River for 200 miles, are obviously incorrect. The length of the river from the Four Corners all the way to its mouth at the Colorado River is less than 200 miles, and the Baker party did not go that far. Stanton proposed different distances, and White vaguely agreed that Stanton's figures might be correct. My calculations are that it is a little more than fifty miles from the mouth of the Mancos to Comb Ridge, where the trio might have left the San Juan River, and it is about 200 miles from Silverton to Comb Ridge. White's statements about mileages would provide several points for disputing his story. After pressing for more precise information in his interview with White, Stanton abruptly asserted to White that he could have been lost after they left the mouth of the Mancos River, and White conceded, "Maybe I was."[13]

Information presented by White to Stanton did no concur with what White said a decade later when he was nearly eighty years old. In kindness to White, it must be granted that the memories of aging people often falter. In addition, Stanton's manner was like that of an inquisitor, possibly contributing to White's confusion when he felt pressed for facts. Such considerations, however, do not account for the contradictory information White gave in late 1867 and in early 1868, as we shall see.

Nonetheless, the party's intention to go down the San Juan River seems inarguable. It is possible that they did a little panning as they proceeded, despite the unpromising appearance of the sandy, eroded banks of the river and its tributary washes along the way. Encouraging them, Baker suggested to his companions that gold could have washed down the river from the mountains. When the trio reached the point beyond which they could not take their horses, many researchers believe that they were at Comb Ridge, a short distance below Bluff, Utah. Near Comb Ridge, the river enters the San Juan Canyon,

76

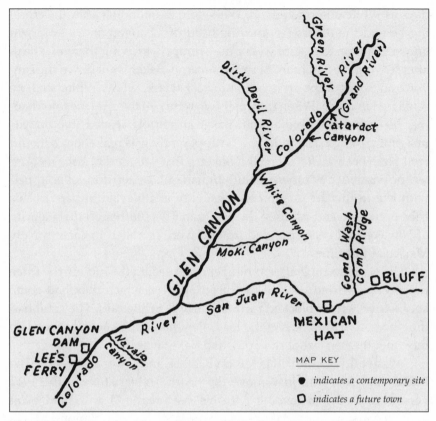

The Colorado River, from the confluence with the Green River to Lee's Ferry.

although Lime Ridge, a mile downstream, would unquestionably be the final limit to further progress downstream with horses. Unless the group had made previous crossings upstream, they still were on the left bank, from which they would have forded to the right, or north, bank, but White told Stanton that they went south. White also said that they swam their horses across the river and that they then headed to the Grand (or Colorado) River.

After fording the river, the Baker party most likely headed up Comb Wash or Butler Wash in a northeasterly direction, the opposite of what White told Stanton. If they had actually headed south from the river, they could have gone down Cane Valley and Chinle Creek, but this route does not jibe with the events that occurred in the next few

days as White described them. White told Stanton that after the crossing he and the others went to the head of a canyon and then down
another canyon to a place where they camped, arriving there two days
after leaving the San Juan.[14] From this camp, Baker went down the canyon and Strole went up it, searching for water, while, White said, he
remained in camp. When the other two returned to camp, he told them
that he had seen an Indian, but Baker and Strole argued that he was
imagining things. The Indian, who apparently was real enough, could
well have been a Ute, since the Baker party was in that tribe's country, or possibly a Southern Paiute Indian, whose territory overlapped
with Ute in this area. Another possibility is a Navajo Indian, as this
tribe occupied land south of the San Juan River, although the majority
of Navajos had been rounded up and were corralled in eastern New
Mexico at this time.

The next morning after White reported seeing the Indian, the three
prospectors started back in the direction from which they had come
because the terrain blocked further passage, White said. They still had
their horses. With Baker in the lead, they had gone about halfway up
the canyon when a shot rang out, and Baker was hit.

White told Stanton, "He fell on his face and never answered. The
Indian had shot him just above the heart." A variation in the 1917
version finds Baker gasping with his last breath, "I am killed." Yet
another version adds Baker's last words to his companions, "Save
yourselves."

The absence of concrete evidence has not deterred considerable
debate about what occurred in mid-August and the following days.
White related in his letter to his brother Josh on September 26, 1867,
his own version, as of that date, about what happened then and in the
next few days:

> Dear Brother it has ben some time senCe i have heard from you I
> got no anCe from the last letter that i rote i Went prospeCted with
> Captin Baker and gorge strole in the San Won montin Wee found
> vry god prospCk but noth that Would pay. then Wee stare Down
> the San Won river wee travel down a bout 200 mils then Wee Cross
> over on Coloreado and Camp We lad over one day Wee ["found
> that," *deleted*] found out that Wee Cold not travel down the river
> and our horse Wass sore fite and Wee had may up our mines to
> tureen back When Wee Was attacked by 15 or 20 utes indes they

kill Baker and gorge Strole and my self tok fore ropes off from our hourse and a ax ten pounds of flour and our guns We had 15 milles to woak ["before," *deleted*] to Colarado Wee got to the river Jest at ["dalk," *deleted*] night Wee bilt a raft that night Wee saile all that night Wee had good Sailing fro three days and the ["third days," *deleted*] fore day gorge strole Was Wash of from the raft and down that left me alone. . . .[15]

Considering the fact that the leader had led his followers on a prof-itless venture and now was surely lost, it is not unrealistic to wonder whether a quarrel could have broken out among the three men with deadly consequences. Baker's companions might have become con-vinced that he was not merely "somewhat enthusiastic," as one earlier acquaintance described him, but a "maniac," as another called him. Several writers have implied that White, rather than Indians, might have killed Baker. The most pointed insinuation was made by P. T. Reilly, a well-known river-runner and historian, who wrote that some students of this episode will contend that "the quick-tempered White probably killed his companions Baker and Strole during a camp quar-rel and offered the stories of the Indian ambush and drowning to cover his crime."[16] Lacking evidence, such an argument can never be proved today.

The voyage described by White in the rest of his letter to Josh was perilous from the start. As White described the original raft to Stanton, it consisted of only four cottonwood logs, six to eight inches thick and eight to ten feet long, lashed together with lariats. Scarcely an ade-quate vessel, it was replaced after four days, according to White, with a sturdier one, eight feet wide and consisting of cedar logs a foot in diameter and fifteen or sixteen feet long. From this second raft, White said that Strole was thrown, never to reappear in the waters of the Colorado River nor in historical evidence.

The name of Charles Baker, however, would reemerge again and again, not only in history but also in figments of narrators' imagi-nations. Of course, in view of the popularity of treasure tales in the West's lore, it is not surprising to find a story that the prospectors had left a cache of gold when they evacuated the San Juan Mountains in 1861 and that some returned to recover it but it was gone. As the lore goes, Baker was blamed for taking it. Still, because "he was presum-ably killed by Indians as he was preparing to lead an exploring party

Navigation of the Big Canon

A terrible voyage

Callville   September 26 1867.

Dear Brother it has ben some time sence i
have heard from you i yet no ancer from the
last letter that i roat to you for i left soon
after i rote i went prospected with Captin Baker in
the San Won montin wee found very god prospeck but
noth that wold pay then wee stare down the San Won river
wee travell down a bout 200 miles then wee cross over
on Colorado and Camp wee lad one day wee
found out that wee cold not travel down the river and
our hors wars sow fite and wee had may up ous mines to
turene back when wee was all to gethy 15 or 20 miles inder thay
kill Baker and yorge strole and my self took fore ropes
off our hourse and a ax ten pounds of flour and ous
gunns wee had 15 milles to wak to Colarado wee got
to the river bext at night wee bilt a raft that
night wee got it bilt abot teen o clock the night
wee saile all that night wee had good saileing fr
three days and the fore days yorge strole was wash
of from the raft and down that left me alone i though
that it wold be my turne next i then pool off my
boos and pands i then tide a rope to my hose i wend
over falls from 10 to 15 feet me my raft wold
tip ous three and fore time a days the thard day
wee loss ous flour flour and fore seven days i
had to eat to rathhide nife cabes the 8 days i got some
muskit beens the 13 days a party of inder frendly thay
wold not giue me noth eat so i giue my pistols
for hine pards of a dog i ead ous of for super and the
other breakfast the 14 days i rive at Collville whare i was

Letter from James White at Callville, Nevada, to his brother Joshua, September 26, 1867. Courtesy, The Bancroft Library, University of California, Berkeley, microfilm, Rich: 547.7.

Letter from James White to his brother Joshua (continued).

into the Grand Canyon, the gold may still be buried somewhere along the Animas River."[17]

Early settlers of the area around Durango, Colorado, had a special talent for inventing such fantasies about Baker. Causes of their errors might have been the faulty memories of the aging pioneers who recounted oral history late in their lives or the pleasure they derived from being sought out as authorities, deservedly or not. In any case, an absence of verifiable evidence did not prevent old-timers from telling bogus narratives and undiscerning publishers from printing them. One such questionable storyteller was Robert Dwyer, a former sheriff from Durango, Colorado. In his story about Baker, recorded several years after the episode he was describing, Dwyer and John Moss were in the Blue Mountains (near Monticello, Utah) in 1875, when they met Ute Indians who claimed to have known Baker and pointed toward the junction of the San Juan and Colorado Rivers as the place where Baker had been killed. Dwyer's story scarcely offers reliable evidence, for the "junction" is a very big area, some hundred miles southwest of the Blue Mountains. In addition, there is no explanation about how these Indians "knew" Baker. And finally, Dwyer destroyed his own credibility by describing "Col. Baker" as a man from Georgia who was a civil engineer in government service.[18]

A particularly discombobulated statement full of misinformation about Baker appeared in the *Durango Herald,* which said: "Col. Baker and two men, a Mr. White and a Mr. Steward whose first names we are unable to obtain, passed through the southern portion of Animas Valley in 1876 when en route to Southern California. At the mouth of the San Juan river, Col. Baker was killed by Indians."[19]

Although Charles Baker had no headstone to mark his passing, he deserved a proper eulogy. It was provided in the prodigious *Works of Hubert Howe Bancroft,* which have been considered by some readers to be authoritative sources but by many others to be unreliable. Depending on paid interviewers to gather and write material, these volumes often contained the fanciful accounts of raconteurs and creative furbelows. The volume *History of Nevada, Colorado, and Wyoming, 1540–1888,* which is replete with inaccuracies, wrote about Charles Baker (called "John Baker" therein) and James White, as follows:

> Baker was a mountaineer of note. He had heard from the Navajos and other Indians that the royal metal existed in the mysterious upper regions of the Sierra Madre, proof of which was exhibited in ornaments and bullets of gold. More than these pretended revelations no one knew, when Baker determined to prove the truth or falsity of the Arabian tales of the Navajos, who had frequently received bribes to disclose the new Golconda, but evaded making the promised disclosure. Finding at Pueblo a considerable number of prospectors who had passed an unprofitable season in looking for placer mines, and who yet had the courage for new undertakings, Baker raised a company variously stated at from "a few" to 1,000 and even 5,000, who set out on their crusade as gaily as knights of old, albeit their banners were not silken, and their picks and shovels were not swords. Proceeding into New Mexico, they entered the San Juan valley; from there, by the way of the Tierra Amerillo and Pagosa, they penetrated the country as far as the headwaters of the Rio de las Animas, where, in anticipation of the future populousness of the country, they laid out a town, calling it Animas City, which was seen longer on the maps than on the ground. Some placer

diggings were found along the various streams and in the vicinity of Baker park, but nothing which promised to realize the exaggerated expectations of the discoverers. Small garnets and rubies were also picked up, and indications were believed to be seen of diamonds. The main portion of the company went no further than Animas City, but a few penetrated to the Rio Grande del Norte. Reinforcements with provisions failed to arrive as expected, and the conditions of the adventurers became critical. Anxious to avoid the long journey back through New Mexico, the company separated into squads, each of which sought according to its judgment a shorter way out of the maze of cañons and peaks than the one by which they came. Many perished of starvation, cold, and Indians, and those who survived suffered the pangs of death many times over before they found egress from the imprisoning mountains. *Baker lived to become a wealthy cattle owner* [emphasis added] and to organize an expedition to explore the grand cañon of Colorado. He was killed at the entrance to the cañon, with all his party save one, a man in the prime of life, who reached the outlet after days of indescribable suffering, with hair bleached like snow, and both hands and feet blistered, in which condition and insensible he was finally rescued. He had devoured his shoes, his leathern belt, and buckskin pouch. So suffered, and often so died, the vanguard of civilization on the continent. Before the inexorable laws of nature, an heir of centuries of intellectual growth is no more than the jelly-fish to the sea, which casts it upon the sand to rot in the sun![20]

Thus, "before the inexorable laws of nature," Charles Baker, George Strole, and Joe Goodfellow had vanished like "jelly-fish to the sea," leaving James White as the only known survivor among the four drifters who left Kansas in 1867.

FIVE

THE ACCIDENTAL CELEBRITY

On September 7, 1867, like flotsam on the waters of the Colorado River, a log raft drifted down to Callville, Nevada, below the Grand Canyon. Clinging to it was James White—his skin, sunburned to a crisp, hanging on an emaciated body. He was about to become a celebrity.

Although tens of thousands of rafters now cruise the Grand Canyon annually, White's emergence from it might best be compared to Lawrence of Arabia's arrival at Aqaba from the desert. No one had done it before. Jacob Hamblin and a couple of companions had descended from Grand Wash during that same year, and Lieutenant Joseph C. Ives had seen it from land at Diamond Creek in 1858, but the Colorado River remained essentially a mystery above the mouth of the Grand Canyon, just as it was below its entrance far upstream. White undoubtedly had learned a little about the Lower Colorado while he

was at Fort Yuma a few years earlier, but he knew no more than anyone else about the Grand Canyon. As for Callville, it did not yet exist
when White was at Fort Yuma.

Callville, also known as Call's Landing, was approximately 300 air
miles, or about 500 by land or river, from the location where some have
contended that Charles Baker died and James White and George Strole
embarked on a raft. By my calculations, the date of his reappearance
alone at Callville was nearly a month after those calamities, although
White said two weeks had elapsed. Regardless, no one can know with
certainty what had occurred in the period prior to September 7, but the
absence of firm evidence has not deterred believers and skeptics from
asserting their convictions that James White was or was not the first
white man to traverse the entire length of the Grand Canyon.

Usually, descriptions of White's arrival at Callville say that the first
individual to spot him was L. C. Wilburn, the captain of *The Colorado*,
a barge tied up at Call's Landing. Particulars differ concerning White's
rescue — whether he was hauled ashore by Indian laborers or whether
he made it by himself, whether he could speak, and what he said.
Whether he lay in a heap or was tottering on his feet, all accounts tes-
tified to his emaciated condition. His nearly naked body was burned
and torn, and he appeared to have endured a perilous journey, whatever its origins. The local warehouse owner, James Ferry, and his gog-
gle-eyed employees took charge of White and provided him with a
bed and food. Items of clothing were donated by soldiers in Callville's
small U.S. Army detachment.

The encampment of soldiers, or those who had not deserted at least,
were supposed to be keeping an eye on things, especially on the Paiute
Indians who hung around the landing, loading and unloading Wilburn's
barges in exchange for food. The permanent population of Callville,
never large but increasingly meager when James White appeared
in 1867, seldom saw more excitement than the occasional arrival or
departure of one of Wilburn's barges that hauled salt and lime from
St. Thomas, near the confluence of the Virgin and Muddy Rivers, and
that brought supplies from downstream to Callville and small Mormon
settlements beyond it. Ferry, besides overseeing Callville's warehouse,
has also been said to have been the mail agent at Callville.[1]

The only land routes to Callville were by way of the Virgin
River, the mouth of which was forty miles upstream, or by way of

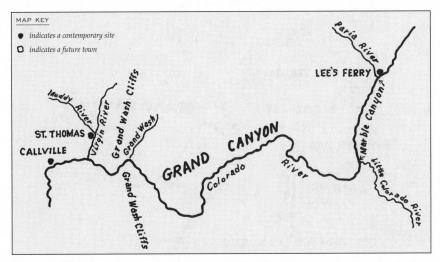

The Colorado River, from Lee's Ferry to Callville, Nevada.

Las Vegas Wash, which was a short distance downstream of Callville. Between these two entryways lay ferociously hot desert and deep gullies backed by dry, fang-like mountains that threatened to eat intruders alive. Comparatively, the Colorado River between Callville and the Virgin River, with the exception of Boulder Canyon, posed only minor difficulties for barges.[2] Little wonder that White's arrival created excitement for, if he actually had come down the river through the unexplored Grand Canyon, his transit might prove that it could be navigable or, at the very least, disprove myths about the river flowing over great waterfalls and through underground tunnels.

A dream persisted that the river system might be an avenue for transportation from the Gulf of California, up the Lower Colorado, through the Grand Canyon, and thence up the Green River, believed to be a suitable artery above its confluence with the Grand. In 1866 the commandant at Fort Bridger in Wyoming was entertaining the notion that a steamer could navigate all the way to Fort Bridger in Wyoming, and in early 1867 the *Daily Rocky Mountain News* carried a brief item that a "boat is being built to explore the Colorado river from Fort Mohave up to the mouth of the Green, and up that stream, as far as it can go."[3]

While James White lay recovering at Callville, the astonishing story about his emergence from the Colorado River spread rapidly.

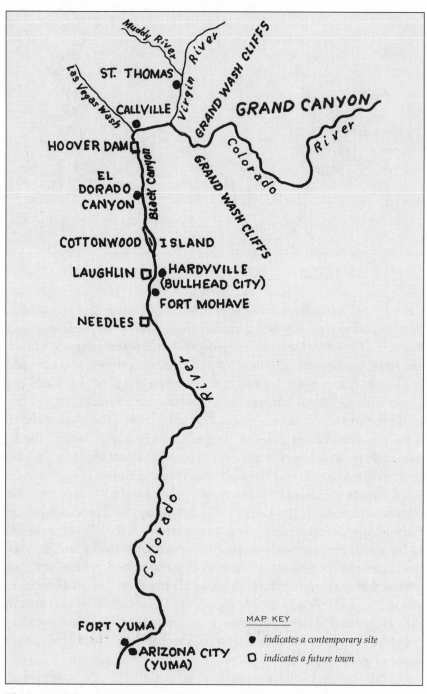

The Lower Colorado River, from Callville to Yuma.

First, Wilburn and his barge crew, delivering a load of salt and lime from St. Thomas to the silver smelter at El Dorado, carried the exciting news. The mining camp at El Dorado Canyon, on Nevada's side of the Black Canyon, had been the scene of mining activity since 1858 and grew to a roistering population of about 500 prospectors along with a small garrison of soldiers and a post office. The place was instantly abuzz with Wilburn's news about James White, and only a day behind Wilburn came Ferry, adding his personal observations. Neither Wilburn nor Ferry, both of whom had seen White's physical state, doubted his story, and neither did others who listened to these first witnesses. One of those hearing the tale on September 9 was E. B. Grandin, the postmaster at El Dorado Canyon. On September 24, Grandin sent a letter to San Francisco that appeared in the *Daily Alta California*, and J. B. Kipp, also hearing the story at El Dorado Canyon, wrote a letter that appeared in newspapers in Los Angeles, San Bernardino, and San Francisco.[4]

On down the river, *The Colorado* carried the news to Cottonwood Island, another mining camp. To prospectors, White's journey meant that it might be possible to reach the camps by way of a water route from the north. In fact, two years later, when Major John Wesley Powell was recruiting boatmen at Green River, Wyoming, for his survey of the Green and Colorado Rivers, two of the crew hoped they could travel with him to Cottonwood Island to prospect.

Next, downstream beyond Cottonwood Island, William Harrison Hardy greeted Wilburn and Ferry at Hardyville, Arizona Territory. In 1865, the year after Callville was founded, Hardy had established Hardyville with a landing, at the present site of Bullhead City, across the Colorado River from today's Laughlin, Nevada. Hardy also operated a ferry and improved the road to Prescott, 130 miles to the east, to facilitate his freighting business. Of course, Hardy and others at the landing and in the dusty little adobe buildings of the settlement hung avidly on every word about James White. Among the chatterers at Hardyville's store, hotel/saloon/billiard parlor, blacksmith shop, and corral was William J. Beggs, a journeyman printer who was drifting around the West.

Despite an alleged fondness for the bottle, Beggs could still recognize a good story, and in those days newspaper editors paid a little for just about any tantalizing item sent in from far-flung places by a correspondent. Scooping the other writers, the *Arizona Miner* at Prescott, Arizona Territory, printed a story by Beggs about White on September 14, only a week after White's arrival at Callville. Hardy's road to Prescott must have facilitated its delivery in such a short time. Without delaying for trifles like verification, Beggs later admitted he had written his story from memory.

Six miles farther down the river on a barren bluff on the Arizona side was the U.S. Army's Fort Mohave, Wilburn's home port. The fort's official role was to protect the stage route and the region from Mohave Indians, and it also offered a safe campsite for expeditions surveying the Southwest after the close of the Civil War. In January 1868, railroad surveyors who were camped at the fort became involved in disseminating the story of James White.

These first printed accounts were thirdhand, from White to Ferry or Wilburn to the writers, and in general the contents were similar, but one cannot help wonder whether White himself, in his sickbed at Callville, had been capable of telling an accurate story or whether some of his story might have been confused, elided, or modified in his own memory. And how accurately were they being repeated by Wilburn, Ferry, Grandin, Kipp, Beggs, and other assorted listeners?

Fairness to James White requires that we begin with the letter written by the hero himself to his brother Josh on September 26, 1867, less than three weeks after his rescue at Callville. Recommencing at the point in the letter when George Strole was washed from the raft and disappeared, White described his journey:

> I though it Wold be my time next I then pool off my boos and pands
> I then tide a rope to my Wase I Wend over folls from 10 to 15 feet
> high my raft Wold tip over three and fore time a day the thurd day
> Wee loss our flour flour and fore ["days," *deleted*] seven days I had
> noth to eat to ralhhide nife Caber [rawhide knife scabbard] the 8.9
> days I got some musKit beens [mesquite beans] the 13 days a party
> of indis frendey [friendly Indians] thay ["walk," *deleted*] Wold not
> give me notheat so I give me ["revl," *deleted*] pstols for hine pards
> of a dog I ead one of for super and the other breakfast the 14 days
> I rive at Callville Whare I Was tak Care of by James ferry I Was tne
> [ten] days With out pants or boos or hat I Was soon bornt so I Cold
> hadly Wolk the ingis tok 7 head horse from us Josh I can rite yu
> Halfe I ender Went I see the hardes time that eny man ever did in
> the World but thank god that I got thrught saft I am Well again and

I hope the few lines will fine you all Well I sned my beck respeCk to all Josh anCer this When you git it

> DreCk you letter to Callville ["Are," *deleted*] Arizona.

Then with much scratching and rewriting, James added the following poignant message, before signing his name with elegant penmanship:

> Josh ass Tom to anCy that letter that I rote him sevel yeas a goe
> James White[5]

Not surprisingly, the stories written by Grandin and Kipp were longer than the letter that White had struggled to write, and the newspaper accounts had a number of factual errors, perhaps attributable to getting their information by word-of-mouth. Beggs's considerably fuller account contains these errors, as well as others, but it became the best-known of the three yarns, and it is quoted here with my notes inserted in brackets:

NAVIGATION OF THE BIG CANON: A TERRIBLE VOYAGE

Wm. J. Beggs, who arrived here today from Hardyville, brings us the following account of the first passage, so far as is known, of any human being through the Big Canon of the Colorado. He derived the particulars from Captain Wilburn of the barge *Colorado*, who arrived at Hardyville on Monday last [September 9], and James Ferry of Callville who arrived on Tuesday [September 10].

In April last a party, consisting of Captain Baker, an old Colorado prospector and formerly a resident of St. Louis, George Strobe [*sic*], also from St. Louis, and James White, formerly of Penosha, Iowa [*sic*], and late of Company H, Fifth California Cavalry, left Colorado City to prospect on the San Juan river, which empties into the Colorado between the junction of the Green and Grand rivers and the Big Canon. [Note that Joe Goodfellow does not appear in this story nor in White's own letter, suggesting that White was sufficiently lucid to select what he chose to tell or omit.] They prospected until the middle of August with satisfactory success, and then decided to return to Colorado City for a supply of provisions and a larger company. They set out to go by the mouth of the San Juan, with the double purpose of finding a more practical route to Green river than the one they had traversed, and of visiting some localities which Captain Baker had prospected some years previously. [No other reference to Baker's earlier prospecting in that region is known.] On the morning of the 24th of August, when encamped about a mile from the Colorado, they were attacked by a band of about fifty Utes.[6]

Beggs provided no source for a date of August 24 for this encampment except White's own statement, and the number of Indians in all the newspaper stories was three times greater than in White's letter. The information presented thus far in the Beggs account differs significantly from much that occurs elsewhere. First, Beggs made no mention of Goodfellow and his shooting. Second, there is no evidence supporting a return to Colorado City after the prospecting had begun. Such a long detour would not be possible within the available time frame. Third, why was nothing said about prospecting in Eureka Gulch? Fourth, if Charles Baker knew anything at all about the Green River area, it is odd he did not know that the most direct way to reach it was to proceed west on the Old Spanish Trail rather than by following the San Juan River. Fifth, how was it determined that August 24 was the date of the Indian attack? There is no support for this date except by deduction since White said he was on the river for two weeks prior to his rescue on September 7. However they were reached, a date of August 23, 24, or 25 was reported in the various accounts that appeared. Sixth, the number of Indians varies in each account.

The Beggs article continues:

Captain Baker was killed, but Strobe and White secured their carbines and revolvers, some ropes and a sack containing ten pounds of flour [and an ax in another account], and ran to the Colorado, where they found a few small drift logs, which they hastily lashed together, and embarking on the frail raft, started down the river in the hope of reaching Callville. [How did White know that Callville existed or where it was?] On the second day they came to the first rapids, in passing over which they lost their flour. On the third day [or the fourth, as White told his brother] they went over a fall ten feet high, and Strobe was washed from the raft and drowned.

White had lashed himself to the raft, which, although shattered by the shock, sustained him, and he hauled it up to an island below the fall, repaired it, and proceeded alone. He had not much hope of getting through, and, being found, furnish a clue by which his friends would learn his fate. He describes the course of the river as very tortuous, with a constant succession of rapids and falls, the latter varying in height from four to ten or twelve feet. [The mention here of a constant succession of rapids and falls is an

important point, because debunkers, taking one of White's subsequent statements out of context, made much of another statement
that there was only one big rapid.] Sometimes, when he plunged
over a fall the raft would turn over on him, and he would have
much difficulty in extricating himself from his perilous position.
For a few days he found on bars and islands in the river sufficient
mezquit [mesquite beans] to allay the pangs of hunger, but for
several days he had nothing to eat but a leather knife scabbard.
He saw a few lizards but was unable to catch them; and he looked
from side to side in vain for any mode of egress from the canon,
the perpendicular walls of which were in many places a mile and
a-half, as well as he could estimate, in height. [Forgivably, many
of White's estimates of the height of canyon walls are incorrect,
but less forgivable are his statements about the sizes of rapids and
his claim that he saw no "mode of egress," for there are several.
Perhaps he believed that the canyon would soon end, or perhaps
he was too weak to undertake leaving the river.] He floated on an
average, about ten hours a day, hauling up at night on the bars
which were formed by the eddies below the falls. For about ten
days he was without hat, pants, or boots, having lost them while
going over a fall. On the afternoon of the 6th inst. [instance], he
passed the mouth of the Virgin river, and a party of Pah-Utes swam
off and pushed his raft ashore. They stole one of two pistols which
he had managed to preserve, and he bartered the other to them for
the hind-quarters of a dog, one of which he ate for supper and the
other for breakfast. On the 7th he reached Callville, and was taken
care of by Captain Wilburn and Mr. Ferry. He was much emaciated, his legs and feet were blistered and blackened by the sun;
his hair and beard, which had been dark, were turned white, and
he walked with difficulty, being unable to stand erect. He remains
at Callville, and although in precarious condition will probably
recover. From his actual traveling time, and the rapidity of the current, it is estimated that the distance through the canon, from the
mouth of the San Juan to Callville, is not much short of five hundred miles. [The distance from the mouth of Moki Canyon, which
has been argued by Eilean Adams as White's point of embarkation,
to Callville is about 470 miles, a close figure.]

Shortly after Beggs's article appeared in the *Arizona Miner,* James
White wrote his letter, dated September 26, 1867, to his brother Josh,
who was still living in Wisconsin. Clearly, Callville's population had
already seen the story in the *Arizona Miner,* for at the top of his letter

White or someone else had printed the banner, "Navigation of the Big Canon/A terrible voyage."

Beggs continued to keep the adventure in circulation for some time for small fees. In December 1868, his story appeared in *Lippincott's Magazine*. Denver's *Rocky Mountain Herald* on January 8, 1869, repeated the story, which an unknown writer said he had obtained in New Mexico.[7] The *Herald's* correspondent offered new variations that appear to have been told to him by someone who had obtained the story indirectly. In this thirdhand, fourthhand, or otherhand version, White was presented in a heroic light, for he is said to have freed himself from the raft's ropes in order to help Strole when he washed overboard, but the drowning man disappeared before White could do anything, so the rescue attempt was aborted. An interesting tidbit for anthropologists is that in the *Herald's* version, White said that one of the "Pahute" Indians at the Virgin River "spoke English." The Indian possibly learned the language as a laborer at Callville or from Mormons who had settled in the area up the Virgin River. If these Indians took two handguns from White, he was better armed than many prospectors, who normally carried only one, and he had done a remarkable job of preserving them during his adventure on the raft. The *Herald* also added that Captain Wilburn had demanded that the Indians return White's property that they seized from him at their camp at the mouth of the Virgin River.

An implausible detail in the *Herald's* story said that White responded feebly when Captain Wilburn hailed him at Callville, "My God, is this Callville?" to which the barge's owner replied, "Yes, come ashore." White then said he was not sure that he could manage to get out of the water, but nevertheless he fastened his raft and under his own power crested a hill near the landing where Wilburn and his workers stood staring aghast at his deplorable condition as he crawled toward them. Like Beggs, this writer mentioned that the poor fellow's hair had turned white, adding that it was long and that he had a white beard besides. A family photograph, made two years later in 1869, shows him with light, but not white, hair. When the men at Callville took him to their camp, the *Herald's* writer said that White "became delirious, but toward evening his wandering senses returned, and he was able to give an account of himself." In conclusion, the writer added, "When I last heard of White he was carrying the mail between

Callville and Mohave."[8] Eilean Adams also mentions a newspaper article that appeared in the *Kenosha Telegraph* on October 1, 1868. This account might have been based on White's letter to his brother or on one of the published stories copying the Beggs article.

The attention resulting from White's adventure brought visitors to meet the celebrity. Within a month or so after his rescue on September 7, White, who to his credit never failed to find paying work wherever he wandered, had recovered sufficiently from his ordeal that he was able to take a job carrying the mail from Callville to locations down-river. But before White was strong enough to go to work, two men from Prescott allegedly arrived at Callville to visit him, or so John Turner claimed. If this incident actually happened, his guests came because of their interest in prospecting at the San Juan River, not because of his heroic voyage through the Grand Canyon. Grandin's letter, published in 1867, had included White's comment that "they were in the vicinity of what will prove to be good mines there, on the San Juan river, judging from the prospects they obtained."

Gossip of this sort undoubtedly spread rapidly afar among prospectors and newspaper readers at Prescott. This town was a center for prospectors who had been congregating there since the early 1860s, some of whom were defectors from the diggings in the San Juan Mountains where they had known Charles Baker. Prescott's population thrived sufficiently that when Arizona Territory was separated from New Mexico Territory in 1863, the town became the new capital. By 1867, however, Prescott was declining to such an extent that the capital moved to Tucson. Diehards still hung around Prescott, though, in hopes that their fortunes would turn, and they believed that the region near the junction of the San Juan and the Colorado was their next hope for striking it rich. It is possible that Charles Baker had been aware of such rumors when he headed for the San Juan River in late spring 1867. Even before Beggs's story was printed in the fall with its mention of the San Juan River and the name of Charles Baker, about 100 of Prescott's men, led by a territorial legislator named Mr. Watkins, were entertaining the idea of undertaking a prospecting trip to the San Juan.

After Beggs's article appeared, some of these men decided it was important to go to Callville to talk to James White and to learn what they could from him. Watkins went to Callville, as did, purportedly,

John Turner. This is the same Turner who had been at Baker's Park in 1861 and later gave a benevolent evaluation of Charles Baker's activities there. After leaving the San Juan Mountains in 1861, Turner had drifted around the Southwest's diggings and married the daughter of another footloose prospector, and, according to Turner's grandson, did "his bit to help populate both the states of New Mexico and Arizona."[9]

Turner's muddled story about the visit to Callville, however, forces one to question whether he actually visited Callville or talked with White at all. Turner could not recall White's first name nor where he was from when he was interviewed by Robert Bruns years later. Turner also offered the impossible information that White was with the Mormon Battalion of 1846–1847. Nevertheless, it seems necessary to include here something about Turner's alleged visit to Callville.

Most accounts imply that soon after his rescue, White was in possession of his mental faculties, but Turner said that White was delirious but able to talk some. According to Turner, White related that Charles Baker had been sure gold would be found down the San Juan River, and their pans were yielding seventy-five cents' worth when the party was attacked by Indians. At the first crack of a rifle, "Baker dropped dead at their feet." White and the "other man" escaped and built their raft. White's "partner crazed by starvation or exposure lost his mind, fell or jumped overboard." Later during Turner's dubious visit, White admitted to Watkins and Turner that at the San Juan the "best results were 2–3c per pan, fine flaky gold," not the previously reported seventy-five cents.[10]

Either because of White's discouraging reports about prospecting or because of the presence of inhospitable Indians, the prospectors from Prescott gave up their plans for an expedition to the San Juan River. Hope lives long, though. Rumors about gold in the area persisted into the 1890s when as many as 2,000 or 3,000 men are said to have arrived in flurries in the area around Mexican Hat but were rewarded with little profit. In the 1880s there also was a rash of prospecting at several diggings along the Colorado in Glen Canyon between White Creek (named for the area's white sandstone) and Lee's Ferry. Later, Robert Brewster Stanton, a significant figure in the White debate, became involved in the Hoskaninni mining enterprise in Glen Canyon.

After the alleged delegation from Prescott, the next individual to meet the celebrity and obtain a story from him was a member of the railroad survey party camped at Fort Mohave. In January 1868 the survey's director, General William Jackson Palmer, was eager that one of his surveyors should learn about White's experiences down the Colorado when they heard he was nearby at Hardyville. For this purpose, Palmer ordered Dr. Charles Christopher Parry to go up to Hardyville. An interview of White by a literate, scientifically minded member of a surveying expedition should have produced the final word on the raft trip and the river. Unfortunately, it did not, as we shall see in the next chapter.

Palmer and his men were part of a well-equipped survey in the Southwest charged with locating a transcontinental railroad route between the Thirty-Second and Thirty-Fifth Parallels for the Pacific Railway, a venture under the corporate umbrella of the Eastern Division of the Union Pacific Railway Company. The survey had begun with three divisions but became five for the work between New Mexico and California. As head of the survey, General Palmer had chosen intelligent, educated men for the work. Although the Grand Canyon was not part of their survey, they were intensely interested in learning about this unknown place that might offer a route for transportation, especially for a railroad.

The person whom Palmer ordered to interview White was a medical doctor by training but a naturalist by inclination. A small but energetic man, C. C. Parry had participated in the border survey following the Mexican War. With wide experience in botany, which earned him a distinguished reputation during his lifetime, Parry was considered capable of working in various scientific fields with or without formal training, so that, besides avidly collecting botanical specimens in his various travels, he was working as an assistant geologist for the railroad survey on the Thirty-Fifth Parallel. The charming demeanor that won him many friends in his lifetime probably assisted him during his interview with White. For his part, White was under the false impression that Parry was actually General Palmer.

Contradicting some accounts that say another survey member, Dr. William A. Bell, attended this meeting, Bell stated that he was not at Hardyville, for his work with the survey was farther south along the Thirty-Second Parallel. Several years later, Bell finally met White, however. Bell was an Englishman, and like Parry and other "scientific men" of their day, he was a sometime medical doctor. Having arrived in America as recently as 1867, he joined up with the survey out of curiosity and fascination with the West. Subsequently, Bell remained a close associate in Palmer's business interests, the Denver and Rio Grande Railway and the founding of Colorado Springs. Parry, Bell, and Palmer were not inconsequential individuals whose reputations could be ignored when the validity of White's voyage through the Grand Canyon was later debated.

Parry's interview with White took place on January 6, 1868, with Parry making sketchy notes during this meeting.[11] Because four months had elapsed since White's rescue at Callville, White by then would have told his story numerous times to captivated listeners and perhaps had corrected or embellished it with each repetition. Based on his notes and memory, Parry wrote his report in the form of a letter that he sent in duplicate to General Palmer and to the president of the Union Pacific Railway. The account that went to the Union Pacific's president, J. D. Perry, was printed in 1868 in the *Transactions of the St. Louis Academy of Natural Sciences,* lending it an aura of authority, and it also appeared in slightly shorter form in Palmer's report of the railroad survey in 1869. For the latter printing, Parry corrected some errors in newspaper reports and some new misstatements that had come in part from White and in part from Parry's false assumptions about the Colorado River and the Grand Canyon. Persistent errors, though, are difficult to justify. Part of Parry's difficulty may have been that the 1858 map, prepared by Friedrich W. von Egloffstein during the Ives expedition, did not cover the Colorado River upstream from the Little Colorado. A survey like Palmer's, presumably, would have possessed a copy of the Egloffstein map. At any rate, Parry's obvious geographical errors subsequently provided grist for the mills of White's detractors, as did those made by others. Parry was responsible for these errors in the end, as Robert Stanton vigorously pointed out when he investigated White's voyage.

Parry correctly gave White's original home as well as the number of companions at Fort Dodge, but much else was less accurate. For instance, Parry called Strole "Henry." Parry said that the fourth man (Goodfellow) left at Colorado City after local people warned the party about the rashness of their plan. Most damaging, he specified that the point of embarkation was fifty miles from where they left the San Juan and that it was on the Grand River above the confluence of the

Colorado and Green, which would have been about 140 miles away, not 50. Parry was sublimely ignorant of the fact that a short distance below this confluence lies a long, wild stretch of white water in the aptly named Cataract Canyon that could not possibly have fit with White's journey. Parry, it appears, is also the person who placed the Little Colorado as entering the Colorado from the right, not the left, and injected the name of Colorado Chiquito (the Little Colorado) and the dramatic story about a whirlpool that allegedly captured White there. Parry gave the date of White's arrival at Callville as September 8, instead of September 7, a relatively minor point when compared to his other errors.

In contrast to his report, Parry's notes, made in January 1868, were quite brief.

> James—White—Kenosha Wisconsin—Started from Ft. Dodge—
> 13 April—with a prospecting party under Capt Baker—Came to
> Colorado City—left 20th May—for San Juan—struck Animas—
> Dolores—Mancos Cañon followed to San Juan down that 200 miles
> crossed to north side crossed over Mts to Colorado [River]—50
> miles went up 12 miles to Cañon. went down to Colorado—12.
> Henry Strole, Capt. Baker killed—went back into Cañon unpacked
> took 10lb flour & coffee—24 Aug fight—went to mouth of Cañon.
> built raft—8 inch 10ft 3. tied up with lariats—river wide & still small
> bottom. 25.th stopped. and repaired raft passed Green 30 miles—
> after leaving Green Cañon traveled 40 miles to San Juan. Laid up
> night 26th traveled all night 40 miles 27th all night—28th 4th—came
> to rapids and Strun was washed off & drowned 3 PM lost provisions
> kept passing rapids—25 or 30 a days passed Colorado Chiquito 4th
> in evening continuous rapids—to 100 miles above Callville—Rock
> in Cañon. White Sand Stone 2 days in foot of Cañon Volcanic reach
> Callville 8th Sept—line of high water mark 30 to 40 ft height 300ft
> rapids caused by fallen rocks on fall 10 ft?—many whirlpools &
> eddies stopped in an edy mouth of Chiq 2 hours prayed out.shape
> of Cañon perpendicular for several 100 ft then flares out course of
> river very Crooked—raft bumping on rocks—Same character of
> rock through the main Cañon.[12]

An important point in Parry's notes is that White said the three prospectors crossed the San Juan River to the north side, not to the south as he would tell Stanton in 1907. The question of where and how the crossing of the San Juan took place figures in attempts to determine the route after the crossing and, for that matter, whether White traversed the Grand Canyon at all. The mention of continuous rapids is significant, too, as it contradicts later claims that there was but one big rapid.

After the interview in which Parry made his notes, it is possible that he obtained additional information from conversations with White. Parry might have gone over his notes and asked leading questions, suggesting place names for instance, for he expanded on the notes and included statements about geography that are incorrect. The question is, then, who made such statements first—Parry or White? One must wonder if Parry believed it to be his function to include his own interpretation, despite his obviously inadequate knowledge about the river and its geography.

Equally innocent of knowledge about the Grand Canyon was Alfred Calhoun, who wrote a more widely read account. Calhoun was a journalist who wrote popular narratives. He had served under Palmer in his elite company during the Civil War and had lost a leg in combat. The general's well-known loyalty to his men might have influenced him to include Calhoun in the railroad survey, during which Calhoun sent dispatches to the *Philadelphia Press* to promote the survey's activities. In 1869, William Bell included a tale by Calhoun about White in *New Tracks in North America*, and this same story, with minor editorial changes, appeared in a separate volume of adventure narratives published in 1872 and again in 1875. Not an author of the first rank, Calhoun in later years wrote stories that were acknowledged to be fiction, whereas his creative work about White, which should have been called fiction, was not.

Without having met White but apparently having seen Parry's notes or his published report, Calhoun wrote a story that was published three times, making his the more widely circulated yarn.[13] The version that first was included in Bell's volume contained introductory words that revealed Calhoun's ignorance about the Colorado River, for he stated that it "rises in Idaho territory," but before the account again appeared he had deleted this portion. By then, he had had a chance to learn more about the Colorado River, thanks to the expeditions of Major John Wesley Powell in 1869 and 1871–1872. Calhoun's story, much lengthier than Parry's, was adorned with inventions and flourishes not found in the latter. Calhoun commenced his adventure story with a description of White, a man of modest demeanor and sturdy physique. Calhoun made no mention of white hair or other evidences of physical suffering caused by the ordeal in the canyon. To demonstrate how the legend of White's journey was being perpetuated and changed within a short time after the alleged events, Calhoun's version is repeated here, omitting introductory general remarks:

> While on the survey . . . and while stopping for a few days at Fort Mohave, Dr. W. A. Bell [Bell definitely was not present], Dr. C. C. Parry, and myself [probably not present], met this man, whose name is James White, and from his lips, the only living man who had actually traversed its formidable depths, we learned the story of the Great Cañon.
>
> James White now lives at Callville, Arizona territory [sic], the present head of navigation on the Colorado River. He is thirty-two years of age [thirty, in January 1868], and in person is a good type of Saxon, being of medium height and heavy build, with light hair and blue eyes. He is a man of average intelligence, simple and unassuming in his manner and address, and without any of the swagger or bravado peculiar to the majority of frontier men. Like thousands of our young men, well enough at home, he grew weary of the slow but certain method of earning his bread by regular employment at a stated salary. He had heard of men leaping into wealth at a single bound in the Western gold-fields, and for years he longed to go to the land where Fortune was so lavish of her favours. Accordingly, he readily consented to be one of a party from his neighborhood who, in the spring of 1867, started for the plains and the gold-fields beyond. [It is not possible to know whether it was Calhoun or White who chose to omit the fact that he had been drifting around the West for six years in other pursuits before turning to prospecting for gold with Baker in 1867.] When they left Fort Dodger [sic], on the Arkansas River, April 13th, 1867, the party consisted of four men, of whom Captain Baker, an old miner and ex-officer of the Confederate army, was the acknowledged leader. [This is the first mention purportedly from White or Calhoun that Baker was in the Confederate Army.] The destination of this little party was the San Juan Valley, west of the Rocky Mountains, about the gold-fields of which prospecters [sic] spoke in the most extravagant terms, stating that they were deterred from working the rich placers of the San Juan only by fear of Indians. Baker and his companions reached Colorado "city," at the foot of Pike's Peak, in safety. This place was, and is still, the depot for supplying the miners who work the diggings scattered

through the South Park, and is the more important from being situated at the entrance to the Ute Pass, through which there is a wagon-road crossing the Rocky Mountains, and descending to the plateau beyond. The people of Colorado "city" tried to dissuade Baker from what they considered a rash project, but he was determined to carry out his original plan. These representations, however, affected one of the party [a false reference to Goodfellow] so much that he left, but the others, Captain Baker, James White and Henry [sic] Strole, completed their outfit for the prospecting tour. [Here, as in Parry's account, Joe Goodfellow is dropped from the story. Probably White had avoided explaining the shooting at Brown's Creek by omitting Goodfellow's presence later.]

The journey was undertaken on foot, with two pack-mules [the horses are omitted] to carry the provisions, mining tools, and the blankets they considered necessary for the expedition. On the 25th of May they left the Colorado city, and crossing the Rocky Mountains, through the Ute Pass, entered South Park, being still on the Atlantic slope of the continent. After traveling ninety miles across the Park [this distance is correct only if it includes Colorado City] they reached the Upper Arkansas, near the Twin Lakes. They then crossed the Snowy Range, or Sierra Madre, and descended towards the west. [The crossing is incorrect, and Brown's Creek and the shootout are omitted.] Turning southerly, they passed around the head waters of the Rio Grande del Norte, and after a journey of 400 miles from Colorado "city," they reached the "Animas" branch of the San Juan River, which flows into the Great Colorado from the east. [The more accurate distance from Colorado City to the Eureka diggings on the Animas River would have been about 300 miles.]

They were now in the land where their hopes centered, and to reach which they had crossed plains and mountains, and forded rapid streams, leaving the nearest abodes of the white man hundreds of miles to the east. Their work of prospecting for gold began in the Animas, and though they were partially successful, the result did not by any means answer their search in the sands. They therefore moved still further to the west, crossing the Dolores branch of Grand River to the Mancos branch of the San Juan. Following the Mancos to its mouth, they crossed to the left bank of the San Juan and began their search in the sands.

There was gold there but not in the quantity they expected; so they gradually moved west, along the beautiful valley for 200 miles [an impossible figure], when they found the San Juan disappeared between the lofty walls of a deep and gloomy cañon [presumably this was at San Juan Canyon at Comb Ridge or Lime Ridge]. To avoid this, they again forded the river to the right bank, and struck across a rough timbered country, directing their course towards the great Colorado. Having traveled through this rough country for a distance estimated at fifty miles, they reached Grand River, being still above the junction of Green River, the united waters of which two streams form the Colorado proper. [Calhoun repeats Parry's impossible claim about this point of embarkation and the distance to it.] At the point where they struck the river, the banks were masses of perpendicular rock, down which they could gaze at the coveted water, dashing and foaming like an agitated white band, 200 feet below. Men and animals were now suffering for water; so they pushed up the stream, along the uneven edge of the chasm, hoping to find a place where they could descend to the river. After a day spent in clambering over and around the huge rocks that impeded their advance, they came to a side cañon, where a tributary joined the main stream, to which they succeeded in descending with their animals, and thus obtained the water of which all stood so much in need. [This successful search for water contrasts with the dry side canyon where there was no water and where White told Stanton that Baker was killed. Calhoun made no mention of White's seeing an Indian the day before the attack.]

The night of the 23rd of August [no explanation was given here or in other accounts for how dates were determined] they encamped at the bottom of the cañon, where they found plenty of fuel and grass in abundance for their animals. [Calhoun said that Baker reached the bottom of the canyon.] So they sat around the camp-fire, lamenting their failure in the San Juan country, and Strole began to regret that they had undertaken the expedition. But Baker, who was a brave sanguine fellow, spoke of placers up the river about which he had heard, and promised his companions that all their hopes would be realized, and that they would return to their homes to enjoy the gains and laugh at the trials of their trip. [Still the same old "somewhat enthusiastic" Charles Baker!] So glowingly did he picture the future that his companions even speculated as to how they should spend their princely fortunes when they returned to the "States." Baker sang songs of home and hope, and the others lent their voices to the chorus, till far in the night, when, unguarded, they sank into sleep, to dream of coming opulence and to rise refreshed for the morrow's journey.

Early next morning they breakfasted, and began the ascent of the side canyon, up the bank opposite to that by which they had

entered it. Baker was in advance, with his rifle slung at his back,
gaily springing up the rocks, towards the table-land above. [In this
version, he was no longer mounted, and the description of Baker's
death varies even more significantly.] Behind him came White, and
Strole with the mules [not horses?] brought up the rear. Nothing
disturbed the stillness of the beautiful summer morning, but the
tramping of the mules, and the short, heavy breathing of the climb-
ers. They had ascended about half the distance to the top, when
stopping for a moment of rest, suddenly the war-whoop of a band
of savages rang, sounding as if every rock had a demon's voice.
Simultaneously with the first whoop a shower of arrows and bul-
lets was poured into the little party. With the first fire Baker fell
against a rock, but rallying for a moment, he unslung his rifle and
fired at the Indians, who now began to show themselves in large
numbers, and then, with the blood flowing from his mouth, he fell
to the ground. White, firing at the Indians as he advanced, and followed by Strole, hurried to the aid of his wounded leader. Baker,
with an effort, turned to his comrades, and in a voice still strong,
said, "Back, boys, back! Save yourselves, I am dying." To the credit
of White and Strole be it said, they faced the savages and fought,
till the last tremor of the powerful frame told that the gallant Baker
was dead. Then slowly they began to retreat, followed by the exul-
tant Indians, who stopping to strip and mutilate the dead body
in their path, gave the white men a chance to secure their animals
and retrace their steps into the side cañon, beyond the immediate
reach of the Indians' arrows. Here they held a hurried consultation
as to the best course they could pursue. To the east for 300 miles
stretched uninhabited country, over which, if they attempted escape
in that direction, the Indians like bloodhounds, would follow their
track. North, south, and west was the Colorado, with its tributaries, all flowing at the bottom of deep chasms, across which it would
be impossible for men or animals to travel. Their deliberations were
necessarily short, and resulted in their deciding to abandon their
animals, first securing their arms and a small stock or provisions,
and the ropes of the mules. Through the side cañon they traveled,
due west, for four hours, and emerged at last on a low strip of bottom land on Grand River, above which, for 2,000 feet on either bank,
the cold grey wall rose to block their path leaving to them but one
avenue of escape — the foaming current of the river, flowing along
the dark channel through unknown dangers.

They found considerable quantities of drift-wood along the
banks, from which they collected enough to enable them to con-

struct a raft capable of floating themselves, with their arms and provisions. This raft, when finished, consisted of three sticks of cottonwood, about ten feet in length and eight inches in diameter, lashed firmly together with the mule ropes. Procuring two stout poles with which to guide the raft, and fastening the bag of provisions to the logs, they waited for midnight and the waning moon, so as to drift off unnoticed by the Indians. They did not consider that even the sun looked down into that chasm for but one short hour in the twenty-four, leaving it for the rest of the day to the angry waters and blackened shadows, and that the faint moonlight reaching the bottom of the cañon would hardly serve to reveal the horror of their situation. Midnight came, according to their calculation of the dark, dreary hours; and then, seizing the poles, they untied the rope that held the raft, which, tossed about by the current, rushed through the yawning cañon, on the adventurous voyage to an unknown landing. Through the long night they clung to the raft, as it dashed against half-concealed rocks, or whirled about like a plaything in some eddy, whose white foam was perceptible even in the intense darkness.

They prayed for the daylight, which came at last, and with it a smoother current and less rugged banks, though the cañon walls appeared to have increased in height. Early in the morning (August 25th) they found a spot where they could make a landing, and went ashore. After eating a little of their water-soaked provisions, they returned, and strengthened their raft by the addition of some light pieces of cedar, which had been lodged in clefts of the rock by recent floods. White estimated the width of the river where they landed at 200 yards, and the current at three miles per hour. After a short stay at this place they again embarked, and during the rest of the day they had not small difficultly avoiding the rocks and whirlpools that met them at every bend of the river.

In the afternoon, and after having floated over a distance estimated at thirty miles from the point of starting, they reached the mouth of the Green River, or rather where the Green and the Grand unite to form the Colorado proper. Here the cañons of both streams combined into one of but little greater width, but far surpassing either in the height and grandeur of its walls. At the junction the walls were estimated at 4,000 feet in height, but detached pinnacles rose 1,000 feet higher, from amidst masses of rock confusedly piled, like grand monuments to commemorate this meeting of the waters. The fugitives felt the sublimity of the scene, and in contemplating its stupendous and unearthly grandeur, they forgot for the time their own sorrows.

For an uncritical reader, this description of the confluence of the Green and the Colorado Rivers in Calhoun's story might suffice, but the geography for the raft's route is impossible. Calhoun's story claimed that from the confluence White and Strole drifted along for forty miles, but they actually would have been headed into Cataract Canyon, hardly a serene place. Parry and Calhoun were ignorant of the fact that this forty-one-mile-long fearsome canyon, filled with fifty-seven rapids, rocks, holes, and standing waves, lay only a short distance downstream from the junction, directly in the path of the raft. Well-equipped, experienced boatmen still fear Cataract Canyon, where so many upsets and deaths have occurred that it has been popularly called the Graveyard. If we are to believe Calhoun, though, White and Strole merely enjoyed the sublimity of the scenery as their raft floated along. Beyond it, the river is transformed in Glen Canyon, a place of mostly tranquil water, even before Glen Canyon Dam created the immense Lake Powell.

Calhoun's story continues:

> The night of the day upon which they entered the Great Cañon, and indeed on nearly all the subsequent nights of the voyage, the raft was fastened to a loose rock, or hauled up on some narrow strip of beach, where they rested till the daylight on next morning. As they floated down the cañon, the grey sandstone walls increased in height, the lower section being smooth from the action of floods, and the rugged perpendicular walls rising towards the far-off sky, which seemed to rest on the rugged glistening summits. [The faulty descriptions of geology here and elsewhere in White's, Parry's, and Calhoun's accounts became an important focus for White's and Parry's critics.] Here and there a stunted cedar clung to the cliff-side, 2,000 feet over head, far beyond which the narrow blue streak of sky was perceptible. No living thing was in sight, for even the wing of bird which could pass the chasms above never fanned the dark air in those subterranean depths—nought to gaze on but their own pale faces, and the cold grey walls that hemmed them in and mocked at their escape. Here and there the raft shot past side cañons, black and forbidding, like cells set in the wall of a mighty prison. Baker had informed his comrades as to the geography of the country, and while floating down they remembered that Callville was at the mouth of the cañon, which could not be far off—"such wonderful walls could not continue much further." [There is no explana-

tion of how they knew about Callville's existence.] The Hope came, with the prospect of deliverance from their frightful position. A few days would take them to Callville; their provisions could be made to last five days. So these two men, thus shut in from the world, buried as it were in the very bowels of the earth, in the midst of great unknown deserts, began to console themselves, and even to jest at their situation.

Forty miles below their entrance into the great cañon, they reached the mouth of the San Juan River. [The distance below the confluence of the Green and the Colorado to the San Juan is nearly 100 miles greater than this estimate, whereas the San Juan River's mouth is forty miles below the mouth of Moki Canyon.] They attempted to enter it [the San Juan River], but its swift current cast them back. The perpendicular walls, high as those of the Colorado, with the water flowing from bank to bank, forbade their abandoning their raft to attempt escape in that direction. So they floated away. At every bend of the river it seems as if they were descending deeper into the earth; the walls came closer together above them, thickening the black shadows and redoubling the echoes that went up from the foaming water.

Four days had elapsed since they embarked on the frail raft; it was now August 28th. So far they had been constantly wet, but the water was comparatively warm, and the current more regular than they could have expected. Strole had taken upon himself to steer the raft, and, against the advice of White, he often set one end of the pole against the bank, or some opposing rock, and then leaned with the other end against his shoulder to push the raft away. As yet they had seen no natural bridge spanning the chasm above them nor had a fall or cataract prevented their safe advance. But about three o'clock in the afternoon of the 28th they heard the deep roar as of a waterfall in front.

If Calhoun had reported that the rafters floated along for another eighty miles or so below the mouth of the San Juan River and past the Paria River toward Marble Canyon, his readers might have been able to believe that White and Strole heard a "deep roar as of a waterfall." It was still only the fourth day of the voyage, though, when Calhoun describes that the river turned sharply and poured through a narrow space between huge rocks. No such place exists in Glen Canyon. Below the Paria River, Badger Creek and Soap Creek are the first major rapids after Cataract Canyon.

Calhoun then wrote:

[White's] comrade stood up for an instant with the pole in his hands, as if to guide the raft from the rocks against which it was plunging; but he had scarcely straightened himself, before the raft seemed to leap down a chasm, and amid the horrible sounds White heard a shriek that thrilled him. Turning his head, he saw through the mist and the spray the form of his comrade tossed for an instant on the water, then sinking out of sight in the whirlpool.

White still clung to the logs, and it was only when the raft seemed to be floating smoothly, and the sound of the rapids was behind, that he dared to look up; then it was to find himself alone, the provisions lost, and the shadows of the black cañon warning him of the approaching night. A feeling of despair seized him, and clasping his hands he prayed for the death he was fleeing from. He was made cognizant of more immediate danger by the shaking of his raft—the logs were separating; then he worked, and succeeded in effecting a landing near some flat rocks, where he made his raft fast for the night. After, he sat down, to spend the long gloomy hours in contemplating the horror of his situation, and the small chance of completing the adventurous voyage he had undertaken. He blamed himself for not having fought the Indians till he had fallen by the side of Baker. He might have escaped through the San Juan Valley, and the mountains beyond, to the settlements. Had he done so, he would have returned to his home, and rested satisfied with his experience as a prospector. But when he thought of "home," it called up the strongest inducements for life, and he resolved "to die hard, and like a Man."

Gradually the dawn, long perceptible in the upper world, began to creep down into the depths of the chasm, and gave him light to strengthen his raft and launch it again on the treacherous river. As he floated down he remembered the sad fate of Strole, and took the precaution to lash himself firmly to the raft, so as to preclude the possibility of his being separated from it. This forethought subsequently saved his life. His course through the cañon was now down a succession of rapids blocked up by masses of rock, over which his frail raft thumped and whirled, at times wholly submerged by the foaming water. At one of these rapids, in the distance of about a hundred yards, he thinks, the river must have fallen between thirty and forty feet. In going over this place the logs composing the raft became separated at the upper end, spreading out like a fan, and White was thrown into the water. He struggled to the side by means

Below the Paria River, the Colorado River enters Marble Canyon. In the foreground is Soap Creek Rapid, where George Strole may have drowned in August 1867. Courtesy, Denver Public Library, Western History Collection, no. Z-2723, Timothy O'Sullivan photo, 1872.

Cliffs in Marble Canyon of the Colorado River. Photo by author.

of his rope, and with a desperate strength held the logs together till they floated into calmer water, when he succeeded in re-fastening them.

White's trials were not yet at an end, and in relating the following incident he showed the only sign of emotion exhibited during his long narrative. About four miles below where the raft separated he reached the mouth of a large stream, which he has since learned was the Colorado Chiquito. [In Parry's account, this stream entered from the right, not the left as it actually does. When he was eighty years old, White insisted that is was on the right. Parry was blamed by critics for suggesting this and other incorrect data.] The cañon through which it enters the main river is very much like that of the San Juan, and though it does not discharge so large a body of water, the current is much more rapid and sweeps across the great Colorado, causing, in a deep indentation on the opposite bank, a large and dangerous whirlpool. [No whirlpool of this description exists at the mouth of the Little Colorado.] White saw this and tried to avoid it, but he was too weak for the task. His raft, borne by the current of the Colorado proper, rushed down with such force, that aided by his paddle he hoped to pass the waters that appeared to seep at right angles across his course from the Chiquito. When he

110

reached the mouth of the latter stream the raft suddenly stopped, and swinging round for an instant as if balanced on a point, it yielded to the current of the Chiquito, and was swept into the whirlpool. White now felt that all further exertion was useless, and dropping his paddle, he clasped his hands and fell upon the raft. He heard the gurgling waters around him, and every moment he felt that he must be plunged into the boiling vortex. He waited, he thinks, for some minutes, when, feeling a strange swinging sensation, he looked up to find that he was circling around the whirlpool, sometimes close to the vortex and again thrown back by some invisible cause to the outer edge, only to whirl again towards the centre. Thus borne by the circling waters, he looked up, up, up through the mighty chasm that seemed bending over him as if about to fall in. He saw in the blue belt of sky that hung over him like an ethereal river, the red-tinged clouds floating, and he knew the sun was setting in the upper world. Still around the whirlpool the raft swung like a circular pendulum, measuring the long moments before expected death. He felt a dizzy sensation, and thinks he must have fainted; he knows he was unconscious for a time, for when again he looked up the walls, whose rugged summits towered 3,000 feet above him, the red clouds had changed to black, and the heavy shadows of night had crept down the cañon. Then, for the first time, he remembered that there was a strength greater than that of man, a Power that "holds the ocean in the hollow of His hand." "I fell on my knees," he said, "and as the raft swept round in the current, I asked God to aid me. I spoke as if from my very soul, and said, 'O God! If there is a way out of this fearful place, guide me to it.'" Here White's voice became husky, as he narrated the circumstance, and his somewhat heavy features quivered, as he related that he presently felt a different movement in the raft, and turning to look at the whirlpool, saw it was some distance behind, and that he was floating down the smoothest current he had yet seen in the cañon. [The actual absence of a whirlpool at the mouth of the Little Colorado is one of the most obvious points providing fuel for White's critics.]

Below the mouth of the Colorado Chiquito the current was very slow, and White felt what he subsequently found to be the case — viz., that the rapids were passed, though he was not equally fortunate in guessing his proximity to Callville. The course of the river below this he describes as exceedingly "crooked, with short, sharp, turns," the view on every side being shut in by flat precipitous walls of "white sand-rock."

Hance Rapid, one of the demanding rapids in the Grand Canyon for boaters, has a gradient of thirty feet in a half mile and is filled with boulders the size of small automobiles. When Powell's first expedition portaged this rapid in 1869, one of Powell's ablest boatmen, George Bradley, wrote about James White's claims in his journal: "I am convinced that no man had ever run such rappids on a raft. . . . I pay little heed to the whole story." Courtesy, Colorado Historical Society, no. J3053, William Henry Jackson photo.

White's guess that the cliffs were sandstone was only one error of many, and his depiction of the river is vastly incorrect. Below Lee's Ferry at the Paria, the Colorado River flows for sixty-two miles through Marble Canyon with a dozen and a half rapids before reaching the Little Colorado. Below the Little Colorado, the distance to the Grand Wash Cliffs is 214 miles. In those miles lies the Grand Canyon with cliffs of many hues and scores of rapids, several being far more extreme than those above the Little Colorado. Yet, of this awesome passage, Calhoun's account said merely that the "current bore White

Although Lava Falls has changed somewhat since 1867, it is doubtful that anyone on a log raft could have survived its abrupt thirteen-foot drop, rocks, and holes. Photo by author.

from the Colorado Chiquito slowly down the main river" for four days. Seemingly, his biggest problem was hunger that he attempted to assuage with "green pods and the leaves of bushes." He tried unsuccessfully to open a vein in his arm to drink his own blood, according to one account. At last he came to an encampment of "Yampais Indians," or Yavapai Indians, at Grand Wash:

> On the afternoon of the eleventh day of his extraordinary voyage he was roused by hearing the sound of human voices, and, looking towards the shore, he saw men beckoning to him. A momentary strength came to his arms, and grasping the paddle, he urged the raft to the bank. On reaching it he found himself surrounded by a band of Yampais Indians [not Pah-Ute, as White originally said] who have lived on a low strip of alluvial land along the bottom of the cañon, and the trail to which from the summit of the plateau is only known to themselves. One of the Indians made fast the raft, while another seized White roughly and dragged him up the bank. He could not remonstrate; his tongue refused to give a sound, so

he pointed to his mouth and made signs for food. The fiend pulled him up the bank, tore from his blistered shoulders the shreds of a shirt, and was proceeding to strip him entirely, when one of the Indians interfered, and to the credit of the savage be it said, pushed back his companion. [In Beggs's account, White's clothing was lost in a rapid several days earlier.] He gave White some meat, and roasted mezique [mesquite] beans to eat, which the famished man devoured, and after a little rest he made signs that he wanted to go to the nearest dwellings of the white men. The Indians told him he could reach them in "two suns" on his raft. Early the next morning he tottered to the bank, and pushed into the current. [Calhoun's version of the encounter with the Indians differs in most particulars from those in Beggs's article and in the letter written to Josh White. Without the Indian who could speak English, communications between White and the Indians was difficult in Calhoun's account, and the distance to Callville was no longer an overnight cruise, as Beggs said.]

Three more long days of hope and dread passed slowly by, and still no signs of friends. Reason tottered, and White stretched himself on the raft, all his energies exhausted; life and death were to him alike indifferent. Late in the evening of the third day after leaving the Indians, and fourteen from the time of starting his perilous voyage, White again heard voices, accompanied by the rapid dash of oars. He understood the words, but could make no reply. He felt a strong arm thrown around him, and he was lifted into a boat, to see many bearded faces looking down upon him with pity. [Calhoun's readers should be relieved to learn that White did not have to haul himself ashore without assistance in this version, nor did he utter the greeting that Beggs provided in his story.]

In short, Callville was reached at last. The people of this Mormon settlement had warm generous hearts, and like good Samaritans, lavishly bestowed every care on the unfortunate man so miraculously thrown into their midst from the bowels of the unknown cañon. His constitution, naturally strong, soon recovered from its shock, and he told his new-found friends his wonderful story, the first recital of which led them to doubt his sanity.[14]

And so James White survived and became a celebrity, although he did not remain long at Callville. Perhaps a handful of sober Mormons, fulfilling an obligation to abjure strong drink, might have endured the tedium of the barren outpost, but it did not appeal to the soldiers and civilians who were deserting the outpost, nor did it appeal for long to

White. With Callville's hopes of prosperity withering, even the "good Samaritans" who had succored him were themselves pulling out, and, not surprisingly, White also would drift on during the early part of 1868 with some acquaintances he had made there.

DRIFTING AGAIN

In its short life, Callville experienced two dramatic events. One was the arrival in 1866 of a paddlewheel, *The Esmeralda,* and the other was James White's appearance in 1867 on a log raft. No other steamboat ever succeeded in forging a passage this far upstream, and no one else ever repeated White's exploit.

James White could not foresee that the remainder of his life would be a denouement. For the moment, both the residents of Callville and White might have imagined that fame and its attendant blandishments would last forever, but such were not their lots. Attention and job opportunities alike were waning by spring 1868, and before the summer's searing heat descended upon the sandy hills and washes around Callville, White prepared to move on, teaming up with others who were abandoning the desolate outpost at Call's Landing, where

117

The ruins of Callville, Nevada, shown in 1950 prior to their disappearance under the waters of Lake Mead. Courtesy, Cline Library, Northern Arizona University, no. NAU.PH.96.4171.1, Bill Belknap Collection.

not even occasional jugs of valley tan or Dixie wine could make life exciting.

White's next perambulations were stated briefly in his life story that appeared in Dawson's *The Grand Canyon.* Although this account focused on White's Colorado River experience, it also offered a little information about his activities at Callville and his next destinations.[1]

White said that he had carried mail between Callville and Fort Mohave for James Ferry for three months, a period that would extend roughly from mid-autumn 1867 until mid-winter 1868. When Ferry decided to pull out of the desolate place, he sold his mail contract to Jim Hinton, who also chose to depart before long. When Hinton left, White and a soldier named Jeff Stanford went with him, intending to head north to prospect in Wyoming's Sweetwater country. In preparation, White said, each man purchased a horse and a pack animal. At St. George, Utah, where the trio stopped to outfit, Hinton decided to pursue a different plan, leaving White and Stanford, who then drifted north by way of Salt Lake City.

Along the way, White and Stanford also changed their plans. Construction of the transcontinental railroad was offering paying jobs to thousands of laborers, and White, already having learned something about the unrewarding labor and risks associated with prospecting for elusive gold, decided that cutting ties for the Union Pacific Railroad was more rewarding. They began working for the transcontinental railroad at Bear River about a year before the golden spike was planted at Promontory Point on May 10, 1869.

The Mormon experiment of plying the Lower Colorado to Call's Landing illustrates how desperately landlocked Utah needed transportation, especially rail transportation, which was slow in arriving despite the interest of investors and surveyors. The Civil War had interrupted development of a transcontinental railroad, and across the Great Plains and in the Southwest, Indian troubles also halted railroad construction. As soon as the Plains Indians were conveniently corralled, however, railroad investors made up for lost time and sent out their surveyors again. Construction crews soon were laying tracks west from Kansas City and Omaha and east from San Francisco. The surveyors who had been camped at Fort Mohave in early 1868 were seeking a southern route as well. Meanwhile, the long-awaited rails were snaking across the plains.

When White and Stanford reached the Bear River, west of Green River, Wyoming, the Union Pacific was constructing its line through Echo Canyon toward Ogden, Utah. White took on a tie contract, but Stanford dropped out. Cutting timber in the mountains, dressing rough-hewn ties, and hauling them to flatcars on the railroad grade were not easy jobs, and before long White, also reconsidered this line of work. He then found a job more to his liking as a teamster.

Although other construction jobs paid better, this was an occupation for which White was well prepared by his experience in the quartermaster corps and around stage stations; and this employment was available, whereas others were not. As tracks entered northeast Utah, they were in Mormon territory, and Brigham Young had obtained contracts with both the Union and Central Pacific companies for grading and masonry work through this domain. He subcontracted the work to bishops, who, in turn, hired members of the Church's wards. This

After James White left Callville in 1868, he found work with the construction of the Union Pacific Railroad. Courtesy, Denver Public Library, Western History Collection, no. Z-5921.

arrangement did not preclude other lower-paying work for Gentiles, as White found.

Restrictions of the Church of Jesus Christ of Latter-day Saints also constrained the social life of construction gangs. Normally, as rails were laid, tents and wooden structures came off the flatcars and temporary end-of-line camps sprang up instantly. Popularly known as "Hell-on-Wheels" for good reason, these towns were populated at the end of each day's labor by hundreds of men thirsting for assorted forms of refreshment and entertainment. One of the last end-of-track towns before rails cut through the mountains to the valley of the Great Salt Lake was Bear River City. Like others, it had dozens of saloons, equal numbers of liquor stores, gambling parlors, and dancehalls, and scores of ladies of the night. Beyond Bear River City and the mountains, railroad workers found themselves in Utah and in dire straits for amusement. As a result, north of Ogden, an end-of-track camp called Corinne sprang up with Gentiles occupying it and operating its enterprises to the exclusion of Mormons. Eilean Adams's biography of her grandfather reported that White went to Corinne and that he owned a saloon there.[2] Although he was not a teetotaler, this venture in entrepreneurship was unique. If White had remained longer, he might

With the completion of the transcontinental railroad, celebrated with the driving of the last spikes at Promontory Point in Utah, rails connected the continent from coast to coast and changed the nation's transportation. Courtesy, Denver Public Library, Western History Collection, no. Z-3258, printed in *Lesley's Weekly,* June 5, 1869.

have prospered, for Corinne continued to greet workers and travelers with open arms even after the rails met at Promontory Point. By 1870, Gentiles formally incorporated their community of about 1,000 non-Mormons, and for a time Corinne became a railroad town threatening to outstrip Ogden. White missed these developments, however, for he sold his saloon in November 1868, and with a little money jingling in his pockets, he headed to Wisconsin to visit his family.

Later, White asserted that he barely missed meeting Powell when the major's first expedition was at Green River City, Wyoming, preparing to start down the Green and Colorado Rivers. Such a claim would seem to be impossible, for White traveled east in the fall of 1868, while Powell was in Colorado preparing to spend the winter studying Ute Indians.[3]

White's stay in Wisconsin did not last long. His father had died in 1865, and James found his mother, sister, sister-in-law, and brother

Josh living in the family home. Josh seems to have become the head of the household. Sitting around the kitchen table or in one of Kenosha's bars, James had a lot to tell about his experiences in the West, if he was feeling loquacious. In the nearly seven years since our picaro began his episodic journey, he had traveled on foot with an emigrant caravan across the plains; had visited mining towns of Colorado Territory and Nevada; had seen the Pacific Ocean and sailed on it, too; had served in the cavalry in California and the Southwest; and was court-martialed in Texas and imprisoned in New Mexico Territory before getting out with an honorable discharge and a bonus. He could tell about working for Barlow, Sanderson and Company in hostile Indian country; stealing Indian ponies; shooting a companion in a gunfight; prospecting (albeit unsuccessfully); losing one companion in an Indian attack and another in the rapids of the Colorado River; and being heralded as the first white man to traverse the Grand Canyon. He had carried mail, helped build the transcontinental railroad, and operated a saloon in Utah.

The letter he had written to Josh, together with C. C. Parry's report and the newspaper story that the *Kenosha Telegraph* had printed, surely must have elicited curiosity about the prodigal son's activities, but one Wisconsin winter was enough. By spring 1869, the old home had become too confining for a seasoned drifter, and he was again ready to leave family and former friends. They probably were ready to let him go, too, as they had become accustomed to his absence. James White packed up and headed back to the open spaces and the freedom of the West.

He traveled to Chicago, Leavenworth, Kansas City, and Junction City, where he again took a job with Barlow, Sanderson and Company. He appears to have remained with the stage company for the next eight years, although he did not stay in any one location for long. During this period, White has said that he drifted from place to place. With the relocation of Indians and the laying of railroad tracks across Kansas, much had changed in the two years since he had last worked for Barlow and Sanderson. While he was cutting ties at Bear River and pouring drinks in Corinne, the stage route along the Arkansas River was shrinking, as Barlow and Sanderson eliminated most stage service when rails reached its stations, leaving only local connections in many locations. By 1869, Fort Lyon was the stage company's eastern

A group portrait with James White, on left, was made during his reunion with his family in Kenosha, Wisconsin, in 1869. His physical condition appears to have restored fully since his ordeal in 1867. Courtesy, Cline Library, Northern Arizona University, no. NAU.PH.93.34.1, James White Collection.

terminus, although service continued to Santa Fe and to some other western destinations.

According to the account in Dawson's *The Grand Canyon,* White drove stage out of Goose Creek, which, I believe, was located in south-central Kansas. Next he was transferred to Fort Lyon and Five Mile Point, although Eilean Adams wrote that he was "tending stock and coaches" at Half Mile Station near Bent's Old Fort. The name "Half Mile" appears to have come from a letter written by General William Jackson Palmer to his "Darling Queen" on August 9, 1869, about meeting

White there.[4] The stage line's premiere authority, Morris Taylor, lists neither Five Mile Point nor Half Mile Station, so this location might have been a temporary swing station, with White possibly its only employee. Tasks in such a place would have involved repairing harnesses and other trappings and taking care of the horses, changing them, cooling down those that had just come in, and feeding and watering them.

No explanation is given for Palmer's knowing about White's presence at Half Mile Station/Five Mile Point, but it is not difficult to imagine that White quietly had been letting his acquaintances know about his exploits, and the word spread in idle chatter from person to person. He even might have carried a tattered newspaper account in his pocket to show to incredulous coworkers and stage passengers, just to prove that his stories were true. Palmer—the employer of chroniclers Parry, Bell, and Calhoun—assuredly was interested when he discovered White's presence nearby.

After seeing White, Palmer wrote his letter to Queen while he was en route to today's Sheridan Lake in Colorado, near the Kansas state line, where Palmer's Kansas Pacific Railroad was being built from the east. Describing his meeting White, Palmer wrote:

> When Mr. Carr and I reached Bent's Fort on the Arkansas yesterday, we found unexpectedly that there was no coach to Sheridan until Monday morning—so we stopped at the Fort all night—took a delightful and refreshing bath in the Arkansas River the next morning, and after breakfast got the stage people to drive us down in a buggy to Fort Lyon (18 miles). [At this time the river, which later changed its course, flowed past the main gate of the fort.] On the way we stopped at a stage station known as "1/2 mile Point," where we had an interview of three hours with a very remarkable character. I do not know that you have ever heard me tell of James White—the man who came through the Colorado Canon alone on a raft just two years ago.—and whom our surveying party met in Arizona shortly after—when we learned his story[.]—The account he gave was so wonderful and dramatic that very few people in the United States have ever believed the story or the fact that he ever really traversed this terrible canon. . . . I did not get to see White in Arizona, so I was very glad to have the opportunity of meeting him here. . . . There were many interesting points brought out as we sat on the sill of the stable for which he was acting as stock tender.[5]

From the letter, one infers that White described his voyage down the Colorado River to Palmer and Carr. Palmer would have been a sympathetic listener, for he had good reasons to defend not only White but also Charles Christopher Parry, his former employee in the railroad survey, whose report Palmer had ordered and endorsed. Although he did not attempt to repeat lengthy details in this personal letter, he did include something about the party of four prospectors who had left Fort Dodge together in the spring of 1867. After Palmer noted that one man had been killed by Indians and another by drowning in the river, Palmer asked White about the fourth man, Goodfellow, whom White had omitted from his previous stories. In reply, Palmer got a straight answer about the shooting at Brown's Creek. During this conversation, however, White made his obviously false claim about having narrowly missed an opportunity to meet Powell. Equally implausible was White's statement that he was willing to make another trip down the Colorado. Palmer wrote in his letter: "White said that Professor Powell had endeavored to see him before starting on his expedition this Spring, to induce him to go along—but they had failed to meet. He said he would have gone willingly—and would have gone again through the canon, as he thought from his experience he could make the trip safely."

In 1869, newspapers were covering the expedition of Major John Wesley Powell, and few, probably, were more interested in the expedition than James White. Powell had set out at Green River, Wyoming, in May 1869 with four boats and a crew of eleven to descend the canyons of the Green and Colorado Rivers. Ninety-eight days later, on August 30, 1869, two of the boats and six of the men reached the mouth of the Virgin River. At the time of General Palmer's meeting with James White at Half Mile Station/Five Mile Point in eastern Colorado, Powell and his crew were still in the Inner Gorge of the Grand Canyon, where White supposedly nearly perished, and the public was as yet uninformed about the final outcome of Powell's expedition. Perhaps General Palmer brought up the subject during his conversation with White, eliciting his cocksure remarks.

In 1906, thirty-seven years after meeting White, Palmer wrote a letter to Robert C. Clowry about the earlier occasion. Palmer's memory or White's account was faulty, as the letter demonstrated:

During his second expedition, Major John Wesley Powell rode in an armchair on a bulkhead of his boat, the Emma Dean, *a means of transportation that, like James White's log raft, understandably did not attract imitators among later river runners.* Courtesy, Denver Public Library, Western History Collection, no. Z-2181, John K. Hillers photo.

White begins his narrative with reference to four men, while it will be observed that he only accounts for the fate of three, including himself; one Capt. Baker was killed by Indians; one "Henry Stro e" [George Strole] was washed from the raft at the first rapid. He [White] explained to me, when I asked about this, in the summer of 1868 [1869], by saying that one of them did not get beyond Canon City, on their way to the San Juan country. . . . The fourth man was killed in a drunken fight at Canon City. [The nonfatal gunfight occurred at Brown's Creek.][6]

Despite White's candid admission in 1869 about shooting Goodfellow, discrepancies were beginning to accumulate in White's stories. Why had he not told other interviewers the truth about Joe Goodfellow? What about Powell's easily refuted attempt to meet White? White was not precise about details, such as saying he was driving a stage at Goose Creek, although it is clear that he was a stock tender instead of a driver when Palmer met him at Half Mile. It seems possible that over the years, as White told his stories again and again, they became progressively more self-aggrandizing and White came to believe them. Palmer's letter acknowledged that some people already were beginning to doubt the story about White's traverse of the Grand Canyon but that he was convinced by White's manner that he was telling them the truth.

After Half Mile Station/Five Mile Point, the next station where James White worked, as reported in Dawson's *The Grand Canyon*, was Bent Canyon. There, White said, he "kept home station." A home station was a point where drivers changed, meals were served, and a little more activity and responsibility occurred than at a swing station, such as Half Mile/Five Mile. At Bent Canyon, passengers and drivers would have milled around when a stage came through, and local ranchers who lived in the sparsely populated region would have dallied there, gawking at the goings-on and exchanging gossip when they came around to pick up their mail or delivered a wagonload of hay.

Bent Canyon lies between La Junta and Trinidad, Colorado. The Mountain Branch of the Santa Fe Trail generally followed Timpas Creek in this area, and Barlow and Sanderson's coaches did so as well. Originally, a stage station was located at Iron Spring, a historic site located by a marker today, but in 1871 the route was moved slightly away from Iron Spring, down to the head of Bent Canyon, to better serve the scattered ranchers who were beginning to settle in the drainage of the Purgatoire River.[7] Cowboys and pioneers in the area simply called this stream the "Picketwire." Bent Canyon Stage Station was on land leased from a rancher named Rourke, at the mouth of a side canyon later known as Stage Canyon.

The next known event in White's life was momentous, for on November 6, 1871, he married Octaviana Johnson at Red Rock, Colorado Territory, as shown on the marriage certificate, with the name of Antonio Johnson, Octaviana's brother, appearing as witness. The bride was sixteen, the groom going on thirty-four. The location of Red Rock was a mystery to White's descendants who possessed the certificate, but in Michael Beshoar's *All about Trinidad and Las Animas County, Colorado* (1882), the place is identified. Beshoar listed Red Rocks (elevation 4,786) at a distance of sixty-five miles from Trinidad, and Bent Canyon (elevation 4,690) at sixty miles from Trinidad.[8] A topographic map of the area shows both Bent and Red Rock Canyons descending in a southeasterly direction toward the Purgatory [Purgatoire] River. Beshoar's booklet also reveals that a post office was located at Bent Canyon.

It is not hard to imagine the Johnson family herding livestock that belonged to them or to some other rancher who hired vaqueros. Perhaps one or more of the Johnson family worked at the Bent Canyon Stage Station. Johnson is a common surname, and several Johnsons were listed in southeastern Colorado Territory in the U.S. Census of 1870, but none was from Red Rock Canyon or its neighborhood, and the names of Antonio and Octaviana are not listed. Eilean Adams wrote that Octaviana's family was ethnically mixed, as her given names implies. On separate occasions, Otis R. Marston told Eilean Adams and me that Octaviana's brother was executed for a crime, but Marston provided no verification for this statement. At any rate, in the lonely Picketwire country, romance blossomed and James White became a married man.

The next known occurrence in the lives of James and Tavvy, as the young girl was called by her family, was the arrival in 1872 of a son, Edward, who died soon after his birth. Another son, Benjamin, was born in 1875. The White family usually called him "Ven," reflecting the pronunciation of his Hispanic mother, for the consonants *b* and *v* are interchangeable in Spanish.

In the account of his life that White signed in 1916, he said that he was "in Las Animas County and other minor places" until he settled in Trinidad, Colorado, in 1878.[9] Possibly one of the "other minor places" was Fort Garland, for much later, perhaps in a lapse of memory, he said he was married there. Barlow and Sanderson's stage line ran through Fort Garland, and White might have worked there. Another slim clue to his whereabouts is found in the *Rocky Mountain News* story of November 1877 that was reprinted in Frank Hall's *History of Colorado*. In this article, the newspaper correspondent mentioned in passing that James White had been at Lake City in May.

Lake City was a thriving mining town where silver was discovered in 1874, and the place became a center of activity during the San Juan silver mining boom. Charles Baker had investigated this very area when he crossed the high mountains into the Animas River drainage in 1860 in search of gold. Two of the people quoted by the newspaper correspondent in 1877 had been in the San Juans during the mining excitement of 1860–1861, and here they were at Lake City, still enamored with mining, wherever it might be. These two were Tom Pollock's recently widowed wife, Sarah, and Stephen B. Kellogg, "both formerly of Lake City, Colo.," who were in Lake City at the time of the interview, or so the writer said.

Although the newspaper story was primarily concerned with the Baker Expedition of 1860–1861, a few lines alluded to the prospecting trip of 1867, Baker's death at the hands of Indians, and James White's transit of the Grand Canyon. The article said: "In May last White was in Lake City, and it is believed that he is now in the southern part of the state. He is about 35 years of age [thirty-nine, actually], a plain, matter-of-fact, practical adventurous man. There is not a shadow of a doubt about his wonderful adventures and his marvelous escape through the Canyon of the Colorado."[10]

No other leads about White's connection with Lake City have been found, but one is tempted to speculate that he might have been there as an employee of Barlow and Sanderson, perhaps on the line that ran through the San Luis Valley and Antelope Spring to Lake City. Equally puzzling is the presence of Sarah Pollock at Lake City. She and Tom had been living in the San Luis Valley and in the Animas country in the 1870s before Tom died in 1876.

As for Kellogg's reemergence in Lake City, where the article said that he "is now justice of the peace," his name does not appear in Hinsdale County's tax records, newspaper index, cemetery index, or census records for that location. Without mentioning a stay at Lake City, a Bancroft manuscript reported that in 1870, "Judge Kellogg" left Granite and Cache Creek, where he had been working "the since famous 'Yankee Blade' mine—finally selling out entirely for $10,000." He then went to Manitou Springs where he operated a hotel. In 1879 he was at Ouray, Colorado, "whence learning of the 'Leadville' excitement—he went joining the mining fever's excited lords. Reaching the spot where he had been 19 years before—he found every available foot of ground located—so he moved with his family to this spot now 'Buena Vista.' He is now quietly living—enjoying excellent health—filling the positions of 'Justice of the Peace' and 'Police Magistrate.' He is in moderate circumstances—owns some supposedly valuable mining claims—and yet hopes to be a millionaire."[11] At Buena Vista, Mrs. Kellogg must finally have put down her foot, insisting that her husband, who now was in his sixties, should stop his drifting from place to place.

White's nomadic life also ended soon thereafter when he and Tavvy moved to Trinidad, Colorado, in 1878. Trinidad was a place that

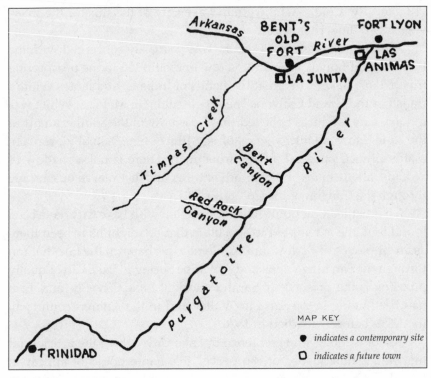

Trinidad, Colorado, region.

still had a few rough edges, not unlike White himself. Drifter though he may have been for seventeen years, he seldom had lacked employment, and he seems to have settled down to domestic life with little chafing under the yoke of husband and family provider. He lived in Trinidad for the remaining half century of his life.

When he and his family arrived at Trinidad, the town was in transition from its origins as a stage station on the Mountain Branch of the Santa Fe Trail to a railroad town on the Atchison, Topeka and Santa Fe Railroad. In its early years, Trinidad had been a rough place, sometimes a violent one, and it still had some maturing to do. Many of the first people living there were Hispanic, but ever-increasing numbers of tough "gringos" had joined them. In late 1867, a "war" broke out between the Spanish-speaking people and the "Americans," after a drunken stagecoach driver shot a popular resident. The victim most likely was equally drunk. Muache Ute Indians showed up at about this time to add to local tension. To end the fracas, soldiers were summoned, although they proved to be as unpopular as the feuding parties.

As the rails approached, Barlow and Sanderson's routes continued to shrink, for the railroad obtained the mail contracts that once kept the stage line economically viable. The mail route between Trinidad and Santa Fe continued for a while, until the arrival of the Denver and Rio Grande Railway at El Moro near Trinidad in 1876, followed by the Atchison, Topeka and Santa Fe Railroad into Trinidad in the fall of 1878. These changes in transportation ended the jobs of many stage company employees like James White, while the railroad spurred rapid growth of Trinidad's population and commerce. The most important source of work was in the area's numerous coal mines, and by the late 1870s, the railroad town's population was approaching 3,000, with a melting pot of Eastern European, Italian, Hispanic, Black, Anglo, and Jewish, along with "Americans" like White. As the town grew, it remained a lively place, with Bat Masterson and circuit gamblers operating there.

Work was plentiful for a husky man like James White. Wagons hauled coal, wool, beer, farm and ranch products, building materials, and commercial goods, offering an opportunity for an individual who needed only a wagon and a team of horses to establish a drayage business to support a growing family in which babies were arriving every year or two. Despite great changes in transportation in the following decades, White continued to operate his express business, with interruptions caused by a broken arm and the loss of an eye. A broken hip finally forced his retirement in 1915, when he was in his late seventies.

White's homelife did not differ greatly from that of other working-class families of the late nineteenth century. Tavvy bore a total of ten children, eight of whom survived. Most were girls, with boys serving as bookends as the eldest and youngest of the eight. Religion does not appear to have played an important role in the family's life. Although Spanish-speaking people such as Tavvy were traditionally Catholic, as were many foreign-born laborers who lived in the Trinidad area, White's children attended public schools rather than parochial, and family members were not buried by Catholic churches or interred in Trinidad's Catholic Cemetery.

Once he was settled, White's only known long trip away from Trinidad was a visit to Kenosha in 1890, twenty-one years after leaving in 1869. He again had contact with a relative twenty years later in 1910, when, carrying a treasured newspaper clipping about White's Grand Canyon story, Joshua White traveled from his current home in North Dakota to see his brother in Trinidad.

Outside the home, occasional nips from the bottle and poker games seem to have been White's pastimes. His card games suggest that his mind was capable of focusing on poker, even if his memories about his Colorado River adventure tended to drift as the years passed. He claimed to have played every week at Bloom Mansion, one of Trinidad's finest houses on brick-paved Main Street. Perhaps so, but in terms of social pretensions and monetary worth, Main Street's residences were a long way from White's modest neighborhood.

The Whites lived in a series of small homes within a couple of blocks of each other in a working-class area, lacking ostentation but conveniently located for his drayage business. The sequence of family homes was located within one small neighborhood on the west side of the river, on the narrow flats bounded on the east by the Santa Fe's railroad tracks and on the west by hillsides where the campus of Trinidad State Junior College is located. One home that he built for his family was repossessed when he broke his arm and was unable to work for a period of time, Eilean Adams wrote. I found the land of another home to be occupied by the parking lot of a fast-food restaurant in 2004, immediately adjacent to the noisy, once-smoky railroad tracks.

The publications in the 1870s of Alfred Calhoun's tale about White's alleged adventure down the Colorado River brought a little notoriety to Trinidad's resident, but his fame was overshadowed by Powell's celebrated exploits in the Grand Canyon in 1869 and 1871–1872. The wider world was about to forget James White until 1907, when *The Outing Magazine* printed an article about him under the title "The Story of James White, First Explorer of the Grand Canyon."[12] This widely circulated magazine, which published stories about sports and adventure worldwide, was read by William H. Edwards, an individual who had once bumped into White.

Edwards was a former boatman on a railroad survey led by Robert Brewster Stanton. Edwards had worked for a mining outfit on the Green River, and he kept up contacts with acquaintances like Stanton who had an interest in the canyon. When Edwards saw the article in

Outing, he wrote from Pueblo, Colorado, to Stanton that around 1894 he had met White, who was then living in Trinidad, Colorado. White and Edwards had had a long conversation, Edwards said, and based on this meeting, he did not believe that White went through the Grand Canyon and also thought it would be impossible to make such a trip in fourteen days because of "the way a raft would drift around in the eddies."[13]

In his letter, Edwards gave White's address to Stanton. This coincidence brought Stanton to White's doorstep, beside the Atchison, Topeka and Santa Fe Railroad's right-of-way, for an interview that became an important part of the ongoing James White saga.

FAME WITHOUT FORTUNE

DURING THE FOUR DECADES BEFORE THE ARTICLE ABOUT JAMES WHITE APPEARED in *The Outing Magazine,* his title as first through the Grand Canyon, in 1867, had been debated, with debunkers by far outnumbering his original advocates at Callville and Hardyville, his family, and his acquaintances in Kenosha and Trinidad. Some Coloradans who did not know White personally were inclined to accept his claim, whereas elsewhere in the nation most believed that John Wesley Powell's expedition of 1869 was first and had forgotten the name of James White.

Back in 1869, however, White and his alleged voyage was a topic of conversation among Powell's crew when they undertook their own Colorado River adventure. Much as they wanted to believe that White had proved that it was possible to survive a transit of the Grand Canyon, and therefore so could they, they were skeptical that he had actually done so, especially on a raft. Some of Powell's recruits for his first expedition were ordinary drifters, men who could not be easily gulled. They had been prospecting, hunting, trapping, and mule skinning long enough that they could spot fakes and phonies a mile away. When they faced the Colorado's heavy rapids that tested their own great strength and courage to the limit, they ridiculed the stories of White and his raft. In the Upper Granite Gorge, with nearly three dozen big rapids in half as many miles requiring the utmost effort of Powell's men, they heartily doubted White's claims of having survived on a raft.[1]

Although Powell remained silent about White during the expedition, he later gave a White supporter a scrap of satisfaction. In his letter to Robert C. Clowry, dated December 27, 1906 (a portion of which is quoted in Chapter 6), General William Jackson Palmer asserted that he met Major Powell on a train in 1870, after his first expedition ended. During their conversation, Palmer showed Powell the railroad survey's report, which included the C. C. Parry account. According to Palmer, in his letter to Clowry, Powell conceded that the White-Parry description of the river's walls was correct, although there is no way to know how carefully Powell read it or how thoughtfully he contemplated it. For his part, Palmer felt vindicated in his belief that White's account was accurate because of Powell's hasty stamp of approval, which overlooked inexact descriptions of geography and geology.[2] When Palmer said that the major concurred with the descriptions, one can only speculate whether Powell had studied them closely. Palmer was satisfied, however, that White was still the first down the Colorado and Powell was second, although Powell continued to be hailed as first by the world at large. The issue about who was first spawned an argument that has lasted for well over a century and still has not been resolved to everyone's satisfaction, but not for want of trying.

Ignored is the fact that witnesses were absent to prove that White did or did not make the journey as he and others portrayed it. Attempting to overcome this lack of reliable information, debaters have resorted to arguments based on wishful thinking, guesswork, deductions, and non sequiturs, none of which answered the question, did he or didn't he go through the Grand Canyon on a raft two years prior to Powell's expedition? In some regards, the debate was like one of the river's whirlpools, sucking yea-sayers and nay-sayers alike into its waters, spinning them round and round, and finally spitting them out, a little dazed by the experience but otherwise unchanged. The only lesson learned is that it is better to stay out of whirlpools. I will attempt to follow that dictum by describing the whirlpool as impartially as possible from the safety of the shore.

First into the whirlpool were those in 1867 and 1868 who met White at Callville and Hardyville or who wrote about him after meeting someone who had met him. Newspaper stories about White's supposed adventure were reaching the public as early as fall 1867, and they continued to circulate the tale. Parry's contributions appealed to a readership with a desire to open transportation in the West, even down the Colorado River. Within a couple of years, with another version Calhoun was helping to keep the White saga alive by entertaining readers who enjoyed adventure tales for leisure reading.

For his part, Powell had nothing to say about White publicly. Despite all the notoriety that Major John Wesley Powell had earned because of his expeditions on the river in 1869 and 1871–1872, he was an enigma. Clearly intelligent, Powell was not formally educated in science, and his need to raise funds for his work complicated both his public relations and his relations with his coworkers, even with his crews on the river. Only three years older than White when each embarked on the river, Powell was a man of ambition, energy, tenacity, curiosity, rudimentary scientific knowledge, and contacts in the academic world on which to build a foundation for his work. Compared to Powell, White was a nonentity, a fluke or a fraud, and, leaving others to assert his claim, Powell dealt with the question of White's raft trip by simply ignoring him.

While he was in Colorado in 1868, Powell had had ample opportunity to hear about White's alleged trip through the Grand Canyon, and it has even been said that Powell visited White to question him before his exploratory expedition embarked in May 1869, but there is no evidence that such a meeting took place. In the early months of 1869 Powell was at Fort Bridger, which is close to Bear River, where White had previously been supplying railroad ties in 1868, but White had left Wyoming and Utah by late 1868 to visit his family in Wisconsin.

Questions about White's raft trip continued to receive attention, thanks to people like Palmer and his colleagues, and in consequence, the achievements of Powell's river exploit also were argued by a few who wondered whether Powell actually was first. The debate captured the attention of Robert Brewster Stanton, a man driven by energy and determination who relished digging into controversies and possessed utmost confidence that he could resolve them. Perhaps Stanton developed such self-assurance from his father, a Presbyterian clergyman, or by observing his aunt, Elizabeth Cady Stanton, a leader in the woman suffrage movement. Perhaps he was overcompensating because of the effects of childhood polio or an accident (accounts differ) that left him with a crippled arm, not unlike John Wesley Powell, who had lost an arm in the Civil War. In any case, after conquering the Grand Canyon himself, Stanton undertook the delicious task of investigating Powell's flaws and foibles, particularly Powell's idiosyncratic report of the "first" expedition that presented incidents from the second expedition as if they had happened in the first and omitted the names of the second's personnel. Stanton was not a man to be dismissed casually, as James White's champions later discovered when Stanton turned his attention to the man on the raft, like an insect in a collection of rare specimens. In their personal traits, methods, and conclusions, Stanton and the later investigator Otis R. Marston had much in common.

Stanton had a proprietary interest in the Colorado River because in 1889, a dozen years after White's alleged transit and a decade after Powell's first expedition, Stanton traversed part of the Colorado with a railroad survey for the Denver, Colorado Canyon, and Pacific Railway Company and subsequently boated the river successfully. During the first, inadequately equipped and poorly planned survey, which quickly turned into a disaster, Stanton steadfastly performed his job as chief engineer. The company hoped to construct a railroad down the Colorado from Grand Junction, Colorado, and through the Grand Canyon to California. The railroad's president Frank M. Brown, who was in charge of the expedition, brought along guests, whom he hoped to impress favorably to encourage their investments in his company. They made it downriver from Grand Junction, Colorado; past Moab, Utah; through Cataract Canyon, where their supplies were lost; through Glen Canyon; and into Marble Canyon. There President Brown drowned, and a little farther on in Marble Canyon, so did one of the crew, Peter Hansbrough, and the outfit's black cook, Henry Richards. Stanton then took charge and led the party to South Canyon, where they could climb out, although a debris flow came close to destroying them there.

That expedition was aborted, but, confident that he could conclude the survey with improved boats and planning, Stanton returned as director of the project. His party embarked in Glen Canyon in spring 1890. During the voyage, the survey's photographer, Frederick Nims, suffered a broken leg, resulting in his evacuation on an improvised stretcher over the precipitous walls of Marble Canyon. Afterward, with Stanton taking photographs at half-mile intervals down the river, the survey succeeded in reaching the Gulf of California, but Stanton's decisions had caused some difficulties, and the Nims incident produced bad press for the expedition and for Stanton. Despite his survey's ultimate success, he was accused of suffering "exceedingly from an aggravated attack of the big head," which estranged his crew.[3]

Stanton later doggedly contended that it would be possible to build and operate a railroad through the canyons, an engineering feat that would have rearranged geography at immense financial and aesthetic cost, but at least he had proved his ability to consummate an extremely difficult transit through the Grand Canyon. He took seriously the title he claimed as the *second* leader of an exploration of the Grand Canyon and zealously strove to discredit White and his supporters, even ignoring or altering evidence. Powell's only acknowledgment of Stanton's Grand Canyon transit was a casual mention that others had attempted to emulate his own achievement of 1869. Stanton was not amused. (The temptation to psychoanalyze these obsessive-compulsive gentlemen is another whirlpool that I will avoid.)

Nameless prospectors in the plateau country heard about these adventures on the water and hoped that boats might provide a faster, easier mode of transportation through the rugged canyons than their feet and pack animals had provided. Others just wanted to see if they could accomplish the same deed. One man, a drifter much like White, was George "Trapper" Flavell, who in 1896 recruited a companion, Ramon Montez, and others to go down the Green and Colorado to the Gulf of California, hunting as they went. They succeeded in traversing the canyon and running all the rapids, as Flavell said. Nathaniel "Than" Galloway later corrected Flavell's statement, saying that they ran all except for Soap Creek Rapid, where they lowered the boat with ropes through the rapid.[4]

In 1897, Galloway, a prospector, gave the river a try and succeeded by employing an innovative technique of running rapids stern first so he could attack them head on before they ate him alive, and he used a flat-bottomed boat instead of keeled hulls. Others later adopted his new way of running fast water. After his own successful run to Needles, Galloway judged White's raft trip impossible.[5]

Meanwhile, Stanton was stewing about Powell. During the railroad survey, Stanton encountered Jack Sumner, Powell's first assistant on the expedition of 1869. Drifting around southeastern Utah, Sumner was prospecting, hunting, and swapping gossip with anyone who passed his haunts. According to reliable accounts, Sumner had become mentally ill. He was nursing a grievance about Powell, who, Sumner believed, had cheated him and others of their share of pay and reimbursements. Also, Sumner's contribution of supplies had been substantial, but his complaints appear to have been based in part on some incorrect notions about Powell's funding. Sumner enjoyed the support of his brother-in-law, William Byers of the *Rocky Mountain News,* which printed Sumner's fulminations about Powell. Another ax to be ground concerned the controversy over the departure of Oramel Howland and two others from the expedition at Separation Rapid and their subsequent deaths. Howland had been employed by the *Rocky Mountain News* prior to Powell's first expedition. A by-product of Sumner's anti-Powell campaign was Stanton's scrutiny of the major's expeditions. (Stanton's tenacious digging produced Powell's long-lost journal from under a piece of furniture in Powell's own Bureau of American Ethnology and also the surviving portion of Sumner's journal. So much literature is available on Powell and his surveys that it is unnecessary to add more to its volume here.[6])

The appearance in 1902 of a book by Frederick S. Dellenbaugh also inspired Stanton to probe James White's raft trip. As a youth, Dellenbaugh had accompanied the second Powell expedition in 1871–1872, and although he was a loyal friend of the major, he believed that Powell's 1875 report had falsified the facts about the first expedition and had been unjust to the second expedition's men. When Dellenbaugh expressed his wish to write an account of the second expedition, Powell concurred. It was published in 1902 as *The Romance of the Colorado River.* In this account, Dellenbaugh mentioned the White saga and pointed out, among other things, that White could have escaped the river at many places in Glen Canyon and at Lee's Ferry. Dellenbaugh concluded:

> We have seen various actors passing before us in this drama, but I doubt if any of them have been more picturesque than this champion prevaricator. But he had related a splendid yarn. What it is intended to obscure would probably be quite as interesting as what he told. Just where he entered upon the river is of course impossible to decide, but that he never came through the Grand Canyon is as certain as anything can be. His story reveals an absolute ignorance of the river and its walls throughout the whole course he pretended to have traversed.[7]

Perhaps in response to the negative views being circulated by Dellenbaugh's popular book, a four-page article about James White's raft trip appeared in 1907 in *The Outing Magazine*. Pointedly, the article about White bore the title "The Story of James White: First Explorer of the Grand Canyon." It consisted of a three-paragraph introduction, a copy of the published report by C. C. Parry, and a photocopy of James White's letter to his brother Joshua, along with a separate, transcribed copy of the letter with minor editing for clarity. The article gave no author's name, so it is unclear whether the editor-owner of the magazine, Caspar Whitney, a prolific writer, had simply happened upon the material and decided to run it, or whether it was submitted by members of C. C. Parry's family who wished to refute Dellenbaugh's opinions. Parry was unable to fight the battle himself, as he had died in 1890, but his family, who had his papers, cooperated with *Outing* at the very least. The introductory paragraphs in the article read:

> The expedition led by Major Powell which descended the Colorado River through the Grand Cañon is generally credited with the first authentic passage of that perilous region. This daring feat was accomplished in 1868 [1869]. A year before that date, however, a prospector named James White went down the Colorado on a frail raft, and after incredible suffering and dangers, reached a settlement and lived many years thereafter to tell the story which has been hidden away in the dusty files of a geological report.
>
> There has been preserved also a letter from this humble hero, written to his brother shortly after he passed through the Cañon. This letter which is reproduced herewith, together with the official report of the adventure, form a remarkable chapter in the history of the discovery of the unknown west.

In January 1868, C. C. Parry, an assistant geologist of the
Union Pacific Railroad Survey, happened to meet James White at
Hardyville on the Colorado, and in a report to the president of the
company he included the following narrative as he received it from
its hero.[8]

Seeing the article, William Edwards wrote his letter to Stanton
and offered his own opinion that White's trip was impossible.[9] With
White's address provided by Edwards, Stanton was off and running.
After taking a look at the article in *The Outing Magazine,* Stanton asked
the Parry family for a copy of White's letter to Joshua and had a photographer verify its authenticity. The Parry family later might have
rued their cooperation with Stanton, who eventually accused Parry of
suggesting faulty geographical information to White and creating the
false legend of his successful raft trip.

In 1907, Stanton wrote a letter to properly introduce himself to
James White and traveled to Trinidad by train to interview him. On
September 23, 1907, Stanton found White and a companion riding
in a wagon that bore the sign "James White, Express" on a street in
Trinidad. White, the driver of the wagon, already knew that Stanton
wanted to talk about the voyage down the Colorado. At this first street-
side encounter, White made it clear that he expected to be paid for his
trouble, warning Stanton that he had sent away some newspapermen
from Denver and St. Louis without their stories when they refused to
pay. He also wanted to have their conversation after six o'clock so that
he would not have to "put my horses in the barn and lose my day's
work."[10] Stanton consented to these conditions and at the beginning of
the interview paid White twenty-five dollars.

It is doubtful that White understood the intensity of the man, who
arrived that evening at the family's modest doorstep by the railroad
tracks. Even though Stanton was accompanied by a local public stenographer, Roy L. Lappin, chances are that White would not have
been very worried had he known. He had become a mellow chap, a
bit foggy in his nearly seventy-year-old head. His interests were cir-
cumscribed by his habitual rounds with his delivery wagon, providing for his wife and children, regularly enjoying games of poker with
his friends, and reminiscing about his adventure for the diminishing
number of people who still were interested. His navigations had long
since been confined to the streets of Trinidad, and the wider world

The transfer wagon belonging to James White resembled these high vehicles belonging to his competitors in Trinidad's drayage business, Trinidad. Courtesy, Colorado Historical Society, Aultman Collection, no. A-836 (1900–1916).

through which he had traveled years before was now a fading memory even for White. Stanton described his appearance at the time of the meeting as vigorous, with the physical appearance of a man no more than fifty except for his thinning gray hair.

That evening Stanton listened to White's story and then proceeded to cross-examine him. White began with the prospecting trip that brought Baker, White, and Strole to the San Juan River but called Charles Baker by "Jim." Stanton questioned White's mileages and locations from the time that they started down the San Juan River. Not very consequential were slips like saying that Strole drowned on the fifth day instead of the fourth, but as Stanton asked questions to double-check White, he became increasingly befuddled. Concerning the canyon, White gave descriptions of the walls, of the raft rolling over many times, of a place where a waterfall came right out of the rock, of the red water flowing out of the Colorado Chiquito. Of particular interest to Stanton was White's insistence that the point of embarkation on the river was on the Grand River—that is, above the mouth of the Colorado and the Green and that White, Baker, and Strole had gone south when they left the San Juan River. When Stanton attempted to correct White's erroneous statements about an absence of rapids below the confluence of the Grand and Green, where Cataract Canyon exists, or about the Little Colorado flowing into the Colorado from the right, White become adamant and at one point wanted to know why he was being asked so many questions if Stanton already knew so much. White said he knew his facts because "General Palmer," meaning Parry, said they were so. The confusion about Parry's identity had existed in White's mind since 1868, but that error was not so damaging as his revelation that Parry had prompted White. Such matters were bad enough, but worse in Stanton's mind was White's observation that the rapids on the river did not seem terribly big, except that on the ninth day a rapid caused his raft to fall apart and he had to tie it together again. On the tenth day he went over a big rapid with a fall of twenty feet, perhaps more. After that rapid, on the twelfth day he came upon seventy-five Indians and got dog meat, and on the fourteenth day, White said, he reached Callville. After the rescue, White related that he had told his story to General Palmer, and so the interview went, straying again and again from known facts and from previous versions in large and small ways.

In his grilling, Stanton took some statements out of context, as occurred most importantly in the exchange about the "big rapid." Stanton pointedly asked, "How many big heavy rapids were there on the Colorado River that you passed over in your journey?" and White fell into Stanton's trap by replying: "In all the journey there was only one big rapid, the one with the twenty-foot fall. All the other rapids were small ones." Although this statement contradicted descriptions of rapids that White had given in 1867 and 1868, Stanton used White's comment about one big rapid to demolish White, and other debunkers would pick up this line of argument later. Stanton knew firsthand that hundreds of rapids existed, and, furthermore, the hazards of navigating some of these rapids increased during periods when the water level is low, as it is in late summer. Today's visitors can no longer see the most severe rapid in the Lower Canyon at that time, which was Lava Cliff Rapid, inundated by Lake Mead since the 1930s.

In the end, Stanton arbitrarily concluded that White actually had gone south from the San Juan River and entered the Colorado River at Grand Wash, below the Grand Canyon. It has been asserted that Stanton could have altered the stenographer's record of the interview to say that White, Baker, and Strole went south, not north, from the San Juan, but this accusation cannot be proved. The embarkation point proposed by Stanton necessitated an overland trip of some 400 miles from the San Juan River to the Grand Wash Cliffs. Stanton bluntly dismissed White's transit of the Grand Canyon with these words: "It is my conviction that at the time White wrote his letter [to his brother Joshua] he knew neither where he had been, how far he had come, or how long he had been on the river — only that he had been for a while on a raft, somewhere on the Colorado." Stanton concluded that "beyond a shadow of a doubt the honor and distinction of having been the first conqueror of the Colorado River" belongs to John Wesley Powell.[11] Apparently, Stanton did not mind being second to Powell so much as being third to White. Meanwhile, in a second, undated edition of *The Romance of the Colorado River*, Dellenbaugh struck another blow at both White and Parry by asserting for the first time in print that White had rafted only from the foot of the Grand Canyon to Callville.

Painstaking as always, Stanton prepared a lengthy report about the Colorado River, his railroad survey, and his investigations of both Major John Wesley Powell and James White, including more than thirty pages of White's interview. The cost of printing Stanton's two-volume opus was prohibitive, so it failed to attract a publisher during his lifetime. Moreover, no sane investors were interested in the notion of building a railroad through the Grand Canyon. Meanwhile, the controversy about White continued to simmer and occasionally let off plumes of steam. Eventually, a decade after Stanton's death in 1922, Julius F. Stone paid James M. Chalfant to edit the portions of Stanton's manuscript about White and Powell, and in 1932 these pages were published at last under the title *Colorado River Controversies*.

Stone was an industrialist from Ohio who was president of the Hoskaninni Company, a gold-mining operation in Glen Canyon that was organized in 1897, with Stanton as superintendent of field operations. During its short, unprofitable life, Stanton was able to convince Hoskaninni's investors to install an immense dredge that now lies under the waters of Lake Powell. Although the life of the mining operation played out by 1902, Stone had become so captivated by the river that he hired Nathaniel "Than" Galloway to take him down the Colorado in 1909. With a crew including Seymour Dubendorff, another of the hoary names in Colorado River lore, the expedition made it to Needles, California, with Stone, the underwriter of the trip, riding along as the first known tourist through the Grand Canyon. Stone then declared that White's trip was impossible: "[In] 1867 James White was taken from a raft after having, as he claimed, passed (on that precarious platform!) through all the canyons from a point some-where above the junction of the Green and Colorado in thirteen days — a claim so manifestly incredible as not to win the belief of anyone who has passed through either the Marble or the Grand Canyon."[12]

During the years while Stanton's manuscript was languishing, Dellenbaugh's prestige was growing, giving him the reputation at that time as the chief historian of the Grand Canyon. As a bright lad and promising artist who was still a teenager in 1871–1872, Dellenbaugh had traversed the rivers with Powell, making sketches, participat-ing in the land survey after the water transit, and keeping excellent personal records, which provided the material for his second book. Dellenbaugh was a likeable individual who in his lifetime earned con-siderable respect as an explorer, lecturer, writer, and founder of the prestigious Explorers Club. His opinions carried weight among elite outdoorsmen in the Eastern establishment, who, not incidentally, regarded Powell as a giant in American science, the hero of the Grand Canyon, the founder of the U.S. Geological Survey, its second director, and director of the Bureau of American Ethnology. In contrast, White was generally dismissed, except when someone happened to mention that his raft trip was impossible.

In 1908, Dellenbaugh's second book, *A Canyon Voyage: The Narrative of the Second Powell Expedition,* was published. In this volume, Dellen-baugh acknowledged the existence of James White by saying, "One James White was picked up (1867) at a point below the mouth of the Virgin in an exhausted state, and it was assumed that he had made a large part of the terrible voyage on a raft, but this was not the case, and the Colorado River Canyons still waited for a conqueror."[13] Agreeing with Stanton, with whom he had had some correspondence, Dellenbaugh went on to contend that White had not been in the Grand Canyon but had traveled overland from the San Juan River and entered the raft at the Grand Wash Cliffs, only sixty miles above Callville.

Otis R. "Dock" Marston, Colorado River historian and James White critic, 1969. Photo by author.

Years later, Otis R. Marston, who knew the Colorado River and all the literature about it exceedingly well, evaded contradiction of the theory put forth by Stanton and Dellenbaugh by writing in 1979: "The numerous excursions into legendary conception provide entertainment, but careful analysis fails to reveal any reason to reject White's

147

raft voyage as starting at Grapevine Wash and ending at Callville."[14] There is no evidence anywhere of a cross-country journey by White. Moreover, the argument that White said he encountered only one big rapid was contrary to his description of numerous rapids in his letter to Josh and in Parry's notes. Such selectivity in reporting White's statements causes one to conclude that the aforementioned writers had no objective except to discredit White's claim of a transit through the entire Grand Canyon.

White's other early critics were men who could attest that they had gone through the Grand Canyon and, as a result of their firsthand experience, did not believe the trip could have been accomplished on a raft. Thanks to the detailed, accurate information in *A Canyon Voyage*, Dellenbaugh had produced the equivalent of a river-runner's guide, which Emery and Ellsworth Kolb carried with them in 1911 when they made their long water voyage from Green River, Wyoming, to Needles and on down to the Gulf of California.[15] After their transit, the Kolbs agreed with Dellenbaugh's assessment that White could not have made his transit on a raft. Ellsworth visited White at Trinidad in 1914 and wrote about this visit in a letter to Lewis Ransome Freeman in 1922: "[White] was so childish it was impossible to make head or tail of his story. He may have gone through the Canyon but he certainly never drifted through in low water, in <u>two weeks</u> as he said. He told me he did not travel at night and did not think it was so very bad except for a couple of falls."[16]

By the second decade of the twentieth century, when Ellsworth Kolb met him, White was clearly in the grip of old age. After almost forty years as a drayman, the once-strong fellow's working days finally ended when he broke a hip around 1915, and he was in poor health until his death twelve years later. When his daughter Esther wrote to Thomas F. Dawson in 1916, she commented that her father's memory was diminished, but some might argue that it was drifting erratically as early as Stanton's interview in 1907.

Indirectly, agriculture and irrigation were the factors that returned James White to the public's attention in 1917. To understand this late reemergence, the year 1902 is important, and not simply because Frederick S. Dellenbaugh published his book then with his disparaging comment about White. First, it is noteworthy that the life of John Wesley Powell, the popular hero of the Grand Canyon, came to a close

John Wesley Powell, undisputed organizer in 1869 of the first scientific exploration through the Grand Canyon. Denver Public Library, Western History Collection, no. F-45234.

in 1902, and he became an apt candidate for immortalization. His many admirers were anxious to restore the reputation of Powell, who had been forced to retire as head of the U.S. Geological Survey a few years earlier. Second, Western water interests, Powell's foes, ironically succeeded in 1902 in achieving one of Powell's own long-range goals—the storage of water for irrigation—when the Newlands Act, or Reclamation Act, created the Reclamation Service, later known as the Bureau of Reclamation.

For several years Powell's path had been far from smooth. His *Report on the Lands of the Arid Region* in 1878 and his proposals for reforming the way public lands were allocated earned him the opposition of Westerners, particularly those with vested interests and the politicians they supported. Powell contended that the way land was mapped and allocated in grids defied topography, climatic reality, and irrigation. Drought in the late 1880s brought many Westerners around to Powell's views about the need for water storage and distribution systems for irrigated agriculture, and they began to think in terms of headwaters and catchment basins from which water could be diverted to irrigable land, but Powell was insisting on the need for time-consuming topographical mapping, during which all nonirrigable land should be withdrawn from sale, entry, settlement, or occupation while an irrigation survey was made. Such a moratorium looked as if it might last for as long as thirty years if it were implemented.[17]

Powell also envisioned a utopian future for the irrigated land, with management by communities, much as early Hispanic settlers in New Mexico and southern Colorado governed their acequias. But most of Colorado's practices were immensely different from those of the first Spanish-speaking tillers who had arrived about 1850 to settle land grants. Under Colorado law, unappropriated water belonged to the state, not to the federal government, and the doctrine of prior appropriation had been established by law, whereby the rights of water users were based on a first-filed, first-served system. Furthermore, water districts and divisions already were administering water use. By means of private projects (and over-appropriation) of surface water, irrigation was making agriculture possible in large portions of the land that Stephen Long had once described as the Great American Desert. The Western states wanted irrigation, yes, but without meddling with their own way of doing things, although they liked the proposition of the federal government's assuming the initial cost of big projects. In the 1880s and 1890s, farmers, railroad and mining interests, bankers, and industrialists in the arid states were not about to surrender their power and future growth to a dreamer like Powell in Washington. Not surprisingly, then, his populist ideas had strong opponents among Western politicians like Senator William Stewart of Nevada and Senator Edward Wolcott of Colorado. In 1892 they forced the termination of the Irrigation Survey, and in 1894 they won Powell's resignation as head of the U.S. Geological Survey, although he remained unchallenged as director of the Bureau of American Ethnology at the Smithsonian Institution.

The above digression may help explain why Powell was not a popular man in Colorado. It also helps explain why James White — an ailing, retired drayman in Trinidad — happened to be resurrected by the U.S. Senate in 1917 as a hero, the *first* man through the Grand Canyon. After years of benign neglect, Colorado's boosters wanted to honor their resident, while also striking a blow against Powell and all he had come to represent on the West's political scene.

Back East, Congress had appropriated $10,000 for a Powell memorial to be placed at Grand Canyon National Monument, so Colorado's delegation in Washington was well aware that Powell was going to be honored. In fact, by 1915 the bronze plaque already was sitting on the porch at El Tovar Hotel on the South Rim while the National Park Service sought an appropriate place to install it. One Ralph Cameron, for whom Cameron, Arizona, is named, was blocking their chosen location because he had mining claims there.[18] He also was obstructing park planning with his "toll road," later called the Bright Angel Trail. Finally, however, the memorial would be placed at Powell Point along the West Rim in 1918.

The plaque reads, "Erected by the Congress of the United States to Major John Wesley Powell first explorer of the Grand Canyon who descended the river with his party in row-boats traversing the gorge beneath this point August 17, 1869 and again September 1[,] 1872." Also inscribed are the names of the men who completed the traverses in 1869 and 1872, with the deliberate omission of anyone who had left the expeditions before their conclusions.

The phrase *first explorer* comprised, of course, fighting words among White's champions in Colorado, who had gone to great lengths to substantiate his claim as first down the Colorado. Today the National Park Service circumvents this controversy by scrupulously referring to Powell's expedition of 1869 as the first *scientific* expedition. Another way the dispute has been avoided is by calling Powell's trip the first

The Powell Memorial, dedicated in 1994 at Powell Point on the South Rim of Grand Canyon National Park, commemorates the 125th anniversary of Powell's first expedition. Photo by author.

organized expedition, which is not the same thing as saying that White was *first*, a distinction that his supporters would have preferred.

In a vain attempt to derail installation of the plaque, Thomas F. Dawson was charged in 1916 by Colorado's Senator John Shafroth to gather the necessary material to show that James White, not Powell, was first. The results of Dawson's work were adopted in 1917 by the U.S. Senate, 65th Congress, 1st Session, Document No. 42, by Senate Resolution 79. It was printed as a sixty-seven-page booklet by the Government Printing Office that year under the title *The Grand Canyon: An Article Giving the Credit of First Traversing the Grand Canyon of the Colorado to James White, a Colorado Gold Prospector, Who It Is Claimed Made the Voyage Two Years Previous to the Expedition under the Direction of Maj. J. W. Powell in 1869.*

The explicit statement in the title about White's preceding Major Powell makes clear the motivation of Document No. 42, and the argument was pressed further within the document:

WHEREFORE.

The erection by the National Government of a monument to the memory of Maj. John W. Powell, as "the first explorer" of the Grand Canyon of the Colorado, has had the effect of raising a question among pioneers of the West as to whether the honor conferred upon Maj. Powell in connection with the early navigation of the Canyon should not be shared with another. Mr. Powell's friends claim for him the distinction of being not only the first to "explore" the canyon but also that of being the first to pass through it under any circumstances. This claim is challenged in behalf of one James White, a mining prospector, who, they contend, went through the canyon two years previous to the time of the Powell expedition. Powell made his voyage in 1869; White claims to have made his in 1867."[19]

A gracious, careful, and intelligent gentleman, Dawson was well-qualified for his assignment. He had a genuine interest in Colorado history and had written articles and books, even a biography of one of Powell's antagonists, Senator Edward Wolcott. Before becoming a secretary for Senator Henry Teller in Washington, Dawson had been a newspaper owner and editor at *Denver Times*.[20] His employment as executive clerk of the U.S. Senate gave him entrée to political contacts, and he availed himself of the Senate's impressive letterhead to gain access to important people, including James White's family. For several months, Dawson carried on a vigorous discourse by mail with the Whites but did not visit them in Trinidad. For her biography of her grandfather, Eilean Adams had access to letters that Dawson wrote to her cooperative and capable mother, Esther. This information, as well as much more of Dawson's correspondence relating to the James White project, can be read in one of the scrapbooks Dawson compiled after he became the curator and historian of the State Historical and Natural History Society of Colorado, now the Colorado Historical Society.[21]

Although Dawson tried to be thorough while preparing his material for the Senate, White created many problems for Dawson and later investigators. On July 21, 1916, in a letter to James White, Dawson pointed out apparent discrepancies in early accounts of his raft trip, such as distances and the description of the Little Colorado, but the old man stubbornly insisted on his own version as it appeared in an account that Dawson acquired in 1916. Surreptitiously, Dawson had solicited this signed autobiographical account that Esther and others in the family helped White prepare and that Esther sent to Dawson on

September 8, 1916. In this story, White briefly recapped his early life and then retold his raft trip, much as it had appeared in print in the 1860s, with a few additions and corrections, some of them puzzling. By November 24, when Esther was writing to Dawson that her father's memory was "not the best" and his health was "failing rapidly," she nevertheless said that he "definitely recalled the whirlpool at the Little Colorado." When U.S. Geological Survey work was being conducted in 1922, however, Lewis Freeman observed that there was nothing at the mouth of the Little Colorado resembling a whirlpool like White had described.[22] Further evidence of White's deteriorating condition was the comment by Esther White to Otis R. Marston that her father always called Charles Baker "Jim" when speaking to the family about him. Also, James White's crabbed signature under his story did not resemble in any way the elegant one on his letter to his brother Joshua in September 1867.

During Dawson's work, Stanton learned about his project, and in a letter, handwritten from New York City on graph paper and dated November 22, 1916, Stanton insisted that he personally knew White's story and denied its validity. Dawson began to work under pressure to head off sabotage by Stanton. Besides the correspondence with the White family, Dawson was gathering all the early accounts he could find — newspaper reports, the stories by Parry and Calhoun with their additional statements, White's corrections, his signed story, and testimonials by Mayor Taylor, a state senator, and a vacuous former governor. There were discussions about individuals like General Palmer and authors like Hubert Howe Bancroft, who supported the story of the raft trip. Included was T. J. Ehrhart's letter to Dawson, dated November 22, 1916, with details about the gunfight at Brown's Creek when Goodfellow was shot. Attempting to appear both thorough and objective, Dawson even provided a summary of the dispute about whether White was first.

The document, accepted by the Senate on May 25, 1917, was a conscientious job, although it did not end the controversy. Dawson sent out copies of his booklet to friends, acquaintances, anyone with a connection to the Grand Canyon, and even Robert Stanton, who read it closely, made a list of Dawson's errors, and sent his critique to the author. Dawson diligently incorporated even this letter in his scrapbook.

In response to his widespread mailing of the booklet, Dawson received other letters with new pieces of information. He incorporated these in his article "More Light on James White's Trip through the Grand Canyon," which was published in *The Trail* in 1919.[23] This magazine was merely the organ of the Society of Sons of Colorado, of which Dawson was an active member. Therefore, Dawson's addendum to *The Grand Canyon* was not widely read and thus has not been a part of the ongoing James White debate. In this article, Dawson noted that he had not known about White's letter to Joshua in 1867 when he was preparing his material for the Senate, and he now compensated for that omission by printing it, with editing for correct English. Dawson also reported that he had heard from Stanton and Dellenbaugh, both of whom argued in favor of White making an overland journey as far as the Grand Wash Cliffs. The secretary of the Kansas State Historical Society had written, too, with some biographical data about the tramp printer William J. Beggs, whom he described as "a simple, likeable man, and a sort of genius, his only fault being his use of intoxicating liquor to excess."[24]

In his article, Dawson also reported that William A. Bell contacted him and said he had visited the Grand Canyon three times, the most recent time being in 1917. During a trip, Bell stopped at Trinidad to see White. He commented that White was mistaken in his belief that he met General Palmer in 1867, but they actually met in 1869 at Fort Lyon, with Palmer coming away convinced of White's reliability. Bell's remarks made it clear that he, like his late friend and associate General Palmer, had continued to support White's raft trip. As a result of the meeting with White, Bell also reported that he had increased confidence in C. C. Parry's narrative, although this opinion seemed to be based more on his admiration for Parry's scientific mind than on the report itself. About Calhoun, Bell believed that the journalist never had seen White in person but would have had an opportunity to talk to Parry and people at Callville and Fort Mohave. Of course, some critics might disregard testimony like Bell's, because it relied so heavily on informal impressions and the prestigious reputations of his associates.

An interesting letter to Dawson, reprinted in *The Trail* article, came from one of the most famous of the Colorado River's steamboat captains, J. A. Mellon, who was then retired and living at Coronado,

California. The contents of this letter, dated December 31, 1918, warrant quotation herein. After acknowledging receipt of Dawson's booklet, Mellon launched into a defense of White:

> I never met White, but was personally acquainted with two men who were at Callville at the time White was rescued — O. D. Gross and Hans Godforson, both reliable men; they never doubted White came through as stated by him, and I don't doubt it. About the same time (1869) that Powell came through, a raft of railroad ties broke adrift on Green River, and eighteen days after, I passed some of them at Castle Dome, 410 days below Callville. Some of those ties came down every high water for five years.
>
> White's chances for coming down on the raft were better than Powell's with the class of boats Powell used. They were keel boats and would strike on a hundred rocks in the river that the raft would pass over. I owned one of the boats and used it at tidewater at the mouth of the Colorado. They were well built but entirely unsuited for swift water navigation. [Most likely, the boat owned by Mellon was the *Kitty Clyde's Sister*, given by Powell to his crew members Andy Hall and Jack Sumner when the expedition ended at the Virgin River in 1869. They rowed it to the mouth of the Gulf of California to complete the odyssey that had begun at Green River, Wyoming.]
>
> A friend of mine, Clark Flevell [George Flavell], some time about 1895, went to Green River crossing [Wyoming], and there built a boat suited to the river. He and another man made the trip from Green River crossing to Yuma in six weeks. Clark never got out of his boat in any of the rapids — he ran every one of them [except Soap Creek, it is believed]. White's coming through was no miracle, but Powell's was, on account of the model of boats he used. And the same can be said of Stanton.[25]

Support for White seemed to be gaining momentum at this time, and some of it came from the new Grand Canyon National Park, site of the finally erected plaque honoring Powell. Tourists, whose numbers were increasing after the close of World War I, relished Colorado River lore and the spectacular scenery. The Kolb brothers at their photographic studio on the South Rim did not promote James White's claim as first down the river, but guide William Wallace Bass did. To augment his livelihood, this former asbestos miner set up a camp, guided visitors on trails, and entertained his guests with tales about

During the half century of James White's residence at Trinidad, electric lighting, street-cars, a thriving commercial district, and automobiles transformed the city. Courtesy, Colorado Historical Society, Aultman Collection, no. A-632 (1900–1916).

the canyon. He also produced a book, *Adventures in the Canyons of the Colorado,* to sell to tourists. Bass had concluded after reading James White's letter to his brother Josh, that it was possible for someone tied to a raft to have made it through the canyon, and Bass pronounced James White to be the first through the canyon in a story he printed in his booklet.[26]

How aware White was of such developments cannot be certain, for he was now an octogenarian, but his insistence that he had made the raft trip all the way through the canyon never wavered. His family and friends in Trinidad remained steadfast in their conviction as well. In the 1920s his champion, Dawson, died, but so did Stanton, White's most persistent antagonist. By the time Julius F. Stone picked up the cudgel and got *Colorado River Controversies* published ten years after Stanton's death, White also was gone.

The obituary of James White appeared on the day of his death, January 14, 1927, on the front page of the *Trinidad Chronicle-News*:

James White, 89 years old, pioneer resident of Trinidad and Civil war veteran, an outstanding figure in the early day history of southern Colorado and the southwest, died at 1:30 this morning at his home 309 Prospect street after an illness of 17 months. Mr. White had resided in this city since 1874 [1878] had conducted the first drayage and transfer service in the city and was credited with having been one of two men who successfully explored the Grand Canon of the Colorado [the other being Powell].

Mr. White, some 12 years ago, suffered a broken hip which caused his retirement from active work of any sort and had been more or less ailing for years. His six daughters and two sons had visited him at intervals during his last illness and two daughters, Mrs. Richard Smith and Mrs. W. B. Armond, were with him when the end came. These six children and his wife survive him. [In Mrs. Smith's obituary in 1970, her husband's name appeared as Daniel A. Smith. Only one of James White's children, his youngest son, Arnold, was still living at the time of her death.]

Mr. White served with the first California volunteers in the Civil war. After the war he came west and was married at Fort Garland, Colo., 1871, coming to Trinidad in 1874. [As I pointed out previously, the marriage certificate said Red Rock, and the move to Trinidad was in 1878.]

Mr. White talked but little of his early day experiences while he lived, hence an interesting story is not available here. He was a member of Trinidad lodge No. 181 B.P.O Elks and his funeral will take place on Sunday afternoon at 2:30 from the R. G. Sipe funeral parlors. Rev. C. L. Rampie of the Lutheran church officiating and interment in the Odd Fellows cemetery. The Elks will have charge of the grave.[27]

The Odd Fellows Cemetery is a portion of the Masonic Cemetery in the northwest corner of Trinidad. People who were neither Odd Fellows nor Masons are interred in this cemetery, Trinidad's principal burying ground. White's modest marble headstone is engraved with his name; his last military assignment, Company E, First California Infantry; and the dates of his birth and death, November 19, 1837, and January 14, 1927. With a mature tree now growing between their graves, Octaviana lies beside him, with an identical stone and the name for Octavia White, with the date 1855–1938.

Although today's residents of Trinidad rarely recognize James White's name, he was still a noteworthy individual in 1930, when a

James White at age seventy. According to White family statements, Robert Brewster Stanton requested that White pose for this studio portrait in 1907, the year when he would have turned seventy. Comparison with another picture, made with his family at the same time, supports this date. A caption for this portrait, appearing in 1917 in Dawson's The Grand Canyon, *incorrectly identifies the age of the subject as eighty.* Courtesy, Denver Public Library, Western History Collection, no. F-22876.

lengthy newspaper account told of his life and featured the Grand Canyon traverse. This article boasted that he had been an "intimate friend" of Trinidad's late Mayor D. L. Taylor, although Eilean Adams wrote that Taylor once had repossessed her grandfather's home. The newspaper story concluded:

> No man in Las Animas county had lived a more adventurous life in his younger days than James White. He had served the Union in the Civil war. He had fought Indians out west in frontier days, and he had driven stage for the old Barlow and Sanderson line. And back in 1867 he had survived an exploit of hazard and adventure, the like of which was only claimed by one other man [a reference to Major John Wesley Powell]. White had explored the Grand Canon of the Colorado river and traversed its perilous waters on a raft, and it was not until later that he was given the national recognition that was his due for this exploit.[28]

One of three testimonials that Thomas Dawson published in *The Grand Canyon* in 1917 might serve as a eulogy, summing up White's life in Trinidad. In it, state senator S. W. De Busk of Trinidad attested to White's good character and contributed additional biographical information, notwithstanding an error concerning the year when White came to Trinidad. De Busk's statement is presented here in part:

> I have known James White since 1872 [1878]. He was in 1872 engaged in general labor with a team and wagon for a long while. Later, when age began to show on him, he reduced his labor to light hauling with a small spring wagon and one horse. By lighter labor he earned a livelihood for some years.
>
> Since I met White he has occupied his own residence in Trinidad; has paid his taxes like any other good citizen; has discharged his obligations to society; has been careful to educate his children; and has many friends. I think he has no enemies.
>
> In 1887 to 1895 White's children and my children attended the same school or schools in Trinidad. All the time we have been fast friends and neighbors.
>
> For 20 years we have had an Early Settlers' Society, of which I happen now to be the secretary and local historian. This position has caused me to seek information from White concerning the pioneer times. For more than a decade past White has given me information as to various matters. Subjecting his statements to the usual tests, I have found him to be truthful. He is not a "prevaricator" or a

"romancer." He has not the mental character or mental habit of the romancer—in other words, of the common liar.[29]

Unlike Trinidad's history, where James White eventually faded from memory, Grand Canyon's lore kept his name alive. As the national park attracted more and more visitors, boat trips began to lure tourists with curiosity and a yen for adventure. Primitive affairs, some of the early river trips, nonetheless, managed to tote camera gear, a dog, a bear cub, and movie actors and actresses in the hope of producing documentaries and cinematic thrillers. And, like their predecessors, most early tourists became instant authorities concerning the probability or improbability of White's having survived the rapids on a raft.

This tendency intensified after commercial river trips were introduced in the late 1930s under the aegis of Norm Nevills. One of his customers in 1940 was the future U.S. senator Barry Goldwater, who later wrote with the charity and tact of a successful politician:

> To those who say that such a voyage could not be made on a raft,
> I answer that men in desperate circumstances have accomplished
> more dangerous feats than running Colorado River rapids on a raft,
> although I would never, in my weakest moments, venture such a
> trip. To those who say that White is wrong on certain points, I say
> to imagine yourself starved, cold, and scared as hell in the mid-
> dle of the Colorado River on a raft, and then ask yourself whether
> you would give a tinker's damn about the scenery or details of it. I
> repeat that nothing has yet been brought forward to make me accept
> anyone other than White as the first through here.[30]

After World War II, the scene on the river changed rapidly. Surplus military equipment became available, with inflatable rafts making float trips comparatively safe and comfortable. Only 100 people, Otis R. Marston among them, are known to have gone through the Grand Canyon before the late 1940s, but as the numbers of boaters swelled, interest in the Colorado's history increased. Spellbound by the canyon and the river, many wrote about it and few omitted the tale of James White.

Although the verdict often was negative, some published material supported White's claim. For instance, Edwin Corle, who had not actually made a river journey, wrote a popular book titled *Listen, Bright Angel,* published in 1946, in which he offered his opinion that

White embarked on the river far downstream at Diamond Creek, but in another book, *The Story of the Grand Canyon,* Corle proposed that White possibly could have entered the river 100 miles upstream at Spencer Creek.[31]

Scholars were harder on the legendary man on the raft. Biographies of Powell by William Culp Darrah and Wallace Stegner appeared in the 1950s, and neither was able to ignore James White, who had been popping up in the literature about the Grand Canyon like an annoying stump in the path of history. Without much to go on except some skeptical remarks by Powell's crewmen, Darrah whittled White down a bit with the observation that "no serious support" had been given for White's claims. Stegner's knife cut considerably deeper:

> James White's tale of a wild river journey of eleven days on a crude raft tied together with lasso ropes had some elements of truth in it. At least White had floated out into the edge of civilization at Callville on September 8 [7], 1867, half naked, blackened with sun, starving and demented on a cobbled raft. But he was either so far out of his head that he had lost all capacity to observe clearly and measure distance accurately, and had come a far shorter distance on the river than he thought he had, or he was one of the West's taller liars.[32]

Stegner suggested an overland journey instead, as did Dellenbaugh, Stanton, and in good time Marston, too, but the proposal of a long journey by land to Grand Wash Cliffs found few advocates. If supporters of the river transit were going to insist that it had happened, however, they needed to find an embarkation point. As always, the missing ingredient was reliable evidence. The most easily ruled out was the location above or near the confluence of the Colorado and the Green, as Parry and White had claimed, respectively.

If one accepted White's statement, as reported by Stanton, that he and his companions went south when they left the San Juan River, a seemingly reasonable candidate for entry to the Colorado River was Navajo Creek and Navajo Canyon. This route led to Glen Canyon, from which point the distance down to Lee's Ferry is twenty-six miles, or ten to the present Glen Canyon Dam. Richard E. Lingenfelter offered the mouth of Navajo Canyon as the embarkation point in *First through the Grand Canyon* and defended White's having made the raft trip. Lingenfelter methodically calculated the numbers of days and miles, based on White's statements, and placed Strole's drowning at a point down the Grand Canyon almost as far as Bright Angel Creek. The most conspicuous flaw in Lingenfelter's case was that he sent Baker, White, and Strole around the heads of various canyons to Navajo Creek, passing over terrain that would have been extremely difficult, if not impossible, with horses. Moreover, Navajo Creek did not match White's description.[33] Later, even Lingenfelter gave up this proposition. The suggestion that the prospectors had gone south from the San Juan River persisted, though, and in Marston's mind it justified his idea that White made a long trek overland to Grand Wash.

In contrast, a believer in the raft voyage was Harold A. Bulger, a medical school professor, collector of historical material, and author in 1961 of an article "First Man through the Grand Canyon." By then, both his title and his recounting of White's story were becoming painfully redundant, but Bulger made a good effort. He carefully analyzed various routes north of the San Juan River to possible and impossible embarkation points. Ruling out Dark Canyon, he selected the White Canyon route instead.[34] Others quickly pointed out that this approach to the river was not feasible with horses, although that argument does not hold up because rustlers are known to have used White Canyon.

Moki Canyon, instead, received the endorsement of two important figures, Dr. Robert C. Euler and White's granddaughter Eilean Adams. For a number of years, Dr. Robert C. Euler conducted extensive archaeological investigations of the land surrounding the Grand Canyon and Glen Canyon by horseback, foot, helicopter, small fixed-wing planes, and map study in his work while on the faculty of Prescott College and on the staff of Grand Canyon National Park as its senior archaeologist. Early on, he had been asked to review Lingenfelter's book, which whetted his interest in the White story. Euler disagreed with Lingenfelter that Navajo Creek was White's embarkation point and began looking into the subject. With his knowledge about Indian hostilities in the area in the 1860s, Euler ruled out the possibility that White could have survived the overland journey proposed by Dellenbaugh, Stanton, and Marston. Euler ultimately traced a more likely route, north from the San Juan River by way of Comb Wash to Elk Ridge and finally to Moki Canyon and the Colorado River. (*Moki* is now the accepted spelling of this canyon, although it was spelled *Moqui* by Euler.) In 1973, Euler concluded that "we shall never know, of course, exactly where

White began his raft journey," but Euler believed that White was the first through the Grand Canyon.[35]

When she wrote her book *Hell or High Water*, Eilean Adams felt confident in stating that the correct place of embarkation was the mouth of "Moqui Canyon," adopting Euler's theory as well as his spelling. Adams examined this canyon from the air with Euler and was convinced that it conformed to the topography where Baker, White, and Strole approached the Colorado River.

An embarkation point at the mouth of this canyon would be about forty miles above the mouth of the San Juan River and about 100 above today's Glen Canyon Dam. More than 135 miles downstream from the proposed embarkation point is Badger Creek Rapid, the first major rapid below Cataract Canyon on the Colorado. If White and Strole set out on their raft at Moki Canyon, they would have floated through serene Glen Canyon with its quiet waters, which are now submerged by Lake Powell, ignoring or not seeing conspicuous escape routes like the Crossing of the Fathers and the Paria River. White and Strole would have passed the Paria, and a few miles below they would have come to Badger Creek Rapid and, next, Soap Creek Rapid, the first encounters with any "falls" remotely resembling the one where White claimed Strole had drowned.

Over the years, a handful of authors have gamely raised a different issue — namely, that White might have been running from something when he made his journey in 1867, as Dellenbaugh insinuated. Stanton went further, suggesting that an explanation for White's journey might have been that he had killed his two companions and then fled.[36] I risked dipping my toe into this whirlpool, as did P. T. Reilly, David Lavender, and Donald Worster, each of whom raised the question of White's possible complicity in the disappearances of Baker and Strole, but we all leapt back to the safety of the shore without asserting a definite statement.[37] In the absence of valid evidence and witnesses, no one can make a definitive statement about events that occurred in August 1867. After the shooting of Joe Goodfellow at Brown's Creek in early June and the alleged deaths of Baker and Strole in August, the only survivor of the four original prospectors was James White.

Since the publication of Eilean Adams's *Hell or High Water* in 2001, some of her readers have believed that the controversy is positively settled in her grandfather's favor — that is, he made the raft trip through the Grand Canyon—but this happy resolution remains elusive. In his scholarly work *A River Running West: The Life and Times of John Wesley Powell*, Worster cautiously concluded that there is nothing in White's story to support a long cross-country trek and that even if the raft trip "seems improbable, all other explanations are more improbable still."[38]

Objective conclusions like Worster's may take the sport out of future research and writing about James White, although the question will linger about whether any raft actually could make it through the Grand Canyon. Since 1867, the Colorado's mighty waters have been successfully challenged by keeled and flat-bottomed boats, gasoline-powered motorboats, oar-powered dories, kayaks, sport yaks, swimmers with water wings, and big baloneys wallowing over the rocks and through the waves with tourists numbering 20,000 or more in a year. But no one has succeeded on a raft, although a few are known to have traversed short distances by this means.

Most arguments about White's adventure, pro and con, from Dellenbaugh and Stanton to Dawson and Adams, have been based on hearsay and unverifiable assumptions, with the unreliable support of the words of White, the inventive interpretations of those who wrote about him, the subjective experiences of river runners, and the intellectual pronouncements of scholars. As for Baker, most references to him simply mention him incorrectly as the "discoverer" of the San Juan's gold, sometimes including his demise at the hands of Indians. And so the words have continued to flow and the truth drifts with them.

Simple, if inaccurate, statements are more enjoyable to read, so we might expect that people will continue to hear that Charles Baker discovered San Juan gold and died near the Colorado River, that George Strole was washed off a raft and drowned in a rapid in the river, that James White was the first, bar none, to make it through the Grand Canyon, and that Joe Goodfellow survived to live out his persnickety life somewhere else. The hard-to-accept fact is that no one knows definitely what eventually happened to the four drifters. Baker, a Southerner who achieved some notoriety as a result of his penchant for promotion of placer mining, may have been killed by Indians somewhere between the San Juan and Colorado Rivers and thus vanished from the scene. George Strole, whose origins were unknown, may have drowned in the Colorado River. Like thousands of other drifters, Joe

Goodfellow appeared out of nowhere and disappeared into the historical void. The early background and later life of James White alone are known, although his wanderings during a period of roughly seventeen years still leave many questions. Had he not appeared spectacularly on a raft at Callville, Nevada, for his moment of fame, he would have been an ordinary drifter who became a workingman, husband, and father, attracting no more attention than did vast numbers of emigrants drifting west and eventually settling in growing communities to live out their lives in historical anonymity.

Adrift in Folklore

Many folk tales, whether based on real events or on imagination, have a basis in fact, although they may have drifted far from literal truth in the telling and retelling. With no living witnesses to the disasters in 1867, James White and Charles Baker are especially apt subjects for legendry. Particularly in need of an anchor are writers with a flare for fictionalizing history.

One creative writer has tried to make a place for White in folklore by portraying him as the discoverer of lost treasure. Fantasies about misplaced mines and caches of gold have long inspired fictions about hidden treasure, whereas true believers are content with the more likely rewards of outdoor recreation, and sometimes the two are even combined. Usually, the tales of lost treasure are about prospectors, those marvels of mobility who stumbled upon fabulous discoveries but had to depart from the spot because of some exigency, like a storm or an Indian attack. They frequently made a crude map or remembered a physical landmark, but the lode could never be found again, or so the stories go. Some such stories are deliberate hoaxes, helping their perpetrators sell magazines, maps, and metal detectors to enthusiasts who combine their love of outdoor recreation with dreams of striking it rich.

With the interweaving of a few facts from publications as a foundation, James White's name has become entangled in one such fantasy on the Internet. It is the handiwork of someone who appears to have read Eilean Adams's book about her grandfather, from which the author borrowed just enough detail to give his whimsy an aura of fact. In addition, the creator of this fabrication attempted to augment his credibility by cautioning his readers to obtain proper permissions before entering national park lands and an Indian reservation to undertake the hunt for treasure that he says is out there.

In this bit of nonsense, White, Strole, and "Captain Jim" Baker have been joined by a fourth man, one Ben Dunlap, prior to a raft trip. They steal some horses from Ute Indians somewhere around the Mancos River and soon afterward Baker and Dunlap are killed in an Indian ambush. White and Strole escape, build a raft, and Strole disappears in a rapid. Somewhere in the Grand Canyon, White tries to climb out. High on the walls, he finds a cave with three large bags, too heavy to lift, containing turquoise and gold nuggets. They were hidden there centuries ago by Zuni Indians, the reader is told. Weak with hunger, White can carry no more than one nugget of gold when he retreats to the river again. After his rescue at Callville, he shows people the nugget, inspiring treasure seekers to hunt for the cave, where tragedy rather than reward awaits them. White never goes back, but in his old age White still has the gold nugget as proof of his finding the treasure cave.

Charles Baker and the Animas River region also engendered folklore. An egregious example is a theatrical triumph, a pageant presented with utter seriousness to celebrate the opening of the second replacement of Baker's Bridge in 1930, although it provides hilarious entertainment for readers today. Printed by Durango's *Herald Democrat* on June 9, 1930, the opus deserves to be preserved for posterity as an example of the way history can be transformed and distorted by local folks who overvalue the merit of creativity and undervalue the merit of historical research. The following copy of the pageant omits the list of characters and the local, amateur actors' names but is otherwise complete.

PAGEANT OF BAKER'S BRIDGE GIVEN AT SERVICES IN UPPER VALLEY ON SUNDAY, WRITTEN BY LOCAL WOMAN

The pageant, "Baker's Bridge," presented at the official opening of the new Baker's Bridge and the unveiling of the marker showing the location of the first bridge constructed by the Baker party, was written and directed by Miss Florence Wilson, a popular Durango school teacher. Mrs. Russell Berry, dressed as a belle of the '60's, was the reader. Special credit for the staging of the pageant is due to the men and women who took part in it and the D.A.R. wishes to publicly acknowledge their indebtedness to them for the services.

Reader:

> Once long ago on the banks of the Animas
> Roamed the Ute Indians, haters of white men.
> Palefaces had not yet dared to come near it,
> Dared to dispute the sole right of the red man.
> Theirs was this valley of richness and plenty;
> Theirs was the river with gold in its waters;
> All of this valley was theirs without question.

Captain Baker and miners appear in distance and reader continues as they approach:

> Then from the land of the long-hated paleface,
> Came Captain Baker with some brave companions;
> Searching for gold in the rush of the river,
> Seeking for wealth in the heart of the Animas.
> Armed with their rifles, their knives, and their axes,
> They came seeking gold, to the land of the Indians.

Captain Baker and men look out over the valley, pick up some soil and rub it through their fingers, pick at the rocks with their picks, and confer together with much shaking of heads in approval. Reader continues:

> For many days did these men linger mining;
> Panning the gold from the sands of the Animas.
> Then one fine day, Captain Baker returned
> To his home in Missouri to get more explorers,
> More brave and hardy pioneers for this valley.

Captain Baker and men leave and disappear in trees. One of the miners remains to act as Scout later on. The others mount horses and ride in with wagon. Baker rides ahead as the wagon enters here. Reader:

> Soon he returned leading on a small caravan,
> Many good souls with brave hearts in their bosoms,
> Women whose love for their men led them onward
> Into the heart of the West, into danger;

(Women get out of wagon here and walk forward.)

> Men whose craving, whose thirst for adventure,
> For gold, for possession of wealth led them onward;

(Men step to the foreground here with the women.)

> These were the people whom Baker led westward;
> Led to the banks of the river Las Animas.

All look over the valley and make sign of approval. Then they begin to unload wagon. Men build fire and pretend to establish camp as reader proceeds:

> In the late spring of '61 a pioneer village
> Of log huts and cabins was named Animas City,
> On the east side of the river the village was founded,
> On rocks red and lasting as the Rock of Gibraltar.
> The men built a log bridge across the deep chasm
> In the narrowest part; strong and lasting they built it.
> And when it was done it was named for their leader,
> For brave Captain Baker who had led them far westward.

Scout approaches as reader continues:

> Not many months were endured here together,
> Before peals of war broke the peace of the valley;
> The peals of the strife which had severed the nation;

Scout arrives at camp and people gather around him, listening. Group divides and Baker and two men mount horses and ride away as reader says:

> Within the small village of Animas City,
> There dwelt men of Northern and Southern extraction.
> Captain Baker, a Southerner with several companions
> At once left to join the Confederate forces.
> Those faithful to the Union left shortly thereafter.
> The village was sundered; downhearted they left it;
> And, bidding adieu to the beautiful valley,
> They left it forever to the peace of its beauty;
> Once more to become hunting ground of the Indian.

After Baker leaves the rest pack up the things, get in wagon and drive away as reader is saying above lines. After wagon gets back to starting place, cowboys join in and prepare to come in with the permanent settlers. Musicians, be ready in wagon. They will play at the end after all the talking part is done. Reader goes on while permanent settlers are getting ready.

> When the last of the settlers had gone from the village,
> The sound of the tom-tom was heard in the valley;
> The Utes danced their dances in war paint and feathers;
> The long-hated white men had gone whence they came.
> So for many years did the Indians hold sway;
> No white men came near to dispute their possession.

Wagon appears in distance, draws near, goes down on road and crosses bridge. Scouts ride ahead as before, cowboys bring up rear. Wagon stops just the other side of the bridge as reader draws to close, with these lines:

> Then in [illegible word] permanent settlers ventured
> Into the broad valley of beauty and richness.
> Over the bridge built by Baker, they entered;
> Bringing with them their families, intending
> To make this their home and the homes of their children.
> To these hardy men and brave women, we owe
> All honor, due praise, heartfelt gratitude, love.
> For without their brave spirits of daring and venture
> This valley today might be unknown and barren.
> So hail to the Pioneers from Baker on downward,
> To each man and woman who dared unknown places;
> Who bid civilization remain far behind them;
> Who came to this valley of Rio de Las Animas.

Musicians tune up and play merrily as a close, and the wagon drives on and turns around and returns.[1]

If prospectors of 1860–1861 had been in the audience, their loud hoots might have drowned out the musicians playing merrily. Shaking their heads, some of the bemused gold seekers might have wondered which prospecting venture had been depicted, while others might have shuddered when they witnessed this example of the civilized, polite society they had hoped to escape when they left home in the gold rush. Scowling, a few might have muttered that they should have strung up Baker while they had the chance. Whatever else they thought about him, it was clear that Charles Baker had shot the moon and missed.

NOTES

INTRODUCTION

1. Richard Henry Dana, *Two Years before the Mast* (New York: Penguin Books, 1964 [1840]), 233–34.

2. William H. Goetzmann, "The Mountain Man as Jacksonian Man," *American Quarterly* 15 (1963):402–15.

3. *Rocky Mountain News*, August 27, 1860, 2.

4. Robert F. Hine and John Mack Faragher, *The American West: A New American History* (New Haven: Yale University Press, 2000), 9–11.

5. Elliott West, *The Contested Plains: Indians, Goldseekers, and the Rush to Colorado* (Lawrence: University Press of Kansas, 1998), 12.

6. Ibid., 115–37. In his chapter titled "The Gathering," West discusses the impact of the gold rushes.

7. *Rocky Mountain News*, February 13, 1861, 1.

8. Patricia Nelson Limerick, *The Legacy of Conquest: The Unbroken Past of the American West* (New York: W. W. Norton & Company, 1987), 124. Limerick

contends that mining created a different social condition in America than the founding fathers had envisioned. She states: "Westward expansion was supposed to create a land of independent, agrarian landowners and to prevent the rise of a wage-dependent laboring population. In mining, the opposite happened."

I . SEDUCTION

1. Augusta Tabor, "Cabin Life in Colorado," *The Colorado Magazine* 2 (March 1927): 151. Nathaniel Maxey and Stephen B. Kellogg were Fifty-Niners at Auraria, and Kellogg figured prominently in the Baker Expedition. His reminiscences are found in Colorado Dictations, HHB [P-L 346], in the Stephen H. Hart Library, Colorado Historical Society, wherein he states that his claim at California Gulch was Number 26, "because it was the 'lode' which fell as his portion by being drawn from a hat in distribution." In this interview, it is learned that prior to his arrival in Colorado Territory in 1859, Kellogg was born in Vermont in 1816 and educated in New England. Later his family moved to Cleveland, Ohio. He went to California in 1850, and a journey on a clipper ship in 1851 (destination Hawaii) terminated after a fire aboard ship. Kellogg fit the pattern of many drifters in general, if not in particular details.

2. Ibid., 151–52.

3. Accounts about the discovery of minerals in the Southwest can be found in accounts of Spanish expeditions, such as Rivera's journal, translated and published as Appendix A, "Translation of Incomplete and Untitled Copy of Juan Maria Rivera's Original Diary of the First Expedition, 23 July 1765," in Joseph P. Sánchez, *Explorers, Traders, and Slavers: Forging the Old Spanish Trail, 1678–1850* (Salt Lake City: University of Utah Press, 1997), 141–42.

4. Ted J. Warner Jr., ed., *The Domínguez-Escalante Journal: Their Expedition through Colorado, Utah, Arizona, and New Mexico in 1776*, trans. Fray Angelico Chavez (Salt Lake City: University of Utah Press, 1995), 14–15; Virginia McConnell Simmons, *The Ute Indians of Utah, Colorado, and New Mexico* (Boulder: University Press of Colorado, 2000), 34–37.

5. William Gilpin's speech was printed in 1859 in *Guide to the Kansas Gold Mines at Pike's Peak* (Cincinnati, OH: E. Mendenhall, 1859), reprinted by Nolie Mumey, as William Gilpin, *Guide to the Kansas Gold Mines at Pike's Peak . . . from Notes of J. W. Gunnison* (Denver, 1952), 21–40. Gilpin's geopolitical interests are discussed in Thomas L. Karnes, *William Gilpin, Western Nationalist* (Austin: University of Texas Press, 1970), 212–52. After accompanying Frémont to the West Coast in the 1840s, Gilpin became one of the many ardent expansionists headquartered in St. Louis, Missouri, with Frémont's father-in-law, Senator Thomas Benton as their political leader. Gilpin became Colorado Territory's first governor in 1861.

6. Information about Henry Mercure is found in Robert J. Torrez, "The San Juan Gold Rush of 1860 and Its Effect on the Development of Northern New Mexico," *New Mexico Historical Quarterly* 63 (July 1988): 259–60.

7. Ann Oldham, *Albert H. Pfeiffer: Indian Agent, Soldier and Mountain Man* (Pagosa Springs, CO: Privately printed, 2003), 40–68. Antonia and a teenaged Ute "daughter" were killed in 1863 by Mescalero Apaches while Pfeiffer was in the U.S. Army at Fort McRae, south of Albuquerque, New Mexico.

8. J. S. Newberry, "Geological Report," in U.S. Army Corps of Engineers, *Report of the Grand and Green Rivers of the Great Colorado of the West, in 1859, under the command of Capt. J. N. Macomb* (Washington, DC: Government Printing Office, 1876), 5. Newberry's report included comments about the Abiquiú area. The Macomb expedition continued west, exploring the region around the confluence of the Green and Grand (Colorado) Rivers, and from there they turned toward the San Juan River.

9. *Rocky Mountain News,* November 11, 1859, 2.

10. Contemporary newspaper accounts about prospecting in the San Juan Mountains appeared frequently from Fall 1860 through Spring 1861. D. C. Collier's lengthy report was printed in September and October 1860. Accounts about the expedition in which Charles Baker participated in July 1860 appeared in Golden, Colorado's *Western Mountaineer,* the *Santa Fe Weekly Gazette,* and Denver's *Rocky Mountain News.* The editor of the *Rocky Mountain News,* William Byers, also kept up a steady stream of editorial comment concerning the San Juan mines, usually denigrating the promotion of expeditions to the San Juan country.

11. *Weekly Rocky Mountain News,* November 14, 1877, 4, as repeated in Frank Hall, *History of Colorado,* 4 vols. (Chicago: Blakely Printing Company, 1890), 2:192–97. The content appears to be reliable, although it was gathered from persons who had a personal investment in the events, possibly resulting in personal biases or a desire to put their own lives in a good light.

12. *Santa Fe Weekly Gazette,* October 27, 1860, and *Rocky Mountain News,* January 21, 1861, 2.

13. Marshall Sprague, *The Great Gates: The Story of the Rocky Mountain Passes* (Boston: Little, Brown and Company, 1964), 177.

14. *Rocky Mountain News,* December 10, 1860, 2.

15. *Rocky Mountain News,* December 4, 1860, 2.

16. George Bute claimed that some of "our party" went with Baker to Santa Fe to secure the charter for building the road from Abiquiú to Animas City and that they induced "Mexicans" to invest in it. The Abiquiu, Pagosa, and Baker City Road Company was incorporated as one of the first acts of the New Mexico Territorial Legislature. New Mexico Territorial Legislature, *Laws of the Territory of New Mexico, 1860–1861* (Santa Fe, NM: J. T. Russell, 1861), 6.

17. Wolfe Londoner, among other pioneers, was interviewed for Hubert Howe Bancroft's *History of Nevada, Colorado, and Wyoming*. This interview was reprinted as "Western Experiences and Colorado Mining Camps," *The Colorado Magazine* 6 (March 1929): 67–68.

18. Ibid.

19. *Rocky Mountain News,* January 29, 1861, 3.

20. Ibid.

21. Ibid.

22. My original article "Captain Baker and the San Juan Humbug," authored by Virginia McConnell, appeared in *The Colorado Magazine* 48 (Winter 1971): 59–74. A detailed history of the San Juan Mountain region is Allen Nossaman's *Many More Mountains*, vol. 1, *Silverton's Roots* (Denver: Sundance Publications, 1989), which offers information about the expeditions and activities in the San Juan Mountains from July 1860 to summer 1861, as well as the verifiable names of participants in the Baker Expedition.

23. Robert J. Bruns, "The First We Know: The Pioneer History of the San Juans," based on interviews, including that of John Turner, and compiled in the 1890s many years after the events that were described had occurred. This manuscript can be read at the San Juan County (Colorado) Historical Society's Archive-Research Center in Silverton, but the unreliable contents of the manuscript must be used judiciously. The four-volume *Pioneers of the San Juan Country,* compiled by the Sarah Platt Decker Chapter, Daughters of the American Revolution (Durango, CO: Sarah Platt Decker Chapter D.A.R., 1952, 1961), also contains articles about early residents of the Durango area, some of which must be approached with caution by researchers.

24. *Rocky Mountain News,* June 8, 1861, 3.

25. Londoner, "Western Experiences and Colorado Mining Camps," 68.

26. *Cañon City Times,* June 1, 1861, on handwritten note at Stephen H. Hart Library, Colorado Historical Society, Denver.

2. THE EDUCATION OF A DRIFTER

1. Data about James White's early life is found in a biography written by his granddaughter, Eilean Adams, in *Hell or High Water: James White's Disputed Passage through the Grand Canyon, 1867* (Logan: Utah State University Press, 2001), which contains information provided by White to his family and collected by Adams's mother, Esther White McDonald. Neither White's daughter nor his granddaughter was impartial, and the material provided about his life was selective. An important source about White's life and activities is the compilation in U.S. Senate, Document No. 42, 65th Cong., 1st sess., May 25, 1917, published as Thomas F. Dawson, *The Grand Canyon* (Washington, DC: Government Printing Office, 1917). Among other materials, at the request of Dawson *The Grand Canyon* included "White's Own Story," 39–43, prepared in

1916 by White with the active participation of Esther White and other family members and the signature of James White. Original copies of most of the correspondence between Dawson and Esther White are located in the Thomas F. Dawson Scrapbook, "James White's Trip through the Grand Canyon in 1867," in the Stephen H. Hart Library, Colorado Historical Society, Denver. Another important source about White is Robert Brewster Stanton, *Colorado River Controversies,* ed. James M. Chalfant (New York: Dodd, Mead & Co., 1932), which includes Stanton's interview with James White in 1907 on pages 39–69. *Colorado River Controversies* was reproduced by Westwater Books (Boulder City, NV: Westwater Books, 1982) with the addition of essays by Otis R. Marston and Martin J. Anderson. As published in *The Grand Canyon,* James White stated, "I was born in Rome, N.Y., November 19, 1837, but was reared in Kenosha, Wis. At the age of 23 I left for Denver, Colo., later drifting to California, and there enlisted in the Army at Camp Union, Sacramento, in Company H." Dawson, *The Grand Canyon,* 39.

2. Mark Twain (Samuel Clemens), *Roughing It* (New York: New American Library, 1962), 29–56. The narrative was written in 1871 and 1872 with assistance of notes made by Samuel's brother Orion Clemens during the journey in 1861. Although some information in *Roughing It* may be accepted as factual, Mark Twain, being Mark Twain, offers certain satirical exaggerations that must be savored with a grain of salt. A recommended history of emigration during the early 1860s is Elliott West, *The Contested Plains.*

3. "Song of the Open Road" is the title of an ebullient poem by Walt Whitman, published in *Leaves of Grass* (Philadelphia: David McKay, ca. 1900).

4. Long quotations describing Dyer's journey to Denver in 1861 originally appeared in John L. Dyer, *The Snow-Shoe Itinerant, An Autobiography of the Rev. John L. Dyer, Familiarly Known as "Father Dyer," of the Colorado Conference, Methodist Episcopal Church* (Cincinnati, OH: Cranston & Stowe, 1890), 118–21.

5. Information about military history has become available electronically to assist today's researchers, with the National Park Service and the California State Military Museum providing information about many installations, including Alcatraz, Camp Wright, and Fort Yuma, with articles by military historian Colonel Herbert M. Hart, USMC (retired). Thumbnail histories about forts of the Southwest can be found in *Soldier and Brave: Historic Places Associated with Indian Affairs and the Indian Wars in the Trans-Mississippi West,* vol.12, *National Survey of Historical Sites and Buildings* (Washington, DC: National Park Service, 1971). An additional source is Herbert M. Hart, *Old Forts of the Southwest* (Seattle: Superior Publishing Company, n.d.), which provides a more complete list of forts, posts, and camps with dates of their existence.

6. Jack Rudder of Alamosa, Colorado, who reenacts military life at Fort Garland State Museum, provided insights about military life during the Civil War.

7. Richard E. Lingenfelter, *Steamboats on the Colorado River, 1852–1916* (Tucson: University of Arizona Press, 1978), 16–23.

8. Dan W. Messersmith, *The History of Mohave County to 1912* (Kingman, AZ: Mohave County Historical Society, 1991), 72–74, 80, 91–94, 97–98, 169. Hubert Howe Bancroft, *The Works of Hubert Howe Bancroft*, vol. 17, *History of Arizona and New Mexico, 1530–1888* (San Francisco: History Company, 1889), also includes information about Fort Yuma, mining, and settlements in the Lower Colorado River region.

9. Adams, *Hell or High Water*, 20–23.

3. HORSE THIEVES

1. Henry Brooks Adams, *The Education of Henry Adams: An Autobiography* (Boston: Houghton Mifflin, 1974).

2. Dawson, *The Grand Canyon*, 39; Stanton, *Colorado River Controversies*, 39.

3. The Upper Crossing was near Chouteau's Island and Indian Mound, five miles west of today's Lakin, Kansas. Beyond this river crossing, the Mountain Branch of the Santa Fe Trail continued west on the north side of the Arkansas. Although a longer trip to Santa Fe by 100 miles, the Mountain Branch was popular because of its access to water and trading posts along the way. The route of the Santa Fe Trail and locations along it are identified in Marc Simmons and Hal Jackson's *Following the Santa Fe Trail*, 3rd ed., rev. (Santa Fe, NM: Ancient City Press, 2001), and markers are placed along the trail to identify sites. Detailed maps of the trail were compiled in Gregory Franzwa's *Maps of the Santa Fe Trail* (St. Louis, MO: Patrice Press, 1989). One of several useful histories of the trail is David Dary's *The Santa Fe Trail: Its History, Legends, and Lore* (New York: Alfred A. Knopf, 2000). No reading about travel on the Santa Fe Trail is complete without Josiah Gregg's *The Commerce of the Prairies; or, The Journal of a Santa Fe Trader*, ed. Milo Milton Quaife (Chicago: R. R. Donnelly & Sons, 1926 [1844]). Among other sources offering firsthand descriptions of the experience are W. B. Napton, *Over the Santa Fe Trail, 1857* (Arrow Rock, MO: Friends of the Arrow Rock, 1991), and David K. Strate, ed., *West by Southwest: Letters of Joseph Pratt Allyn, a Traveler along the Santa Fe Trail, 1863* (Dodge City: Kansas Heritage Center, 1984).

4. Two excellent histories of Fort Dodge are David Kay Strate, *Sentinel to the Cimarron: The Frontier Experience of Fort Dodge, Kansas* (Dodge City, KS: Cultural Heritage and Arts Center, 1970), and Leo E. Oliva, *Fort Dodge: Sentry of the Western Plains* (Topeka: Kansas State Historical Society, 1998). A sketch of the sutler's store, drawn by Theodore R. Davis, which appeared in *Harper's Weekly*, May 25, 1867, is included in Oliva's booklet. The fort eventually became the Kansas Soldiers' Home.

5. The names James White and Charles Baker are both so common that researchers have often chased false leads and written incorrect statements

about these men, particularly about Baker. Fifty entries for the name of Charles Baker appear in the National Park Service's Civil War Soldiers and Sailors System Search, Confederate, and various Charles Bakers appear in the U.S. Census of 1860 at many locations. Jerome Smiley, in his *History of Denver, with Outlines of the Earlier History of the Rocky Mountain Country* (Denver: Times-Sun Publishing Company, 1901), identifies two James Whites, neither of whom were the man in this story. Members of Strobe families, also spelled "Straube," appear in William S. Bryan and Robert Rose, *A History of the Pioneer Families of Missouri* (Baltimore: Genealogical Publishing Co., 1984), possibly hinting at another spelling for the surname of Strole, but George remains a mystery.

6. James White's story about the raid at Mulberry Creek appears in Stanton, *Colorado River Controversies*, 39–40, and in shorter form in Dawson, *The Grand Canyon*, 39. Stanton's account said that thirteen Indian horses were stolen, whereas Dawson's said fourteen.

7. In July 1867 a large party of Kiowa Indians surrounded a wagon train in which the Most Reverend Jean Lamy, bishop of Santa Fe, was traveling. In his retinue were several priests, seminarians, and five Sisters of Loretto, whom the bishop had recruited back East for service in New Mexico. Surrounded by threatening Kiowas, the caravan was expecting annihilation momentarily when they discovered that some of their own party were afflicted with cholera. Perhaps the Indians recognized signs of the dreaded disease, for they left the scene without killing anyone. In the bishop's party, one man died of cholera and a sister died from the disease or, as is sometimes said, from fright, and they were buried on the prairie. The other travelers continued safely to Santa Fe, but hysterical reports about this event began to circulate immediately, with one newspaper stating incorrectly that the bishop had died. Letters he wrote to reassure his superiors and friends provided the best account of what really occurred and can be found in Thomas J. Steele, S.J., ed. and trans., *Archbishop Lamy: In His Own Words* (Albuquerque: LPD Press, 2000), 10–11. Another reliable source for this dramatic incident is Paul Horgan, *Lamy of Santa Fe: His Life and Times* (New York: Farrar, Straus and Giroux, 1975).

8. An indispensable source about mail lines and service is Morris F. Taylor, *First Mail West: Stagecoach Lines on the Santa Fe Trail* (Albuquerque: University of New Mexico Press, 1971). Barlow and Sanderson's tenure at Bent's Old Fort, 1861–1880, is discussed in Arthur Woodward, "Sidelights on Bent's Old Fort," *The Colorado Magazine* 33 (October 1956): 280. Seth Eastman, who trained in topographical drawing at West Point, made an excellent pencil sketch of Bent's Old Fort on July 13, 1869; this drawing, in the Carl S. and Elisabeth Waldo Dentzel Collection, is reproduced in Patricia Trenton and Peter H. Hassrick, *The Rocky Mountains: A Vision for Artists in the Nineteenth Century* (Norman: University of Oklahoma Press, 1983), 19.

9. The Starsmore Center for Local History at the Colorado Springs Pioneers Museum has the unpublished manuscripts "The Life and Reminiscences of Anthony Bott," "The Life and Reminiscences of George Bute," and "The Life and Reminiscences of David McShane." Information about these settlers and the early history of Colorado City is also included in Manly Dayton Ormes and Eleanor R. Ormes, *The Book of Colorado Springs* (Colorado Springs, CO: Privately printed, 1933), 6–7, 13, 119. These sources reveal three men who were typical emigrants, drifting from opportunity to opportunity prior to their settling permanently in El Paso County, Colorado, where they were respected pioneers. Bott's migrations began in 1838 when his parents came from France to Buffalo, New York. Twenty years later he was in Kansas City, where he learned of the gold discoveries in the Pikes Peak country and headed west. Bute, from Hanover, Germany, joined the party that included Bott at Westport. Their caravan consisted of fifty men and one woman traveling in "Pennsylvania schooners" with ox teams. Building log cabins, they started Colorado City in 1859 with the intention of creating a supply town for the mining country, with access by way of Ute Pass, to rival Denver, but they left soon to take part in the San Juan excitement. The first Catholic Mass was celebrated in 1860 in Bott's cabin. David McShane, born in Pennsylvania in 1830, went to Iowa in 1851 and to Kansas in 1855 before heading to Pikes Peak in 1859. George Bute became clerk and recorder of El Paso County, and David McShane was chairman of the county commissioners after their failed prospecting ventures in the San Juan Mountains in 1860–1861.

4. DISASTER

1. The popular jingle about seeing the elephant has been attributed to a variety of sources, but most reliably to John Godfrey Saxe.

2. Information about the region through which the prospectors passed— Ute Pass, South Park, the Upper Arkansas River Valley, and the San Luis Valley—is drawn from my previous books. Virginia McConnell, *Ute Pass: Route of the Blue Sky People* (Denver: Sage Books, 1963); Virginia McConnell Simmons, *Bayou Salado: The Story of South Park* (Boulder: University Press of Colorado, 2002 [1966]); Virginia McConnell Simmons, *The Upper Arkansas: A Mountain River Valley* (Boulder, CO: Pruett Publishing, 1990); Virginia McConnell Simmons, *The San Luis Valley: Land of the Six-Armed Cross* (Boulder: University Press of Colorado, 1999 [1979]).

3. T. J. Ehrhart (Thomas Jefferson Ehrhart), letter to Thomas F. Dawson, November 22, 1916, in Dawson, *The Grand Canyon*, 50–51. The original copy of Ehrhart's letter is collected in the Thomas F. Dawson Scrapbook, "James White's Trip through the Grand Canyon in 1867." June Shaputis locates many properties at Centerville, as Brown's Creek became known, in *Where the Bodies Are* (Salida, CO: Arkansas Valley Publishing, 1995). History of Brown's Creek

is also found in June Shaputis and Suzanne Kelly. comps. and eds., *A History of Chaffee County* (Buena Vista, CO: Buena Vista Heritage, 1982). Ehrhart's grandson George Love assisted me by identifying the Ehrhart family home, which was built in the 1880s and still exists with additions on the east side of U.S. 285, across the highway from the sales office of Mesa Antero, a land development. The shooting of Joe Goodfellow occurred on the Ehrhart property. Thomas J. Ehrhart was a state senator prior to and after his employment as highway commissioner. Another grandson, Harvey Donald Love, has written "Rocky Mountain Progressive: Thomas Jefferson Ehrhart and the Making of Modern Colorado" (M.A. thesis, University of Northern Colorado, 2000).

4. Stanton, *Colorado River Controversies*, 41.

5. Dawson, *The Grand Canyon*, 51.

6. William Jackson Palmer, letter to Mary L. ("Queen") Mellon, written at Fort Lyon, August 9, 1869. Queen Mellen was the future wife of Palmer. A photocopy of this handwritten letter is in the author's collections, courtesy of Otis R. Marston. Palmer's indexed papers are in Collection 477, Box 15, at the Stephen H. Hart Library, Colorado Historical Society, Denver.

7. At an elevation of 12,588 feet, Stony Pass's trail followed a twisting trace around boulders and trees to timberline and then slid down the western side's extremely steep slope, dropping a thousand feet per mile in some sections. At the top, rain or shine, bogs greeted weary travelers. An authoritative history of Stony Pass and its environs in the 1870s and later is Cathy E. Kindquist's *Stony Pass: The Tumbling and Impetuous Trail* (Silverton, CO: San Juan Book Company, 1987).

8. After I laboriously worked out this route, I welcomed finding the corroborating opinion of Dr. William A. Bell, who differed only in misplacing the location of Salt Springs. Bell's findings were published in Thomas F. Dawson, "More Light on James White's Trip through the Grand Canyon," *The Trail* 11 (February 1919): 5–14. Richard E. Lingenfelter, *First through the Grand Canyon* (Los Angeles: Glen Dawson, 1958), 94–95, described the same route from Baker's Park to the Mancos River.

9. Dr. Charles Christopher Parry interviewed James White on January 6, 1868, four months after his rescue at Callville, Nevada. Parry sent copies of his report in duplicate, based on notes taken then, to J. D. Perry, president of the Union Pacific Railway, Eastern Division, and to General William Jackson Palmer. J. D. Perry's copy appeared in *The Transactions of the Academy of Science of St. Louis* 2 (1868): 49–53, under the title "Account of the Passage through the Great Canyon of the Colorado of the West, from the Mouth of the Green River to the Head of Steamboat Navigation at Callville in the Months of August and September 1867, by James White, Now Living at Callville." The next year Palmer's copy was included in William J. Palmer, *Report of Surveys across the*

Continent in 1867–68 (Philadelphia: W. B. Selheimer, 1869), with C. C. Parry's report appearing with the title "Story of White's Descent of the Colorado River." The Parry account also was printed in William A. Bell, *New Tracks in North America: A Journal of Travel and Adventure Whilst Engaged in the Survey for a Southern Railroad to the Pacific Ocean during 1867–8* (London: Chapman and Hall; New York: Scribner, Welford & Co., 1870), with the attribution of "with Contributions by W. J. Palmer, Major A. R. Calhoun, C. C. Parry, M.D., and Captain W. F. Colton." Robert B. Stanton, including some of this bibliographical data in his preface to *Colorado River Controversies,* xxii–xxv, blamed C. C. Parry for encouraging White to believe he had traversed the Grand Canyon and for the "yellow journalism" that repeated the claim "through decade after decade." Ibid., xxii–xxiii.

10. Dawson, *The Grand Canyon,* 40.

11. Early descriptions of Mesa Verde appeared in Hayden's reports and were reprinted in William H. Jackson and William H. Holmes, *Mesa Verde and the Four Corners* (Ouray, CO: Bear Creek Publishing, 1981). Ernest Ingersoll's account appeared in *The Crest of the Continent: A Summer's Ramble in the Rocky Mountains and Beyond* (Chicago: R. R. Donnelley & Sons, 1885). A history of Mesa Verde's early explorations, omitting Charles Baker's entourage as do others, is found in Don Watson, *Indians of the Mesa Verde* (Mesa Verde National Park, CO: Mesa Verde Museum Association, 1953).

12. Dawson, *The Grand Canyon,* 39.

13. Stanton, *Colorado River Controversies,* 67.

14. A map showing the complex topography of the San Juan River and its tributaries in southeastern Utah is "Bluff: Utah-Colorado" (U.S. Bureau of Land Management, 1985). Another useful map, including data such as modern roads and trails, is "Southeastern Utah: Utah Multipurpose Map," produced by the Utah Travel Council (n.d.). Having visited and rafted the San Juan River from Bluff, Utah, to Clay Hill Crossing, I agree with other researchers that the Baker party most likely left the San Juan River at Comb Ridge.

15. James White's letter to Joshua White was written at Callville, Nevada, on September 26, 1867. A facsimile of this letter appears in Chapters 4 and 5 herein. A photographic copy of James White's letter was printed in *The Outing Magazine* 50 (April 1907): 48–49. Subsequently, Parry's nephew, John E. Parry, who gained possession of it after Parry's death in 1890, lent it to Robert B. Stanton for examination. When Thomas F. Dawson prepared his material for *The Grand Canyon,* he was as yet unaware of the letter. He later included it in his article "More Light on James White's Trip" in *The Trail,* 11–12. The letter is now in the collections of the Bancroft Library, University of California, Berkeley, in the Charles Christopher Parry Papers, most of which are botanical, geological, and boundary survey reports. James White's letter and Parry's notes are also on microfilm (Rich. 547:7).

16. P. T. Reilly, "How Deadly Is Big Red?" *Utah Historical Quarterly* 37 (Spring 1969): 253.

17. Raymond H. Cooper, "A History of San Juan Country," in *Pioneers of the San Juan Country,* (Durango, CO: Sarah Platt Decker Chapter D.A.R., 1961), 4:12.

18. Bruns, "The First We Know," 34.

19. *Durango Herald,* January 1, 1888. Another example of confusion involving Charles Baker is that he was called the owner of the Animas City, Pagosa Springs and Conejos Wagon Road, chartered in 1877, long after he had disappeared. The Colorado State Archives lists no articles of incorporation for a road with that name in 1877, or in any other year, nor does the four-volume *Pioneers of the San Juan Country* mention such a road. As stated in Chapter 2, the Abiquiu, Pagosa, and Baker City Road Company received a charter in New Mexico Territory in 1860, with Charles Baker being one of its organizers. At that time Colorado Territory was not yet organized. Possibly, an effort was being made in 1877 to legitimize the old road company in Colorado, with the link to Abiquiú in New Mexico dropped from the name. Also, a peculiar reference to Charles Baker is found in the identification of a photograph in the collections of the Colorado Historical Society. This view shows a large log house in the 1870s in Baker's Park and names Charles Baker as its owner, despite the fact that his only known habitation in the area was a brush shelter.

20. Bancroft, *Works of Hubert Howe Bancroft,* vol. 25, *History of Nevada, Colorado, and Wyoming,* 497–98.

5. THE ACCIDENTAL CELEBRITY

1. O. D. Gass, who had drifted with other down-on-their-luck prospectors from El Dorado, California, to El Dorado, Nevada, before he threw in his gold pan and turned to farming at the future site of Las Vegas, also is said in pioneer histories to have been postmaster for Callville from 1867 to 1869. The Army posted a half dozen or so men at Callville in 1867 and early 1868 to deter Indian depredations and also to keep an eye on Mormons, but Callville was dull, barren, and blazing hot in summer, and desertions were common. Although ambitious promoters of the town had managed to obtain the status of county seat of Pah-Ute County, in Arizona Territory originally, the title moved when Callville and its county found themselves in the new state of Nevada. Despite the inhospitable climate, Callville's location was ideal for those who hoped to capitalize on the river as a thoroughfare; however, the advance of transcontinental railroads put a damper on prospects for navigation on the Colorado River. Thus, within only three years of its birth, Callville was dying when James White arrived and briefly revived the notion that the river, if navigable, might offer some economic promise. Nevertheless, Callville was virtually defunct only a couple of years later. Its vestiges disappeared after

Boulder Dam (later renamed Hoover Dam) was constructed in the 1930s and Lake Mead inundated the site. The sole reminder of Callville is a marina at Callville Bay in Lake Mead National Recreation Area.

2. In 1867, three Mormons, including Jacob Hamblin, were sent with a rowboat to investigate the river from Grand Wash Cliffs down to Callville, the head of navigation. Although the Colorado Navigation Company had been running half a dozen steamers north of Yuma as far as the Black Canyon by the mid-1860s, the boats had to cope with the river's fickle nature where currents, sandbars, and water levels constantly changed and required poling by barge crews. In the Black Canyon, bolts were placed in the jagged walls to assist boats, and between the Black Canyon and the Virgin River, the narrow channel and cliffs at Boulder Canyon presented another obstacle to navigation. As a result, the only steamboat to make it upstream to Callville was *The Esmeralda*, towing a barge in 1866, and this vessel went no farther. Above that point, as far as the Virgin, the Colorado was navigated only by barges. St. Thomas, Nevada, was near the confluence of the Muddy and Virgin Rivers, twenty-five miles above the Colorado. The site of St. Thomas now lies under the waters of the Overton Arm of Lake Mead, except during periods of extremely low water when remnants have reemerged.

3. *Daily Rocky Mountain News,* February 11, 1867, 2. The idea of navigating the Colorado and Green Rivers by steamboat to Fort Bridger is found in a letter from First Lieutenant Colonel Anson Mills, Fort Bridger, Utah, to Judge C. S. Eyster, Denver City, Colorado, December 16, 1866, a copy of which is in my collection, courtesy of Otis R. Marston. In September and October of 1871, Lieutenant George M. Wheeler of the U.S. Topographical Engineers, with G. K. Gilbert and others, succeeded in towing, rowing, and portaging boats upstream to Diamond Creek.

4. E. B. Grandin's letter, written to Frank Alling on September 8, 1867, was printed in San Francisco's *Daily Alta California* on September 24, 1867. J. B. Kipp's letter, written to Simon Wolff, was printed in the Los Angeles *News* on September 20, 1867; in the San Bernardino *Guardian* on September 21, 1867; and in the San Francisco *Bulletin* on September 27, 1867. Kipp's letter also was published later in his booklet *The Colorado River,* with an introduction by Francis P. Farquhar (Los Angeles: Muir Dawson, 1950).

5. The first appearance in print of White's letter was in *The Outing Magazine* in the April–November issue of 1907.

6. William J. Beggs's story, "Navigation of the Big Cañon: A Terrible Voyage," appeared in Prescott's *Arizona Miner* on September 14, 1867. The text presented herein is from a typescript copy made at the Prescott Historical Society and is in my collections, courtesy of Otis R. Marston. In a footnote to Geo. W. Martin's article "Biography of Thomas Allen Cullinan of Junction City," *Kansas Historical Collections* 9 (1905): 533–40, William Beggs is said to

have been a "tramp printer" who sometimes used "John Clarke" as his nom de plume. This article also claims that Cullinan and others were exploring the Colorado River in 1860 on behalf of merchants in Denver and that he would have been the first explorer of the Grand Canyon had the expedition not been deterred by Ute Indians. A photocopy of the article in *Lippincott's Magazine* is in my collections, courtesy of Otis R. Marston.

7. *Rocky Mountain Herald,* January 8, 1869. The article also was included in Dawson, *The Grand Canyon,* 30–34.

8. Ibid.

9. The John Turner interview is in the Robert J. Bruns manuscript "The First We Knew." John C. Turner's grandson John W. Turner prepared a short article titled "An Early Pioneer Family," in *Pioneers of the San Juan Country* (1952), 3:114–22. A typical drifter in his prime, the elder John Turner finally settled in the Animas Valley. John W. Turner's article makes no mention of the visit with White at Callville.

10. Ibid.

11. C. C. Parry's notes, made on January 6, 1868, were printed in Lingenfelter, *First through the Grand Canyon,* 38–39. John E. Parry was acknowledged therein for permitting the use of the notes. C. C. Parry's narrative report appeared in 1868 and 1869 without the notes.

12. C. C. Parry's notes and James White's letter to Joshua White passed to Parry's family after his death in 1890. When Richard E. Lingenfelter used them, they were in the possession of C. C. Parry's nephew, John E. Parry, of Glens Falls, New York, according to the preface and bibliographical notes in Lingenfelter, *First through the Grand Canyon,* 18–19, 114.

13. William A. Bell included Major A. R. Calhoun's account in 1870 under the title "Passage of the Great Cañon of the Colorado" in *New Tracks in North America.* The same account, with minor corrections, appeared in 1872 and 1875 in Major Alfred R. Calhoun, W. A. Bell, and others, *Wonderful Adventures: A Series of Narratives of Personal Experiences among the Native Tribes of America* (London, 1872; Philadelphia: W. B. Evans and Company, 1875). Minor changes in orthography appear in the various editions.

14. Calhoun, "Passage of the Great Cañon of the Colorado," 1–24.

6. DRIFTING AGAIN

1. Dawson, *The Grand Canyon,* 42.

2. Adams, *Hell or High Water,* 84–87.

3. William Jackson Palmer, letter to Mary L. ("Queen") Mellen, August 9, 1869, written at Fort Lyon, Colorado, William Jackson Palmer Papers, Collection 477, Box 15, Stephen H. Hart Library, Colorado Historical Society, Denver, CO, photocopy in author's collections, courtesy of Otis R. Marston.

4. Ibid.

5. Ibid.

6. William Jackson Palmer, letter to Robert C. Clowry, December 27, 1906, William Jackson Palmer Papers, Collection 477, Box 15, typed copy in author's collections, courtesy of Otis R. Marston.

7. Taylor, *First Mail West*, 153.

8. M. [Michael] Beshoar, M.D., *All about Trinidad and Las Animas County, Colorado, Their History, Industries, Resources, Etc.* (Trinidad, CO: Trinidad Historical Society, 1990 [1882]), 116.

9. Dawson, *The Grand Canyon*, 43.

10. *Weekly Rocky Mountain News*, November 14, 1877, 4. Hinsdale County files that I have investigated are archived at the Hinsdale County Museum in Lake City, Colorado.

11. The relocations of the Stephen B. Kellogg family are detailed in an interview, cited as Colorado Dictations, HHB (PL-346) in the Stephen H. Hart Library, Colorado Historical Society. Following the Baker Expedition, Kellogg said in this interview that he returned to Denver and sold his original share in the town, the value of which was $350, for ten sacks of flour.

12. "The Story of James White, First Explorer of the Grand Canyon," *The Outing Magazine* 50 (April–September 1907): 46–49.

13. Stanton, *Colorado River Controversies*, 36.

7. FAME WITHOUT FORTUNE

1. William Culp Darrah, *Powell of the Colorado* (Princeton, NJ: Princeton University Press, 1951), 137–38. The journals and letters of George Y. Bradley, Andrew Hall, William Robert Wesley Hawkins, Oramel Howland, Walter H. Powell, and John Colton Sumner from Powell's expedition of 1869 have been published in Michael P. Ghiglieri, *First through the Grand Canyon: The Secret Journals and Letters of the 1869 Crew Who Explored the Green and Colorado Rivers* (Flagstaff, AZ: Puma Press, 2003), wherein James White's story is summarized on pages 70–71, and Bradley and Sumner debunk the raft cruise therein on pages 200 and 206.

2. Palmer, letter to Robert C. Clowry, December 27, 1906.

3. O. Dock Marston, "Water Level Rails along the Colorado River," *The Colorado Magazine* 46 (Winter 1969): 287–303; Dwight L. Smith, "The Nims and Czar Incidents in the Denver Press," *The Colorado Magazine* 48 (Winter 1971): 49–58.

4. David Lavender, *River Runners of the Grand Canyon* (Grand Canyon, AZ: Grand Canyon Natural History Association, 1985), 34–35.

5. Otis R. Marston, "James White's Raft Journey of 1867," in Stanton, *Colorado River Controversies*, 241–42.

6. Biographies of John Wesley Powell with references to James White that have been consulted are Darrah, *Powell of the Colorado*; Wallace Stegner,

Beyond the Hundredth Meridian: John Wesley Powell and the Second Opening of the West (Boston: Houghton Mifflin, 1953), 33–34, 49, 50, 84; Donald Worster, *A River Running West: The Life and Times of John Wesley Powell* (New York: Oxford University Press, 2000), 133–34, 165.

7. Frederick S. Dellenbaugh, *The Romance of the Colorado River* (New York: G. P. Putnam Sons, 1908), 183.

8. "Story of James White," 46.

9. Marston, "James White's Raft Journey of 1867," 241.

10. Stanton, *Colorado River Controversies*, 37.

11. Ibid., 93.

12. Marston, "James White's Raft Journey of 1867," 242; Robert B. Stanton, *The Hoskaninni Papers: Mining in Glen Canyon*, ed. C. Gregory Crampton and Dwight L. Smith, Anthropological Papers No. 54, Glen Canyon Series No. 15 (Salt Lake City: University of Utah Press, 1961).

13. Frederick S. Dellenbaugh, *A Canyon Voyage: The Narrative of the Second Powell Expedition* (Tucson: University of Arizona Press, 1962 [1902]), 2.

14. Marston, "James White's Raft Journey of 1867," 250.

15. As they went, they produced a motion picture film. Until his death in 1976, Emery showed this primitive but remarkable film at the Kolb studio on the South Rim of the Grand Canyon.

16. Marston, "James White's Raft Journey of 1867," 243.

17. Powell's biographers, cited in note 6, discuss his political conflicts concerning land reform and the Irrigation Survey. See also Alvin T. Steinel, *History of Agriculture in Colorado* (Fort Collins, CO: State Board of Agriculture, 1926), 166–244; Thomas G. Alexander, "John Wesley Powell, the Irrigation Survey, and the Inauguration of the Second Phase of Irrigation Development in Utah," *Utah Historical Quarterly* 37 (Spring 1969): 90–206.

18. Horace M. Albright and Marian Albright Schenck, *Creating the National Park Service: The Missing Years* (Norman: University of Oklahoma Press, 1999), 64–65. Establishment of a national park met resistance not only from prospectors who had claims staked on the South Rim and in the canyon but also from entrepreneurs. With the arrival in 1901 at Grand Canyon Village of the Grand Canyon Railway, a spur of the Atchison, Topeka and Santa Fe, tourism was underway. The Kolb brothers were photographing mule trips that carried tourists down Ralph Cameron's toll road, renamed the Bright Angel Trail, and Fred Harvey's luxurious El Tovar Hotel opened in 1905. The original, stone monument in which the Powell marker was set was replaced by an imposing structure, resembling a shrine, at Powell Point in 1994.

19. Dawson, *The Grand Canyon*, 3.

20. Biographical information about Thomas F. Dawson is from E. M. Ammons, "A Tribute to Thomas F. Dawson," *The Colorado Magazine* 1 (November 1923): 3–9, written after Dawson's death in an automobile accident while

accompanying President Warren Harding on an outing near Denver. See also David N. Wetzel, "Thomas F. Dawson: History's Journalist," *Colorado History Now* (February 2002): 3.

21. "James White's Trip through the Grand Canyon in 1867," Thomas F. Dawson Scrapbook, Stephen H. Hart Library, Colorado Historical Society, Denver. The comment about James White's calling Charles Baker "Jim" was made by Esther White McDonald to Otis R. Marston, Mercer Island, Washington, December 19, 1964, according to a note from Marston in author's collections.

22. Marston, "James White's Raft Journey of 1867," 244.

23. Dawson, "More Light on James White's Trip," 5–14.

24. Ibid., 13, confirmed by comments in Martin, "Biography of Thomas Allen Cullinan," 535.

25. Quoted in ibid., 7.

26. William Wallace Bass, comp., *Adventures in the Canyons of the Colorado by Two of Its Earliest Explorers, James White and W. W. Hawkins* (Grand Canyon, AZ: Privately printed, 1920).

27. James White's obituary appeared on the front page of the *Trinidad Chronicle-News,* January 14, 1927, reporting his death that day. Microfilm of this newspaper is in the collections of the Carnegie Public Library at Trinidad, Colorado.

28. *Trinidad Chronicle-News,* May 25, 1930, 4. This newspaper article was preserved in a scrapbook compiled by Dr. J. H. East, now in the collections of the Stephen H. Hart Library, Colorado Historical Society, Denver. (Copy also in author's collections, courtesy of Otis R. Marston.)

29. Authors of testimonials for James White's character, which were printed in Dawson, *The Grand Canyon,* 53–55, include Hon. D. L. Taylor, mayor; Hon. S. W. De Busk, state senator from Trinidad; and Hon. Julius Gunter, Governor of Colorado.

30. Barry Goldwater, *Delightful Journey down the Green and Colorado Rivers* (Tempe: Arizona Historical Foundation, 1970), 186–87.

31. Lingenfelter, *First through the Grand Canyon,* 78.

32. Darrah, *Powell of the Colorado,* 182; Stegner, *Beyond the Hundredth Meridian,* 33.

33. Lingenfelter, *First through the Grand Canyon,* 96–98.

34. Harold A. Bulger, "First Man through the Grand Canyon," *Bulletin of the Missouri Historical Society* 18 (July 1961): 321–31.

35. Robert C. Euler, unpublished manuscript, "First through Grand Canyon: An Ethnohistorical and Geographical Approach to the Saga of James White" (1973), copy in author's collections, courtesy of Otis R. Marston. Dr. Euler's hypothesis about the embarkation point and the aerial reconnaissance of Moki (or Moqui) Canyon by Adams and Euler appear in Eilean Adams, *Hell or High Water,* 121–59.

36. Stanton, *Colorado River Controversies*, 5.

37. Ibid., 5; Reilly, "How Deadly Is Big Red?" 253; Simmons [McConnell], "Captain Baker and the San Juan Humbug," 74; David Lavender, "James White: First Through the Grand Canyon?" *American West* 19 (November/December, 1982): 30; Worster, *A River Running West*, 133–34.

38. Worster, *A River Running West*, 165. Edward Dolnick, in *Down the Great Unknown* (New York: HarperCollins, 2001), 326–27 (note), arrives at the conclusion that White's raft trip was "unlikely rather than impossible." James White's version of the demises of Charles Baker and George Strole is uncritically accepted by Michael P. Ghiglieri and Thomas M. Myers in *Over the Edge: Death in the Grand Canyon* (Flagstaff, AZ: Puma Press, 2001), 133–35. Ghiglieri's *First through the Grand Canyon*, 70–71, also supports the possibility that James White preceded John Wesley Powell through the Grand Canyon.

APPENDIX: ADRIFT IN FOLKLORE

1. *Durango Herald Democrat*, June 9, 1930, 2. In 1930 a dramatic performance of this pageant commemorated the opening of the second Baker's Bridge. In addition to the historical license taken by the author of "Baker's Bridge," confusion later existed in the area regarding the location of the first Animas City. The site of the first settlement of that name was on the east side of Baker's Bridge, but it has been mistaken in some histories as the later town, which was ten miles farther south on the west side of the river, adjacent to the later Durango. This error was set solidly in bronze and erected by the Colorado Historical Society and the Sarah Platt Decker Chapter of the Daughters of the American Revolution near the east end of Baker's Bridge in 1961. When a new span forced relocation of the old marker thirty years later, no one pointed out or corrected this embarrassing error. The plaque, which incorrectly identifies the location of the original and Animas City and states that Baker found gold in the San Juans, reads: "*Baker's Bridge*. Captain Charles H. Baker [no known source exists for the initial "H"], who discovered gold in the San Juan in 1860, led a party of prospectors in this area in 1861. They placer mined on El Rio de las Animas, built the first bridge (300 feet north), and established the town called Animas City. It was a mile and a half north of the present site of Durango."

BIBLIOGRAPHY

Adams, Eilean. *Hell or High Water: James White's Disputed Passage through the Grand Canyon, 1867*. Logan: Utah State University Press, 2001.

Aken, Jean. *Ute Mountain Tribal Park*. Moab, UT: Four Corners Publications, 1987.

Albright, Horace M., and Marian Albright Schenck. *Creating the National Park Service: The Missing Years*. Norman: University of Oklahoma Press, 1999.

Alexander, Thomas G. "John Wesley Powell, the Irrigation Survey, and the Inauguration of the Second Phase of Irrigation Development in Utah." *Utah Historical Quarterly* 37 (Spring 1969): 90–206.

Ammons, E. M. "A Tribute to Thomas F. Dawson." *The Colorado Magazine* 1 (November 1923): 3–9.

Bancroft, Hubert Howe. *The Works of Hubert Howe Bancroft*, vol. 17, *History of Arizona and New Mexico, 1530–1888*. San Francisco: The History Company, 1889.

————. *The Works of Hubert Howe Bancroft*, vol. 25, *History of Nevada, Colorado, and Wyoming, 1540–1888*. San Francisco: The History Company, 1890.

Bass, William Wallace, comp. *Adventures in the Canyons of the Colorado by Two of Its Earliest Explorers, James White and W. W. Hawkins*. Grand Canyon, AZ: Privately printed, 1920.

Beggs, William J. "Navigation of the Big Cañon: A Terrible Voyage." *Arizona Miner* (Prescott), September 14, 1867. Typed copy in author's collections.

————. "A Terrible Journey." *Lippincott's Magazine of Popular Literature, Science, and Education* (December 1868). Copy of clipping in author's collections.

Belknap, Buzz, and Loie Belknap Evans. *Grand Canyon River Guide*. Evergreen, CO: Westwater Books, 1989 [1969].

Bell, William A. *New Tracks in North America: A Journal of Travel and Adventure Whilst Engaged in the Survey for a Southern Railroad to the Pacific Ocean during 1867–8*. London: Chapman and Hill; New York: Scribner, Welford & Co., 1870.

Beshoar, M. [Michael], M.D. *All about Trinidad and Las Animas County, Colorado: Their History, Industries, Resources, Etc*. Trinidad, CO: Trinidad Historical Society, 1990 [1882].

Bott, Anthony. "The Life and Reminiscences of Anthony Bott." Starsmore Center for Local History, Colorado Springs Pioneers Museum, Colorado Springs, CO.

Bruns, Robert J. "The First We Know: The Pioneer History of the San Juans." San Juan County Historical Society, Archive–Research Center, Silverton, CO.

Bryan, William S., and Robert Rose. *A History of the Pioneer Families of Missouri*. Baltimore: Genealogical Publishing Co., 1984.

Bulger, Harold A. "First Man through the Grand Canyon." *Missouri Historical Society Bulletin* 18 (July 1961): 321–31.

Bute, George. "The Life and Reminiscences of George Bute." Starsmore Center for Local History, Colorado Springs Pioneers Museum, Colorado Springs, CO.

Calhoun, Major A. R. "Passage of the Great Cañon of the Colorado." In Major Alfred R. Calhoun, W. A. Bell, and others, *Wonderful Adventures: A Series of Narratives of Personal Experiences among the Native Tribes of America*. Philadelphia: W. B. Evans and Company, 1875 [London, 1872].

Carlson, Dale. "A Defense of Charles Baker." San Juan County Historical Society Archive–Research Center, Silverton, CO.

Colorado Dictations. HHB (PL-346). Wolf Londoner interview. Stephen H. Hart Library, Colorado Historical Society, Denver, CO.

Cooper, Raymond H. "A History of San Juan County." In *Pioneers of the San Juan Country*, 4: 10–12. Durango, CO: Sarah Platt Decker Chapter N.S.D.A.R, 1961.

Dana, Richard Henry. *Two Years before the Mast.* New York: Penguin Books, 1964 [1840].

Darrah, William Culp. *Powell of the Colorado.* Princeton, NJ: Princeton University Press, 1951.

Dary, David. *The Santa Fe Trail, Its History, Legends, and Lore.* New York: Alfred A. Knopf, 2000.

Dawson, Thomas F. *The Grand Canyon* (U.S. Senate, Document No. 42, 65th Cong., 1st Sess., May 25, 1917). Washington, DC: Government Printing Office, 1917.

———. "More Light on James White's Trip through the Grand Canyon." *The Trail* 11 (February 1919): 5–14.

Dellenbaugh, Frederick S. *A Canyon Voyage: The Narrative of the Second Powell Expedition.* Tucson: University of Arizona Press, 1962 [1902].

———. *The Romance of the Colorado River.* New York: G. P. Putnam Sons, 1908.

Dolnick, Edward. *Down the Great Unknown.* New York: HarperCollins, 2001.

Dyer, John L. *The Snow-Shoe Itinerant, An Autobiography of the Rev. John L. Dyer, Familiarly Known as "Father Dyer," of the Colorado Conference, Methodist Episcopal Church.* Cincinnati, OH: Cranston & Stowe, 1890.

Euler, Robert C. "First through the Grand Canyon: An Ethnohistorical and Geographical Approach to the Saga of James White." 1973. Copy in author's collections.

Farquhar, Francis P. *The Books of the Colorado River & the Grand Canyon: A Selective Bibliography.* Los Angeles: Glen Dawson, 1953.

Franzwa, Gregory. *Maps of the Santa Fe Trail.* St. Louis, MO: Patrice Press, 1989.

Ghiglieri, Michael P. *First through the Grand Canyon: The Secret Journals and Letters of the 1869 Crew Who Explored the Green and Colorado Rivers.* Flagstaff, AZ: Puma Press, 2003.

———, and Thomas M. Myers. *Over the Edge: Death in the Grand Canyon.* Flagstaff, AZ: Puma Press, 2001.

Gilpin, William. *Guide to the Kansas Gold Mines at Pike's Peak . . . from Notes of Capt. J. W. Gunnison.* Denver: Nolie Mumey, 1952 [1859].

Goetzmann, William H. "The Mountain Man as Jacksonian Man." *American Quarterly* 15 (1963): 402–15.

Goldwater, Barry. *Delightful Journey down the Green and Colorado Rivers.* Tempe: Arizona Historical Foundation, 1970.

Gregg, Josiah. *The Commerce of the Prairies; or, The Journal of a Santa Fe Trader.* Ed. Milo Milton Quaife. Chicago: R. R. Donnelly & Sons, 1926 [1844].

Hall, Frank. *History of Colorado*, vols. 2 and 4. Chicago: Blakely Printing Company, 1890.

Hart, Herbert M. *Old Forts of the Southwest*. Seattle: Superior Publishing Company, n.d.

Hine, Robert F., and John Mack Faragher. *The American West: A New American History*. New Haven: Yale University Press, 2000.

Horgan, Paul. *Lamy of Santa Fe: His Life and Times*. New York: Farrar, Straus and Giroux, 1975.

Ingersoll, Ernest. *The Crest of the Continent: A Summer's Ramble in the Rocky Mountains and Beyond*. Chicago: R. R. Donnelly & Sons, 1885.

Jackson, William H., and William H. Holmes. *Mesa Verde and the Four Corners*. Ouray, CO: Bear Creek Publishing, 1981.

Karnes, Thomas L. *William Gilpin, Western Nationalist*. Austin: University of Texas Press, 1970.

Kindquist, Cathy E. *Stony Pass: The Tumbling and Impetuous Trail*. Silverton, CO: San Juan Book Company, 1987.

Kipp, J. B. *The Colorado River*. Intro. by Francis P. Farquhar. Los Angeles: Muir Dawson, 1950.

Lavender, David. *Bent's Fort*. Garden City, NY: Doubleday & Co., 1954.

———. "James White: First through the Grand Canyon?" *American West* 19 (November/December 1982): 22–30.

———. *River Runners of the Grand Canyon*. Grand Canyon, AZ: Grand Canyon Natural History Association, 1985.

Limerick, Patricia Nelson. *The Legacy of Conquest: The Unbroken Past of the American West*. New York: W. W. Norton & Company, 1987.

Lingenfelter, Richard E. *First through the Grand Canyon*. Foreword by Otis R. Marston. Los Angeles: Glen Dawson, 1958.

———. *Steamboats on the Colorado River, 1852–1916*. Tucson: University of Arizona Press, 1978.

Londoner, Wolfe. "Western Experiences and Colorado Mining Camps." *The Colorado Magazine* 6 (March 1929): 67–68.

Madsen, Brigham D., and Betty M. Madsen. "Corinne, the Fair: Gateway to Montana Mines." *Utah Historical Quarterly* 37 (Winter 1969): 102–23.

Marston, Otis R. [O. Dock Marston]. "Early Travel on the Green and Colorado Rivers." *The Smoke Signal* (Tucson Corral of the Westerners) 20 (Fall 1969): 231–36.

———. "Foreword." In Richard E. Lingenfelter, *First through the Grand Canyon*, 7–10. Los Angeles: Glen Dawson, 1958.

——— [O. Dock Marston]. "James White's Grand Canyon Cruise?" 1975. Copy in author's collections.

———. "James White's Raft Journey of 1867." In Robert Brewster Stanton, *Colorado River Controversies*, 233–50. Boulder City, NV: Westwater Books, 1982.

——— [O. Dock Marston]. "The Lost Journal of John Colton Sumner." *Utah Historical Quarterly* 37 (Spring 1969): 173–89.

———. "The Points of Embarkation of James White in 1857." *The Branding Iron* (Los Angeles Corral of the Westerners) 75 (December 1965): 1–6.

———. "The Reluctant Candidate—James White, First through the Grand Canyon?" *Brand Book III* (San Diego Corral of the Westerners) (1973): 166–76.

——— [Otis Marston]. "River Runners: Fast Water Navigation." *Utah Historical Quarterly* 28 (July 1960): 291–308.

———. "Water Level Rails along the Colorado River." *The Colorado Magazine* 46 (Winter 1969): 287–303.

——— [O. Dock Marston]. "Who Named the Grand Canyon?" *The Pacific Historian* 12 (Spring 1968): 4–8.

Martin, Geo. W. "Biography of Thomas Allen Cullinan of Junction City." *Kansas Historical Collections* 9 (1905): 533–40.

McShane, David. "The Life and Reminiscences of David McShane." Starsmore Center for Local History, Colorado Springs Pioneers Museum, Colorado Springs, CO.

Messersmith, Dan W. *The History of Mohave County to 1912.* Kingman, AZ: Mohave County Historical Society, 1991.

Napton, W. B. *Over the Santa Fe Trail, 1857.* Arrow Rock, MO: Friends of the Arrow Rock, 1991.

Newberry, J. S. "Geological Report." In U.S. Army Corps of Engineers, *Report of the Grand and Green Rivers of the West in 1859, under the Command of Capt. J. N. Macomb.* Washington, DC: Government Printing Office, 1876.

New Mexico Territorial Legislature. *Laws of the Territory of New Mexico, 1860–1861.* Santa Fe, NM: J. T. Russell, 1861.

Nossaman, Allen. *Many More Mountains,* vol. 1, *Silverton's Roots.* Denver: Sundance Publications, 1989.

Oldham, Ann. *Albert H. Pfeiffer: Indian Agent, Soldier and Mountain Man.* Pagosa Springs, CO: Privately printed, 2003.

Oliva, Leo E. *Fort Dodge: Sentry of the Western Plains.* Topeka: Kansas State Historical Society, 1998.

Ormes, Manly Dayton, and Eleanor R. Ormes. *The Book of Colorado Springs.* Colorado Springs, CO: Privately printed, 1933.

Palmer, William Jackson. Letter to Mary L. ("Queen") Mellen, August 9, 1869. William Jackson Palmer Papers, Collection 477, Box 15. Stephen H. Hart Library, Colorado Historical Society, Denver, CO. Copy in author's collections.

———. Letter to Robert C. Clowry, December 27, 1906. William Jackson Palmer Papers, Collection 477, Box 15. Stephen H. Hart Library, Colorado Historical Society, Denver, CO.

————. *Report of Surveys across the Continent in 1867–68*. Philadelphia: W. B. Selheimer, 1869.

Parry, Charles Christopher. "Account of the Passage through the Great Canyon of the Colorado of the West, from the Mouth of the Green River to the Head of Steamboat Navigation at Callville in the Months of August and September, 1867, by James White, Now Living at Callville." *The Transactions of the Academy of Science of St. Louis* 2 (1868): 49–53.

————. Notes, written January 6, 1868. Original and microfilm (Rich 547.7). Charles Christopher Parry Papers, Bancroft Library, University of California, Berkeley.

————. "Story of White's Descent of the Colorado River." In William J. Palmer, *Report of Surveys across the Continent in 1867–68*. Philadelphia: W. B. Selheimer, 1869.

Pioneers of the San Juan Country, vols. 3 and 4. Durango, CO: Sarah Platt Decker Chapter D.A.R., 1952, 1961.

Reilly, P. T. "How Deadly Is Big Red?" *Utah Historical Quarterly* 37 (Spring 1969): 244–60.

Sánchez, Joseph P. *Explorers, Traders, and Slavers: Forging the Old Spanish Trail, 1678–1850*. Salt Lake City: University of Utah Press, 1997.

Shaputis, June. *Where the Bodies Are*. Salida, CO: Arkansas Valley Publishing Company, 1995.

————, and Suzanne Kelly, comps. and eds. *A History of Chaffee County*. Buena Vista, CO: Buena Vista Heritage, 1982.

Simmons, Marc, and Hal Jackson. *Following the Santa Fe Trail*, 3rd ed., rev. Santa Fe, NM: Ancient City Press, 2001.

Simmons, Virginia McConnell. *Bayou Salado: The Story of South Park*. Boulder: University Press of Colorado, 2002 [1966].

———— [Virginia McConnell]. "Captain Baker and the San Juan Humbug." *The Colorado Magazine* 48 (Winter 1971): 59–75.

————. *The San Luis Valley: Land of the Six-Armed Cross*. Boulder: University Press of Colorado, 1999 [1979].

————. *The Upper Arkansas: A Mountain River Valley*. Boulder, CO: Pruett Publishing Company, 1990.

————. *The Ute Indians of Utah, Colorado, and New Mexico*. Boulder: University Press of Colorado, 2000.

———— [Virginia McConnell]. *Ute Pass: Route of the Blue Sky People*. Denver: Sage Books, 1963.

Smiley, Jerome. *History of Denver, with Outlines of the Earlier History of the Rocky Mountain Country*. Denver: Times-Sun Publishing Company, 1901.

Smith, Duane A. *The Birth of Colorado: A Civil War Perspective*. Norman: University of Oklahoma Press, 1989.

————. *Song of the Hammer and Drill: The Colorado San Juans, 1860–1914*. Boulder: University Press of Colorado, 2000.

Smith, Dwight L. "The Nims and Czar Incidents in the Denver Press." *The Colorado Magazine* 48 (Winter 1971): 49–58.

Soldier and Brave: Historic Places Associated with Indian Affairs and the Indian Wars in the Trans-Mississippi West, vol. 12, *National Survey of Historical Sites and Buildings*. Washington, DC: National Park Service, 1971.

Sprague, Marshall. *The Great Gates: The Story of the Rocky Mountain Passes*. Boston: Little, Brown and Company, 1964.

Stanton, Robert Brewster. *Colorado River Controversies*. Ed. James M. Chalfant. Boulder City, NV: Westwater Books, 1982 [1932].

————. *The Hoskaninni Papers: Mining in Glen Canyon*. Ed. C. Gregory Crampton and Dwight L. Smith. Anthropological Papers No. 54, Glen Canyon Series No. 15. Salt Lake City: University of Utah Press, 1961.

Steele, Thomas J., S.J., ed. and trans. *Archbishop Lamy: In His Own Words*. Albuquerque: LPD Press, 2000.

Stegner, Wallace. *Beyond the Hundredth Meridian: John Wesley Powell and the Second Opening of the West*. Boston: Houghton Mifflin, 1953.

Steinel, Alvin T. *History of Agriculture in Colorado*. Fort Collins, CO: State Board of Agriculture, 1926.

"The Story of James White, First Explorer of the Grand Canyon." *The Outing Magazine* 50 (April–November 1907): 46–49.

Strate, David Kay. *Sentinel to the Cimarron: The Frontier Experience of Fort Dodge, Kansas*. Dodge City, KS: Cultural Heritage and Arts Center, 1970.

————, ed. *West by Southwest: Letters of Joseph Pratt Allyn, a Traveler along the Santa Fe Trail, 1863*. Dodge City: Kansas Heritage Center, 1984.

Tabor, Augusta. "Cabin Life in Colorado." *The Colorado Magazine* 2 (March 1927): 149–53.

Taylor, Morris F. *First Mail West: Stagecoach Lines on the Santa Fe Trail*. Albuquerque: University of New Mexico Press, 1971.

Torrez, Robert J. "The San Juan Gold Rush of 1860 and Its Effect on the Development of Northern New Mexico." *New Mexico Historical Quarterly* 63 (July 1988): 257–72.

Trenton, Patricia, and Peter H. Hassrick. *The Rocky Mountains: A Vision for Artists in the Nineteenth Century*. Norman: University of Oklahoma Press, 1983.

Turner, John W. "An Early Pioneer Family." In *Pioneers of the San Juan Country*, 3: 115–22. Durango, CO: Sarah Platt Decker Chapter D.A.R., 1952.

Twain, Mark (Samuel Clemens). *Roughing It*. New York: New American Library, 1962.

Warner, Ted J., Jr., ed. *The Domínguez-Escalante Journal: Their Expedition through Colorado, Utah, Arizona, and New Mexico in 1776*. Trans. Fray Angelico Chavez. Salt Lake City: University of Utah Press, 1995.

Watson, Don. *Indians of the Mesa Verde.* Mesa Verde National Park, CO: Mesa Verde Museum Association, 1953.

Webb, Robert H. *Grand Canyon, a Century of Change: Rephotography of the 1889–1890 Stanton Expedition.* Tucson: University of Arizona Press, 1996.

Weber, David J. *The Taos Trappers: The Fur Trade in the Far West, 1540–1846.* Norman: University of Oklahoma Press, 1971.

Weber, William A. *King of Colorado Botany: Charles Christopher Parry, 1823–1890.* Boulder: University Press of Colorado, 1997.

West, Elliott. *The Contested Plains: Indians, Goldseekers, and the Rush to Colorado.* Lawrence: University Press of Kansas, 1998.

Wetzel, David N. "Thomas F. Dawson: History's Journalist." *Colorado History Now* (February 2002): 3.

White, James. Letter to Joshua H. White, September 26, 1867. Original and microfilm (Rich. 547.7). Charles Christopher Parry Papers, Bancroft Library, University of California, Berkeley.

White, Laura C. Manson. "Albert H. Pfeiffer." *The Colorado Magazine* 10 (November 1933): 217–22.

Woodward, Arthur. "Sidelights on Bent's Old Fort." *The Colorado Magazine* 33 (October 1956): 280.

Worster, Donald. *A River Running West: The Life and Times of John Wesley Powell.* New York: Oxford University Press, 2000.

INDEX